Emily Herds an Ox

To Live a Life of Meaning in Grace

"A narrative through the ten stages of Zen practice and enlightenment"

Leon Isaac Drucker

This is a work of fiction. Similarities to real people, places, or events are entirely coincidental.

EMILY HERDS AN OX

First edition. April 15, 2024.

Copyright © 2024 Leon Isaac Drucker.

ISBN: 979-8218421069

Written by Leon Isaac Drucker.

Table of Contents

DEDICATION

To my mother's cousin Judyth O. Weaver, the first person to teach me about presence. As a young boy of twelve, I watched Judyth eat a bowl of my grandmothers pea soup. That may sound like a mundane experience however, she was in a state of mindfulness and grace. That moment impacted the rest of my life. I wanted to attain the peace and awareness that Judyth had demonstrated.

Judyth was a member of the founding faculty at Naropa Institute, now Naropa University, (Boulder, CO) in the 1970's, creating it's T'ai Chi Ch'uan program.

A former modern dancer, she lived in Japan 1965-1968, studying classical dance (Kabuki and Noh), tea ceremony, and other aspects of Japanese culture. She then lived and studied at Shofukuji, a traditional Rinzai Zen Buddhist monastery, under Yamada Mumon Roshi. Since 1969 she has taught and led workshops at Esalen Institute in California, Hollyhock in Canada, and other educational centers in the western world, as well as in Russia, Japan, Taiwan, Mexico, and India.

To my first teacher of Zen, I dedicate this book with love to you.

ABOUT THE AUTHOR

Leon Isaac Drucker has been a student of Zen and the Martial Arts since 1964. His Judo Black belt was received in 1970 by his instructor and Legendary Judo Master Professor Takahiko Ishikawa. His close to 60 years of experience also includes training in Northern Shaolin Kung Fu, Yang Style Tai Chi Chuan, and Traditional Japanese Bujutsu.

Additional Published Books:

Preserving Life Through The Study Of The Martial Way, 2012, Budo Taijutsu Training Manual (1)

Preserving Life Through The Study Of The Martial Way, 2013, Budo Taijutsu Training Manual (2)

The Shadow of Death, 2017, "An introduction to Tantric Buddhism"

Yang Lu Chan Old Style Tai Chi Chuan, 2023 "Advanced Training Manual"

Warriors of Wisdom "Arjuna's Tale in a Modern Gita" 2023

www.leonisaacdrucker.com[1] **www.myo-fu-an.com**[2]

---

1. http://www.leonisaacdrucker.com
2. http://www.myo-fu-an.com

FORWARD

The "Ten Ox Herding Pictures," are a series of images and accompanying poems or commentaries that are part of the Zen Buddhist tradition. These pictures and texts symbolize the stages of a practitioner's progress toward enlightenment and his or her subsequent return to society to enact wisdom and compassion.

The ten stages depicted in the ox herding pictures are as follows:

SEARCHING FOR THE OX:

This represents the beginning of the spiritual path, where the practitioner is seeking enlightenment.

DISCOVERING THE FOOTPRINTS:

The practitioner finds traces of the true nature of reality.

SEEING THE OX:

Seeing the Ox: The first glimpse of enlightenment, or true nature.

CATCHING THE OX:

The difficult task of confronting and acknowledging one's own true nature.

TAMING THE OX:

Learning to control one's own mind and passions.

RIDING THE OX HOME:

Achieving harmony with one's true nature.

THE OX FORGOTTEN, LEAVING THE MAN ALONE:

A higher stage of enlightenment, where there is no distinction between the practitioner and the true nature.

THE OX AND MAN BOTH GONE OUT OF SIGHT:

Complete enlightenment, transcending all dualities.

RETURNING TO THE ORIGIN, BACK TO THE SOURCE:

Returning to the world, recognizing that the source of enlightenment is in everyday life.

ENTERING THE MARKETPLACE WITH HELPING HANDS:

Engaging with the world compassionately, with an enlightened perspective.

Each stage in this progression represents a deeper level of understanding and integration of Zen principles into one's life, culminating in the return to everyday life with a new, enlightened perspective on the world.

The Quest Begins
"Searching for the Ox"

"Amidst the rhythms of a digital world, where does the silent mind leap to grasp the essence of satori?"

Emily Nguyen's life was a canvas of routine and comfort, painted in the monochromatic hues of a bustling city life. At 29, she had carved a niche for herself as a software developer in a tech firm that buzzed with the relentless energy of ambition and innovation. Her days flowed in a seamless loop of coding, debugging, and team meetings, punctuated by the occasional laughter and chitchat with colleagues who, like her, were cogs in the grand machine of the digital world.

Yet, beneath the surface of this well-orchestrated routine, Emily harbored a quiet sense of disquiet. The city, with its towering skyscrapers and neon lights, felt like a world teetering on the edge of reality and illusion. She found solace in her solitary hobbies — the gentle caress of book pages and the earthy scent of her small balcony garden. These moments, though fleeting, were windows to a world beyond the digital screens and concrete jungles.

Emily's introverted nature meant her social outings were few and far between, confined to a small group of friends who shared her love for quiet cafes and indie movies. They were like islands in her life, places where she could dock her thoughts and feelings, although briefly. But even amidst these friendly shores, Emily often felt adrift, her mind wandering to the deeper questions of existence and purpose.

In her unassuming apartment, nestled among a row of similarly structured buildings, Emily would often spend her evenings in the company of various philosophical and spiritual texts. The writings of Thich Nhat Hanh, Rumi, and Alan Watts whispered to her from the pages, their words a balm to her restive soul. These moments of reading were not mere pastimes; they were silent quests for meaning in a world that often felt too loud, too fast.

Despite her success in the tech world, a world that celebrated logic and precision, Emily yearned for something more — a bridge between the empirical and the existential. Her heart, a compass of its own, pointed towards a path she had yet to tread, a journey inward that beckoned her with the promise of discovery and self-realization.

One evening, as the city lights flickered like distant stars outside her window, Emily found herself immersed in a book on Zen Buddhism. The concept of 'satori' — sudden enlightenment — leapt from the pages, stirring something deep within her. It was a concept so starkly different from the gradual, logical progressions she was used to in her programming work. This was a philosophy that spoke of leaps, of transcendence, of finding the extraordinary in the ordinary.

As she pondered over these ideas, the familiar sounds of the city seemed to fade into a soft murmur. Emily's mind drifted to the park she often visited on weekends, a patch of green in the concrete desert, where she witnessed the effortless flow of nature. It was in these moments, watching the dance of leaves in the wind or the serene glide of ducks across the pond, that she felt hints of a profound connection, a fleeting glimpse of something vast and unexplored.

Her quest, she realized, was not just in the pages of ancient texts but in the very fabric of her daily life. It was a journey that awaited her, a journey to bridge the gap between her outer world of code and logic, and her inner world of wonder and contemplation.

As the night deepened, and the city embraced its nocturnal symphony, Emily knew that her journey had already begun. In the quiet of her room, surrounded by books and the subtle fragrance of her garden, she felt the first stirrings of a transformation, a slow awakening to the possibilities that lay within and beyond her.

"Amidst the city's digital tapestry, where does the heart find its true echo?"

Emily's world was a tapestry of modernism, woven with the threads of technology and the rhythms of city life. Her apartment, a high-rise sanctuary amidst the urban sprawl, reflected her life: organized, efficient, and digitally connected. The walls were adorned with abstract art, and the shelves held an array of gadgets that orchestrated her daily routines with precision.

From the moment the sun peeked through her blinds — automated to rise at the first hint of dawn — to the time she laid her head on her smart pillow, Emily's life ran on a seamless schedule. Her mornings began with the soft chimes of her phone's alarm, followed by a review of her day's agenda on her tablet. Breakfast was a quick, nutritious affair, often accompanied by a podcast or an audiobook playing through her smart speakers.

Her job as a software developer demanded a blend of creativity and logic, a challenge she relished. She worked in a sleek office downtown, where the clatter of keyboards and the soft hum of conversation filled the air. Her colleagues were a diverse group of tech enthusiasts, each absorbed in their own digital worlds, occasionally intersecting with hers over coffee breaks and brainstorming sessions.

Yet, in this world of high-speed internet and instant messaging, Emily's connections often felt transitory. Her friends, a close-knit group from college and work, were like satellites in her orbit, their interactions often limited to group chats and social media. They met for brunch and movie nights, sharing laughs and stories, but rarely delving beyond the surface of their lives. It was a camaraderie born of convenience and shared history yet lacking the depth Emily secretly craved.

Her family, living in another town, was a constant yet distant presence. Video calls and text messages bridged the miles, but the warmth of physical proximity was unmistakably absent. Her parents, supportive of her career and independent life, often expressed their love and concern through care packages and long phone calls during the weekends. Emily cherished these moments, yet they were bittersweet reminders of the physical and emotional distance that separated them.

In the solitude of her apartment, Emily often found herself reflecting on the nature of her relationships. The digital world offered connections aplenty, but they were like streams that ran wide yet shallow. She yearned for something deeper, more tangible — a connection that transcended the screens and the city's relentless pace.

This longing for depth was also evident in her choice of books, an eclectic mix of philosophy, spirituality, and literature. They were her silent companions, offering glimpses into worlds and ideas far removed from her daily reality. In these quiet moments of reading, Emily found herself engaging in imaginary dialogues with the authors, questioning the nature of happiness, fulfillment, and connection.

Her life, with its modern comforts and conveniences, was like a well-oiled machine, yet Emily couldn't shake off the feeling that she was meant for something more. It was as if she was standing at the edge of a vast ocean, her toes just touching the water, hesitant yet curious to dive into its depths.

As the city lights twinkled outside her window, mirroring the stars above, Emily's thoughts wandered to the park where she found her moments of peace. It was there, amidst the rustling leaves and the gentle whispers of nature, that she felt a glimpse of the serenity she longed for. It was a serenity that seemed to beckon her, promising answers to the silent questions that echoed in her heart.

"In the heart of ceaseless motion, where does one find the stillness that echoes with true joy?"

In the heart of the city, amid the relentlessness of urban life, Emily Nguyen stood at the crossroads of existence and essence. Her life, externally, was a portrait of success - a well-paying job, a cozy apartment, and a social circle to fill her weekends. Yet, internally, it echoed with a profound sense of longing, a void that no amount of material success could fill.

Emily's days at the tech company were a whirlwind of coding and problem-solving, a digital ballet that she performed with both grace and precision. Each project was a puzzle, a challenge that stirred her intellect but seldom touched her heart. The glowing screen of her computer was a window to a world of logic and algorithms, but it offered no view to the horizons of her soul.

As she navigated through lines of code, Emily often found her thoughts drifting to existential questions. What was the purpose of her toils? Was there more to life than this endless cycle of deadlines and deliverables? In these moments of introspection, she felt a disconnect, a nagging sensation that she was skimming the surface of a much deeper existence.

This inner turmoil was a silent companion to her solitary evenings. Her apartment, a neatly arranged enclave in the towering complex, was both her refuge and her cage. The books that lined her shelves whispered tales of enlightenment and transcendence, speaking of realms beyond the tangible. They spoke of a joy and fulfillment that transcended worldly achievements, a state of being that Emily yearned to understand and experience.

Her interactions with friends, though warm and jovial, often left her feeling unfulfilled. Conversations that skimmed the surface of pleasantries and societal norms seemed like missed opportunities to delve into the profound mysteries of life. Emily longed for a connection that went beyond the mundane, a bond that touched the core of her being.

Her family, miles away, remained a reminder of a different life, one rooted in tradition and simplicity. Their loving voices over the phone were a comfort to her restless spirit, yet they also echoed the distance between her current world and the one she had left behind. The warmth of her mother's wisdom and her father's gentle guidance seemed like echoes from a distant shore, urging her to find her own path to fulfillment.

In moments of solitude, Emily often pondered the nature of happiness. Was it a fleeting moment of joy, or was it a deeper, more enduring state of contentment? The city, with its dazzling lights and endless hustle, seemed to equate happiness with success and possessions. But in the quiet of her heart, Emily sensed that true happiness lay in the realms of the spirit, in the unexplored depths of her own consciousness.

It was this spiritual void, this yearning for a deeper understanding of herself and the world, that lingered in her thoughts. Emily realized that her journey was not just one of career and social accomplishments, but also of self-discovery and spiritual exploration. She stood at the precipice of this realization, ready to embark on a journey that promised to bridge the gap between her external world and her inner longing. In this quest, she sought not just answers, but also the questions that would lead her to the essence of her being, to the heart of true happiness and fulfillment.

Traces of the Extraordinary
"Discovering the Footprints"

"In the city's awakening light, where does the ordinary reveal the dance of the extraordinary?"

As the first light of dawn crept into Emily's apartment, painting the room in a soft golden hue, she found herself waking earlier than usual. There was a newfound allure in these quiet hours, a peaceful solitude that the city's daytime bustle could never offer. She began to savor this time, sitting by the window with a cup of tea, watching as the world outside slowly stirred to life.

The light at dawn had a quality that Emily had never noticed before. It was gentle, transforming ordinary objects in her apartment into artworks of shadow and luminescence. The way it danced across the surface of her wooden table, the way it gave her potted plants a silhouette of intricate lace – these details, once overlooked in her morning rush, now captivated her.

This newfound appreciation for the simple beauty around her extended beyond the confines of her home. The city, which she had always navigated with a sense of purposeful haste, began to reveal its hidden rhythm to her. The streets became a canvas alive with the strokes of everyday life – the hurried steps of commuters, the rhythmic sway of trees lining the avenues, the fleeting smiles exchanged between strangers.

One such day, amidst the discord of urban life, Emily found herself drawn to a street musician. His guitar sang a melody that seemed to transcend the noise around them, weaving a moment of serenity. She paused, allowing herself to be enveloped by the music. It was in this simple pause that Emily realized how everyone in the city contributed to its vast, living ballet, each playing their part in an intricate dance of existence.

Her interactions, too, took on a new depth. The barista who greeted her each morning, the elderly neighbor who shared stories of his youth, the young artist painting murals in alleyways – they were no longer mere background characters in her life. They were fellow travelers, each with their own rich story, weaving the diverse tapestry of the city.

This shift in perspective was never more evident than during Emily's visit to the local park. The park was an oasis of tranquility, a stark contrast to the surrounding urban landscape. Here, nature thrived in harmony with the city's heartbeat. Emily walked along the winding paths, surrounded by the lush greenery, feeling the soft grass beneath her feet, inhaling the earthy scent of soil and leaves. The simplicity of nature, its effortless existence amidst the city's chaos, struck a chord within her.

As she sat by the pond, watching the ducks glide gracefully across the water, Emily felt a profound sense of peace. The park became a sanctuary where she could reflect and reconnect with herself. Nature's subtle beauty – the rustling of leaves, the dappled sunlight through the branches, the chorus of birds – spoke to her in a language beyond words, stirring a sense of wonder and curiosity about the world.

This newfound connection with nature and the beauty in everyday life began to influence Emily's interactions and thoughts. Conversations with her friends started to delve into deeper topics, exploring the essence of happiness, the pursuit of purpose, and the interconnectedness of all things. Even her work at the tech company took on new meaning as she began to see her projects as part of a larger picture, each line of code a thread in the digital fabric of human connection.

The transformation in Emily's life was subtle yet profound. She began to view her existence not as a series of isolated events but as part of a larger, interconnected whole. Her journey of mindfulness and observation was about finding beauty in the world around her; it was about understanding her place within it, about recognizing the shared humanity and the common thread that binds all life together.

In this journey, Emily found not just beauty and tranquility but also a deeper understanding of herself. As she navigated her days with a newfound awareness, she realized that the journey was just beginning. It was an ever-evolving path, leading her to new realizations, new experiences, and a deeper connection with the world around her. The city, once a place of noise and haste, had become a world of endless discovery, and Emily, with her awakened senses and open heart, was ready to explore its every color and contour.

"In the city's dawn, where does the mundane reveal the rhythm of a deeper harmony?"

Emily Nguyen's world, once defined by the strict rhythm of a software developer's life in the bustling city, began to unfold into something richer, more textured. Each morning, as she woke to the tender embrace of dawn, her apartment bathed in a soft, golden light, Emily felt a burgeoning connection to the world, a sense of wonder that reached beyond the confines of her usual routine.

The once overlooked details of her surroundings began to captivate her. The way light played on the leaves of her potted fern, casting delicate shadows on the wall, seemed like an intricate dance of nature and urban life. The early morning sounds of the city, from the distant hum of traffic to the muffled footsteps of early risers in the hallway, composed a symphony that spoke of life's continuous ebb and flow.

On her way to work, Emily's senses were heightened. The city, once a backdrop to her focused mind, now engaged her in a different way. She noticed the varied portrait of faces in the subway, each carrying a story untold. The street vendors, with their colorful arrays of goods, no longer blurred into the periphery of her vision; they were vibrant characters in the city's dynamic narrative.

This shift in perception was nowhere more evident than in her interactions at her tech company. Colleagues who had once been mere co-workers began to emerge as individuals with unique aspirations and struggles. Conversations by the vending machine evolved from discussions about deadlines and code to reflections on life's bigger questions. Even in meetings, Emily found herself considering not just the project at hand, but the larger impact of their work on society.

One day, during lunch, Emily opted for a solitary walk in the nearby park, a verdant oasis within the city's concrete expanse. As she sat on a bench, observing the effortless flight of birds and the playful squirrels, she realized how much of life she had missed in her previous haste. Nature, with its unassuming beauty and rhythm, offered a stark contrast to the artificial urgency of her previous existence.

This connection to nature ignited a curiosity about the philosophical underpinnings of existence. Emily found herself pondering the teachings of Thich Nhat Hanh and Alan Watts, drawing parallels between their insights and her own experiences. Her mind, once occupied with code and algorithms, now delved into thoughts about mindfulness, interconnectedness, and the essence of being.

This inner transformation began to influence her relationships. Conversations with friends took on new depths. Emily found herself sharing her observations and listening more intently to their experiences. Even her weekly calls with her family became more meaningful, as she started to appreciate the nuances of their lives and words.

As Emily embraced this new way of seeing the world, she encountered moments of dissonance. Balancing her newfound mindfulness with the demands of her tech career, and reconciling her inner changes with her existing relationships, presented complex puzzles. But these challenges only deepened her resolve to explore this path.

In the evenings, as she reflected on her day, Emily felt a sense of fulfillment that had eluded her before. Her life was becoming an embroidery of experiences, each thread woven with the colors of awareness and discovery. The city, once a place of routine, had transformed into a landscape rich with potential for growth and understanding.

As she journeyed forward, Emily realized that this was just the beginning of a much larger exploration, one that promised to lead her to new horizons of understanding and being. The world around her, once familiar, now held a promise of new insights and revelations. In this journey, she was not just a passive observer, but an active participant in the unfolding story of her life, a life that was becoming a beautiful blend of the mundane and the profound, the logical and the philosophical.

"In the silent awakening of dawn, what truths are whispered to the observer in the city's embrace?"

In the gentle embrace of the morning, Emily found a new rhythm to her life. Awakened by the first rays of the sun, she lay in bed for a few moments, watching the golden light creep across her room, transforming the familiar into something otherworldly. It was as if the dawn whispered secrets in a language only understood by those willing to listen in these quiet hours.

Her apartment, perched high above the slumbering city, became her sanctuary during these mindful mornings. She observed the play of light on the walls, creating patterns that changed with the progression of the sun. The shadows moved like silent companions, telling stories in their dance across the room. Emily found beauty in these simple phenomena, a beauty she had overlooked in the haste of her previous routines.

As the city slowly rumbled to life below, Emily sat by her window, cradling a warm cup of tea. She watched the streets awaken, the early risers beginning their day. The distant sounds of traffic, the muffled voices of pedestrians, and the occasional bark of a dog formed a backdrop to her thoughts. In these moments of solitude, she felt a deepening connection to the world outside her window, a world that was always there, but which she had seldom taken the time to truly observe.

This ritual of greeting the dawn became a sacred time for Emily. It was a period of reflection and anticipation, a time to gather her thoughts and set intentions for the day ahead. She noticed the subtle shifts in the quality of light as the seasons changed, each bringing its own mood and color to her morning vigil.

Emily discovered a space for introspection, a quiet corner in her mind where she could explore her thoughts and feelings without the distractions of her busy day. It was a time to be present, to live in the moment, fully aware of her surroundings and herself. This daily practice became the foundation of her journey towards mindfulness and self-discovery, a journey that transformed not just her mornings but her perception of life itself.

"In the symphony of the city's stride, where does the awakened step find the rhythm of stillness?"

As Emily ventured into the heart of the city each day, her commute transformed from a mundane routine into a journey of discovery. The city, with its pulsating energy became a living, breathing entity, its rhythm resonating with her newfound mindfulness.

Gone were the days when Emily would traverse the city streets with her eyes fixed on the ground, lost in her own thoughts. Now, she walked with a heightened sense of awareness, attuned to the life that thrived around her. The ebb and flow of pedestrians on the sidewalks turned into a graceful dance of humanity, each person contributing to the fluid motion of the crowd.

The sounds of the city, once a background noise to be drowned out, now formed a symphony that captivated her. The rhythmic tapping of shoes on concrete, the distant hum of traffic, the sudden laughter from a group of friends – all these sounds merged into a melody that told the story of the city. Street musicians, with their guitars and violins, added layers of harmony to this urban orchestra. Emily found herself pausing to listen, appreciating the talent and passion that turned street corners into stages.

Even the snippets of conversation that floated to her ears as she passed by people became intriguing glimpses into the lives of strangers. These overheard dialogues – a couple planning their day, a businessman on a phone call, a group of students discussing their studies – were like pieces of a puzzle, each offering a hint of the diverse stories that composed the song of the city.

Emily's daily commute became an exploration of the city's rhythm. She noticed the subtle changes as the day progressed – the brisk, purposeful pace of the morning, the leisurely stroll of the afternoon, and the relaxed saunter of the evening. Each phase of the day brought its own tempo, its own character to the streets she walked.

This newfound connection to the city's rhythm deepened Emily's appreciation for her urban surroundings. She began to see the beauty in the chaos, the harmony in the disorder. The city, once a place she navigated with indifference, now fascinated her with its complexity and vitality.

Through this daily immersion in the city's rhythm, Emily learned to find tranquility in the hustle, to appreciate the individual stories that played out around her, and to embrace the energy of the urban landscape. Her journey through the city streets became a reflection of her journey within, each step an opportunity to connect with the world in a more meaningful, more mindful way.

"Amidst the city's many faces, where does one encounter the mirror of shared existence?"

As Emily navigated the lively streets of the city, her journey of self-discovery intertwined with the myriad lives around her. The people she encountered, once mere passersby in the urban landscape, now piqued her curiosity and compassion. Each face in the crowd, each fleeting interaction, was a rich expression of human experience.

The morning barista, who greeted her with a warm, familiar smile, became more than just a dispenser of caffeine. He was an artist in his own right, crafting each cup with care and precision. Emily noticed the small details – the way his eyes lit up when discussing his favorite blends, the pride he took in perfecting the swirls of milk in a latte. His cheerful demeanor was a daily reminder of the joy found in simple pleasures and the artistry present in everyday life.

On her walks, Emily often passed an elderly man in the square, surrounded by a flurry of pigeons. He was a constant in the ever-changing scene, a serene figure amid the city's hustle. The birds flocked to him, drawn by the gentle rhythm of his hand as he scattered breadcrumbs. Watching him, Emily was struck by the peaceful coexistence of man and nature within the urban chaos. He seemed to exist in a world of his own, a world that Emily found herself longing to understand.

These encounters with strangers sparked a deeper reflection in Emily. She began to ponder the lives of those she met, each person carrying their own story, their own joys, and struggles. The city, she realized, was a living tale, and each person she encountered was a character with their own unique plotline.

Even brief exchanges – a shared smile with a fellow commuter, a quick chat with a vendor at the market, a polite nod to a neighbor – took on new significance. These were not just perfunctory interactions; they were connections, however brief, that wove the fabric of community and shared existence.

Emily's growing interest in the people around her led her to become more present in her interactions. She listened more attentively, observed more keenly, and engaged more openly. With each encounter, she gained a deeper appreciation for the diversity of human experience – the myriad ways in which people navigated the complexities of life.

Through these encounters with strangers, Emily's journey of mindfulness expanded beyond her own inner world. She began to see herself as part of a larger whole, a participant in the collective dance of humanity. Each person she met, each story she glimpsed, added depth to her understanding of the world and her place in it. In the faces of strangers, she found reflections of herself – a shared humanity that transcended the boundaries of individual experience.

"Amidst the city's tumult, where does one hear the serene song of a hidden sanctuary?"

On a particularly energetic afternoon, when the city's relentless pace seemed overwhelming, Emily sought peace in her nearby park. Stepping into this grassy sanctuary, she felt as though she had crossed an invisible threshold, leaving behind the harshness of urban life for a haven of natural tranquility.

The park was an oasis within the concrete and steel. Tall trees stood like sentinels, their leaves rustling softly in the gentle breeze. The air here was fresher, imbued with the earthy scent of grass and soil, a stark contrast to the exhaust fumes of the city. As Emily walked along a winding path, the soft crunch of gravel under her shoes provided a soothing rhythm to her thoughts.

She found a secluded spot, a little nook where the canopy of trees opened to the sky above. Settling onto the lush grass, Emily closed her eyes for a moment, letting the sun's warmth kiss her face. The sounds of the park were a symphony of nature; birds chirping in a melodious conversation, the distant laughter of children playing, the whisper of leaves in the breeze. It was as if each element of nature was performing its part in perfect harmony.

Opening her eyes, Emily watched the play of light and shadow created by the trees. The branches swayed gracefully, giving shape to the wind. She observed the squirrels as they scurried about, the effortless flight of a butterfly, and the serene glide of ducks across the pond. In these simple acts of nature, she found a profound beauty and a sense of peace that she had seldom felt during her daily routine.

This connection with nature, in the heart of the lively city, became a profound experience for Emily. It was a reminder of the serenity that existed beneath the surface of everyday life, a tranquility that could be found in the simplest of moments. The park became a mirror reflecting the calmness she sought within herself, a physical manifestation of the peace that comes with being present in the moment.

As Emily sat there, absorbing the sights and sounds of the park, she felt a deepening of the mindfulness she had been cultivating. The tranquility of nature provided a backdrop against which she could observe her thoughts and emotions, allowing them to flow through her like the breeze around her.

This moment in the park marked a turning point in Emily's journey. It underscored the importance of finding balance in life's chaos and the necessity of reconnecting with nature to find inner peace. The park, with its gentle reminder of the world's natural beauty and rhythm, became a sanctuary she would return to, a place where she could recharge and find clarity.

In the tranquility of this urban oasis, Emily found an escape from the hustle and bustle of city life, but also a deeper connection to the world around her. It was a connection that nurtured her soul, reminding her of the beauty and peace that lay waiting to be discovered in the ordinary moments of life.

"In the city's green embrace, where does the seeker find the echo of her true self?"

The afternoons Emily spent in the park became more than just fleeting escapes; it marked a significant turning point in her journey. The tranquility she found there awakened a deep longing within her – a yearning to reconnect with the natural world and discover the serenity it offered. This experience ignited a transformation in her, as she began to seek out these pockets of nature within the city's concrete landscape.

Emily's weekends, previously occupied with the routine errands and occasional social gatherings, now included regular pilgrimages to various green spaces around the city. She explored hidden gardens, quiet riverbanks, and even small patches of wilderness that defied the urban sprawl. Each location offered a unique experience of nature's beauty and breathing room from the relentless pace of her daily life.

In these natural settings, Emily found a profound sense of peace. Sitting under the shade of a tree, watching the sunlight filter through the leaves, she felt a connection to something larger than herself. The rhythmic rustling of foliage, the gentle flow of water, and the distant call of birds allowed her to tune into a frequency of life that was more subtle, yet more profound than anything she had experienced in her urban routine.

These moments of solitude and reflection became sacred to Emily. With her phone tucked away, she was free from the constant barrage of notifications and the urge to be perpetually connected. Nature's presence became a relief from the noise and distractions that often filled her life. In the stillness, Emily discovered the space to breathe, to think, and to simply be.

Her forays into nature also deepened her mindfulness practice. She became more attuned to her senses – the feel of the earth beneath her, the scent of blooming flowers, the kaleidoscope of colors in the sunset. This sensory immersion brought a heightened awareness of the present moment, each detail a reminder of the world's inherent wonder.

Emily's curiosity and sense of wonder about the world were rekindled in these natural havens. She began to read more about the flora and fauna of her region, the ecosystems of the parks she visited, and the environmental challenges facing these green spaces. Her relationship with nature evolved from one of passive enjoyment to active engagement and learning.

The impact of these experiences extended beyond the moments spent in nature. Back in her apartment, surrounded by the artifacts of her urban life, Emily found herself more centered and grounded. The lessons learned in the quiet company of trees and rivers – patience, resilience, the importance of harmony – began to influence her approach to life's challenges.

This reconnection with nature became a vital part of Emily's journey of self-discovery. It was a catalyst that provided an escape from the stress of her daily life and a lens through which she could view the world with a new perspective. In nature, Emily found tranquility and beauty along with a deeper understanding of herself and her place in the world.

"In the city's quiet corners, how does one light the lantern of wisdom from another's flame?"

Emily, her steps light and purposeful, made her way across the busy street to Mrs. Kaur's apartment building. The air was tinged with the crispness of early fall, carrying with it the promise of change.

As she entered the lobby, Emily's thoughts were a blend of anticipation and the normal hum of everyday concerns. She had volunteered to help Mrs. Kaur with her groceries, a small gesture of kindness towards her elderly neighbor, who had always greeted her with a warm smile.

Ascending the stairs, Emily balanced the grocery bags with an ease born of a routine that had become familiar over the past few weeks. Reaching Mrs. Kaur's door, she knocked gently, the sound echoing in the hallway. The door opened, revealing Mrs. Kaur, her face creasing into a welcoming smile that seemed to light up the dimly lit corridor.

"Ah, Emily, thank you, dear," Mrs. Kaur said, her voice rich with a warmth that immediately put Emily at ease. As Emily stepped into the apartment, she was enveloped by an air of tranquility that seemed to permeate the space. The apartment was a sea of colors, adorned with artifacts and books that spoke of a life rich in experiences and wisdom.

As they began to unpack the groceries, a conversation unfolded naturally between them. Mrs. Kaur's questions were simple yet insightful, gently probing into Emily's life and interests. It was during this exchange that Emily's curiosity about spirituality came to light, a topic that seemed to spark a special interest in Mrs. Kaur.

"You know, Emily, spirituality is not just about seeking—it's about discovering what's already within us," Mrs. Kaur said, her eyes reflecting a depth of knowledge and experience.

Emily, placing a can of soup on the shelf, paused, and turned to Mrs. Kaur. "I've always felt like there's something more, something deeper to understand about life. But I don't really know where to start," she confessed, her voice tinged with a mix of hesitation and earnestness.

Mrs. Kaur nodded, a gentle smile playing on her lips. "The journey of self-discovery is a beautiful one, and it's unique for each of us. I've walked that path for many years, and perhaps, if you'd like, I could share some of what I've learned."

The offer hung in the air, a bridge extending towards Emily, inviting her to embark on a journey that could transform her understanding of herself and the world. In Mrs. Kaur's offer, there was a promise of guidance, of shared wisdom from a life lived in pursuit of spiritual understanding.

As they continued to chat, arranging the groceries in a rhythmic dance of familiarity, the seeds of a deeper relationship were sown. In Mrs. Kaur, Emily found not just a neighbor but a potential mentor, someone who could guide her through the uncharted territories of her own spirit.

The afternoon sun cast a soft glow through the kitchen window, bathing the room in a golden light. In that light, the beginnings of a profound bond shimmered—a bond that promised to unlock doors to new realms of understanding and growth for Emily. This moment marked the start of a journey, for both of them, as teacher and student, mentor, and mentee, bound together by a shared quest for something greater than themselves.

"As tea steeps in ancient cups, how does the seeker's path unfold in the mentor's tales?"

The invitation to Mrs. Kaur's for tea felt like a gentle beckoning into a world unknown, a world that Emily had only begun to glimpse through her recent encounters and curiosities. As she made her way to Mrs. Kaur's apartment, a mingling sense of anticipation and nervousness fluttered within her. The hallway, with its familiar aged carpet and the hum of the city beyond the windows, seemed to resonate with her steps, leading her to a door that opened to realms yet unexplored.

Mrs. Kaur welcomed her with the warmth that Emily had come to associate with her – a warmth that seemed to emanate from a life richly lived and deeply understood. The apartment, a cozy enclave nestled amidst the bustling cityscape, was infused with an aura of tranquility. The walls were adorned with tapestries depicting mystical landscapes, and the shelves were lined with books whose spines bore the names of philosophers and sages.

As they settled into the comfortable cushions by the low tea table, a sense of peace enveloped Emily. The tea, aromatic and soothing, seemed to transcend its physical warmth, radiating a comfort that eased her into the conversation.

Mrs. Kaur began to share her journey, her voice a gentle stream winding through the years of her explorations. She spoke of the early days of her quest, filled with curiosity and a thirst for understanding the deeper truths of existence. Her path had meandered through various philosophies and spiritual practices – from the ancient wisdom of the East to the contemplative traditions of the West, each step a chapter in the larger story of her life.

Emily listened, captivated. The stories were chronicles of places and teachings; they were imbued with the struggles and revelations that had shaped Mrs. Kaur's understanding. She talked of moments of doubt, of profound insights, and of the peace that comes with true acceptance. It was a wealth of experiences, rich with the hues of joy, sorrow, and ultimately, enlightenment.

As Mrs. Kaur described her experiences with meditation, yoga, and other spiritual practices, Emily's world expanded. She realized the vastness of the spiritual landscape, a territory as diverse in its paths as it was unified in its ultimate pursuit. The conversation was an unfolding of wisdom, the passing of a torch from one seeker to another.

In Mrs. Kaur's stories, Emily found mirrors of her own questions and yearnings. The dialogue drifted seamlessly from anecdotes to deeper philosophical discussions, exploring themes of consciousness, purpose, and the interconnectedness of all life. It was as if each story, each philosophical musing, was a thread pulling Emily deeper into her own spiritual journey.

As the evening waned and the room grew dim, only illuminated by the soft glow of the setting sun, a profound sense of gratitude filled Emily. She had come seeking knowledge, but she found more – a mentor, a guide, and a friend in Mrs. Kaur. This meeting a sharing of wisdom was the beginning of a journey, a journey that promised to take Emily beyond the horizons of her current understanding, into a world where every experience, every encounter, was a step towards a greater awakening.

"Amidst the city's endless whisper, how does the seeker's silent breath unfold the map of now?"

Nestled within the walls of Mrs. Kaur's apartment, a new chapter was about to unfold in Emily's journey. The room, bathed in the soft, amber glow of the late afternoon sun, provided a tranquil backdrop to what would be Emily's first foray into the world of meditation.

Mrs. Kaur, with the ease of a seasoned teacher, began to introduce Emily to the basics of meditation. Her voice was soft yet clear, like a gentle stream flowing over smooth stones, as she explained the essence of meditation – not as an escape from reality but as a deeper immersion into it.

"Meditation is about being fully present," Mrs. Kaur said, her eyes reflecting a calm that seemed to transcend the ordinary. "It's about experiencing this moment, fully and without distraction."

As Emily listened, she could feel the weight of her daily concerns begin to lift slightly, as if the very act of listening was preparing her for the journey inward. Mrs. Kaur guided her to a comfortable sitting position, encouraging her to find a posture that was both relaxed and alert.

"Let's begin with your breath," Mrs. Kaur instructed. "Focus on the natural flow of your breath. Feel it enter your body, filling you with life, and then leave, taking with it what is no longer needed."

Emily closed her eyes, her body still, her mind initially restless with the remnants of her day. She focused on her breathing, following the rise and fall of her chest, the air moving in and out of her nostrils. Slowly, the external noises – the distant hum of traffic, the muffled footsteps in the hallway – began to fade into the background.

As she breathed, Emily's mind began to settle. Thoughts continued to drift in and out, but she found herself less attached to them, more willing to let them go and return her focus to her breath. It was a feeling of coming home, a return to a state of being rather than doing.

Mrs. Kaur's voice gently guided her through the session, her words encouragement in the unfamiliar territory of Emily's inner landscape. "Allow yourself to be here, in this moment. Nothing to fix, nothing to change. Just be."

The session continued, time blurring as Emily dove deeper into the practice. When Mrs. Kaur finally signaled the end of the meditation, Emily opened her eyes, feeling as though she had awakened from a deep and restorative sleep. The room looked the same, yet everything felt subtly different – clearer, more vivid.

In those moments of meditation, Emily had touched something profound within herself – a sense of peace and presence she had never known. Mrs. Kaur smiled at her, a knowing smile that spoke of her own journey through the realms of meditation.

As Emily left Mrs. Kaur's apartment that evening, stepping back into the rhythm of city life, she carried with her a newfound tool – a way to connect with the present moment, to find calm amid chaos. It was the beginning of a practice that would become a cornerstone of her spiritual journey, a practice that would teach her the art of presence, of living fully in the now.

This first meditation session was more than an introduction to a technique; it was an initiation into a new way of experiencing life. In the stillness of meditation, Emily had found a gateway to a deeper understanding of herself and the world around her.

"As leaves drift on the city's hidden stream, where does the mind's quiet water reflect the unspoken truth?"

Within the harshness of daily life, a sanctuary of calm and understanding was taking shape. Emily's meetings with Mrs. Kaur had become a much-anticipated part of her routine, a time when the world's relentless pace seemed to slow, allowing her to dig into the realm of mindfulness.

Mrs. Kaur's apartment was a place that felt detached from the noise outside. The apartment, with its warm hues and soft lighting, exuded a sense of tranquility. Each session began with the ritual of brewing tea, the fragrant aroma filling the room, setting a tone of serenity.

As they settled into their comfortable seats, the outside world seemed to fade away, leaving only the space that they shared. Mrs. Kaur, with the patience and wisdom of a seasoned guide, introduced Emily to various mindfulness techniques. Each technique was a tool, aiding Emily in navigating the landscapes of her mind and the complexities of her daily life.

One of the key practices they explored was the observation of thoughts. Mrs. Kaur taught Emily to view her thoughts as if they were leaves floating down a stream – present, acknowledged, but not obstructing the flow of water. This metaphor resonated with Emily, helping her understand the transient nature of thoughts.

"Let them come and let them go," Mrs. Kaur would say gently. "Observe them without attachment or judgment. They are not you; they are merely passing through."

This practice brought a profound change in Emily. She learned to sit quietly, observing her thoughts as they arose and faded. With time, the critical voices in her head – the ones that had always been so quick to judge and analyze – began to quieten. In their place grew a newfound sense of peace and acceptance.

Mrs. Kaur also guided Emily in becoming more aware of her surroundings. They practiced mindfulness exercises that heightened Emily's senses, making her acutely aware of the present moment. The texture of the cushion beneath her, the subtle play of light on the walls, the distant hum of city life – all became vivid and alive.

During these sessions, Mrs. Kaur and Emily often engaged in philosophical discussions about mindfulness. They explored its roots in ancient wisdom traditions and its relevance in contemporary life. These discussions were explorations of life itself, of how to live deeply and meaningfully.

As Emily incorporated these mindfulness practices into her daily life, she noticed a shift in her interactions and experiences. She approached her work with greater focus and less stress. Her conversations with friends and family became more genuine and present. Even in moments of solitude, she found joy in the simple act of being.

In these regular meetings with Mrs. Kaur, Emily was not just learning techniques; she was undergoing a transformation. Mindfulness was becoming an integral part of her existence, changing the way she perceived herself and the world around her. It was as if she was learning a new language – the language of the present moment, of awareness and acceptance.

Each session with Mrs. Kaur was a step on Emily's journey to inner peace and understanding. In the haven of Mrs. Kaur's apartment, with the aroma of tea and the wisdom of ages, Emily was finding her path, learning to navigate life with a calm and mindful heart.

"In the dance of the bustling city, can one still trace the fragrance of tranquility?"

In the tranquility of Mrs. Kaur's apartment, surrounded by an array of plants that thrived in the sunlit space, Emily found herself within another transformative session. The gentle aroma of jasmine tea lingered in the air, a soothing backdrop to their profound dialogues.

"So, Emily, how have you been feeling since our last session?" Mrs. Kaur asked, her voice always infused with a comforting warmth.

Emily paused, reflecting. "I've been feeling... more present, I guess. It's like I'm seeing the world a bit more clearly." She traced the rim of her teacup thoughtfully with her finger. "But I'm also realizing how often I'm not present, how easily my mind wanders."

Mrs. Kaur nodded sagely. "That's the first step, noticing. With mindfulness, we begin to see the patterns of our mind. It's not about stopping thoughts but learning to observe them without getting swept away."

Emily's mind turned inward, recalling instances from the past week. Scenes flickered through her consciousness - a stressful meeting at work, a quiet evening walk, a laughter-filled call with her sister. She saw them all through a new lens, noticing her reactions and emotions with a detachment she hadn't possessed before.

"It's like I'm learning to watch my life as it happens, rather than just being caught up in it," Emily mused aloud.

"Exactly," Mrs. Kaur replied, smiling. "You're becoming an observer of your life. This detachment doesn't mean you care less. On the contrary, it allows you to engage more fully, without the clutter of unnecessary thoughts and emotions."

As they delved deeper into their conversation, Emily felt layers of understanding unfold within her. Mrs. Kaur's words were gateways to self-discovery. The room, with its comforting ambiance and the soft light filtering through the curtains, seemed to cocoon them in a world set apart from the chaos outside.

"Sometimes, I find it hard to maintain this awareness," Emily confessed. "The world is so... busy. It's easy to get lost in the noise."

Mrs. Kaur's eyes twinkled with empathy. "The world will always be busy. The key is to find your center amid that noise. Meditation and mindfulness are not practices for isolation; they're tools to navigate the bustle of everyday life with a calm and centered mind."

Emily's thoughts wandered to her recent struggles at work, the conflicts, and the high demands. She realized that these challenges were not just obstacles but opportunities to apply her new understanding. Each difficulty was a chance to practice patience, compassion, and detachment.

As their session ended, Emily felt a renewed sense of purpose. The insights gained here were more than philosophical concepts; they were practical tools for daily living. She thanked Mrs. Kaur, feeling a deep gratitude for this journey they were on together.

Leaving the apartment, Emily stepped back into the rhythm of the city. The sounds of traffic, the rush of people, the vibrant chaos of life - they all greeted her. But now, she faced them with a different perspective, armed with tools to find peace within the pandemonium, to find clarity amidst the confusion.

In her journey with Mrs. Kaur, Emily was not only learning about mindfulness; she was learning about life. Each step, each revelation, was a piece in the puzzle of her existence, helping her to piece together a picture of who she was and who she could become.

"As infinite echoes weave the tapestry, can a single thread discern its own melody in the symphony of existence?"

In the sanctuary of Mrs. Kaur's living room, surrounded by walls lined with books that seemed to whisper the secrets of the ages, Emily found herself eagerly diving into another realm of her spiritual journey. The book that lay open between them, "Echoes of the Infinite," had become a catalyst for deep philosophical discussions that transcended the boundaries of ordinary conversation.

As they reached into the pages, each chapter provoked thoughts and questions, unraveling the complex knots of spiritual wisdom. The book, a collection of teachings from various traditions, offered a kaleidoscope of perspectives that both challenged and expanded Emily's understanding.

"Mrs. Kaur, this chapter here," Emily pointed to a passage about the interconnectedness of all beings, her finger tracing the lines. "It speaks of the universe as an intricate web where every action affects the whole. How do we reconcile this with our individual experiences?"

Mrs. Kaur sipped her tea thoughtfully, her eyes reflecting a depth of knowledge forged by years of introspection. "Our individual experiences are like threads in that web, Emily. Each one unique but part of a larger pattern. The beauty of it is in the diversity of these threads, each contributing to the strength and beauty of the whole."

The conversation flowed touching upon concepts of destiny, free will, and the nature of consciousness. Mrs. Kaur shared insights from her own journey, intertwining them with the teachings from the book. Her words were invitations for Emily to explore and reflect.

Emily's mind was alight with questions and revelations. The discussions peeled back layers of her preconceived notions, exposing her to new ways of seeing the world. "And what about suffering?" she asked, a question that had long lingered in her mind. "Is it just an inevitable part of this interconnectedness?"

"Suffering is often where we find our deepest lessons," Mrs. Kaur responded gently. "It's not about seeking it out, but about how we respond to it. It's in those moments of challenge that our true strength and resilience are revealed."

As they talked, the room seemed to become a space out of time, a place where philosophical explorations brought them face to face with life's profound mysteries. The dialogues were deeply personal, each concept a mirror reflecting Emily's own experiences and inner transformations.

In these sessions, Emily found herself not only learning but evolving. Her worldview shifted with each discussion, each insight shedding light on her path. The book, with its diverse teachings, served as a map, guiding her through the complex terrain of spirituality.

The discussions with Mrs. Kaur also deepened their bond. In the sharing of wisdom and exploration of ideas, a unique friendship flourished, one rooted in mutual respect and a shared quest for understanding.

As Emily left Mrs. Kaur's apartment after each session, she carried with her more than just the knowledge from their discussions. She carried a sense of being part of something larger, a feeling of connection to the infinite.

The book "Echoes of the Infinite" and her discussions with Mrs. Kaur became touchstones in Emily's journey, anchors that she would return to time and again as she navigated the ebbs and flows of her spiritual exploration. In those pages, and in the wisdom shared between them, lay the echoes of truth, resonating with the very core of her being.

"In the city's dance, where each step weaves the ordinary with the extraordinary, can the soul hear the infinite's whisper amidst the mundane melody?"

The teachings of "Echoes of the Infinite" and the wisdom imparted by Mrs. Kaur began to weave their way into the fabric of Emily's daily life, transforming it in subtle yet profound ways. Each day became a chance for her to apply these newfound insights, turning routine moments into opportunities for growth and reflection.

As Emily navigated the city streets on her way to work, she found herself observing the world with a renewed sense of awareness. The noise of the city, once a mere backdrop to her hurried steps, now played a symphony of life that she engaged with more deeply. She saw the interconnectedness in the flow of people, the rhythm of traffic, and the dance of leaves in the wind – all parts of a greater whole.

In the office, where deadlines and demands had once stirred a sea of stress, Emily now found a space for calm and composed action. She approached her tasks with mindfulness, focusing fully on the task at hand, her mind less cluttered with the anxieties of past and future. Her interactions with colleagues, too, were infused with a new level of patience and understanding.

Conversations with her team, which often treaded the delicate line between professional and personal, were now navigated with a clarity that stemmed from her deeper understanding of human emotions and motivations. She found herself listening more intently, responding to words, and to the unspoken feelings behind them.

The teachings from the book had introduced her to the concept of impermanence, a theme that resonated strongly with her. This understanding allowed her to view challenges and successes at work as transient experiences in her larger journey. This perspective brought a sense of liberation and peace, freeing her from the weight of attaching her identity solely to her achievements.

Emily's internal dialogues, once a battleground of self-doubt and criticism, began to shift. She learned to observe her thoughts with detachment, recognizing them as fleeting clouds in the vast sky of her consciousness. This practice of self-observation led to a greater sense of inner harmony and self-acceptance.

Even her personal relationships began to reflect this change. Conversations with friends and family took on a new depth, as Emily brought an authentic presence to these interactions. She shared her experiences and learnings from the book and her sessions with Mrs. Kaur, sparking meaningful dialogues and mutual growth.

In moments of solitude, Emily reflected on her journey, acknowledging the transformation she was undergoing. She realized that the teachings were not just philosophical concepts to be understood but living truths to be embodied. Each day was an opportunity to practice compassion, mindfulness, and gratitude – the core principles that now guided her life.

As she walked through the park, where her journey of self-discovery had gained momentum, Emily felt a profound connection to everything around her. The rustling leaves, the chirping birds, and the gentle breeze seemed to echo the truths she was learning. It was here, amidst the simplicity of nature, that she found a mirror reflecting her inner transformation.

In this journey of applying the teachings to her life, Emily discovered that the path to peace and clarity was not found in escaping the world, but in engaging with it more consciously, more wholly. She understood that true wisdom was not just in knowing, but in living – in turning the knowledge into action, the insights into experiences.

As she continued to integrate these teachings into her life, Emily became witness to the transformative power of spiritual wisdom. Her journey was not just about personal enlightenment but about bringing that light into the everyday world, illuminating the paths of those she touched with her presence and her story.

"Is the observer who ventures into the depths of consciousness the wave or the ocean itself?"

The journey of self-discovery, once embarked upon, has a way of unfolding in layers, each revealing deeper truths and more profound insights. This was the path Emily found herself traversing, guided by Mrs. Kaur's seasoned wisdom. As her understanding deepened, the practices that once seemed merely exercises transformed into vital components of her daily life.

In the quiet sanctum of Mrs. Kaur's apartment, where time seemed to pause and the outside world faded into a distant hum, Emily sat in eager anticipation. The air was suffused with a sense of tranquility, accentuated by the gentle aroma of incense that Mrs. Kaur had lit, creating an ambiance conducive to deeper exploration.

"Today, we'll delve into a practice that goes beyond the surface," Mrs. Kaur began, her voice soft yet carrying an undercurrent of excitement. "It's about connecting with the essence of your being, the very core of who you are."

Emily listened intently, her heart beating with a mix of curiosity and reverence. The journey so far had been transformative, and she was ready to dive deeper, to explore the realms that lay beyond her current understanding.

Mrs. Kaur guided her through a meditation that was more intricate than any they had practiced before. It was a journey inward, a voyage to the depths of her consciousness. Emily focused on her breath, allowing it to be the anchor that kept her grounded as she ventured into the uncharted territories of her mind.

As she meditated, Emily felt layers of her consciousness peel away. Thoughts and worries that usually clouded her mind began to dissipate, revealing a serene expanse beneath. It was a space of profound stillness, yet alive with a subtle energy that pulsed in harmony with the rhythm of existence.

Mrs. Kaur's voice seemed to float to her from a great distance, a gentle guide in this inner exploration. "Allow yourself to be present with whatever arises. Observe it, but don't attach to it. You are not your thoughts; you are the observer of your thoughts."

In this space, Emily encountered emotions and memories, each surfacing and then drifting away like clouds in a vast sky. She witnessed them with a newfound detachment, understanding their transient nature. This process was not only an exercise in mindfulness; it was a profound encounter with the essence of her being.

The session concluded, but the sense of deep peace lingered. Emily opened her eyes, feeling as if she had returned from a long journey. The room, the familiar objects around her, everything seemed imbued with a new clarity, as if she was seeing them for the first time.

"Thank you," Emily said, her voice infused with genuine gratitude. "I feel like I've discovered a new part of myself."

Mrs. Kaur smiled, her eyes reflecting the joy of a teacher witnessing a student's growth. "That's the beauty of these practices, Emily. They reveal to us the depths of our own being, depths we never knew existed."

As Emily continued to explore these advanced practices, she found them becoming an integral part of her growth and wellbeing. These techniques were pathways to self-discovery, tools that helped her navigate the complexities of life with greater ease and understanding.

The journey with Mrs. Kaur had started as a quest for knowledge, but it had become so much more. It was a journey of transformation, of awakening to the deeper truths of existence. In this journey, Emily found peace and clarity along with the connection to a part of herself that was eternal and unchanging, a connection to the infinite.

Challenges

"As dawn whispers to the bustling city, why does the quest for silence awaken the mind's loudest symphony?"

In her modest apartment, Emily embarked on her maiden journey into the world of meditation. Inspired by Mrs. Kaur's teachings and armed with a burgeoning enthusiasm, she was ready to explore the realms of inner peace and mindfulness.

Settling onto a cushion in a quiet corner of her room, Emily attempted to emulate the serene posture Mrs. Kaur had shown her. She closed her eyes, inhaled deeply, and exhaled, expecting to slip into a state of tranquility. However, as minutes ticked by, she found her mind buzzing with relentless thoughts.

There was a constant stream of to-dos, memories of yesterday's meeting, plans for the day ahead, a grocery list – each thought vying for her attention, refusing to be stilled. Emily's brow furrowed in frustration as her initial excitement about meditation gave way to a sense of inadequacy. "Why can't I quiet my mind?" she thought, her heartbeat syncing with the rhythm of her racing thoughts.

Each time she attempted to focus on her breath, her mind wandered, leading her down a rabbit hole of endless mental chatter. The tranquility and focus that Mrs. Kaur had described seemed like distant, unattainable concepts. Emily's initial enthusiasm wavered under the weight of her struggle, leaving her feeling disheartened.

After several attempts, Emily opened her eyes, the light of the morning now fully illuminating her room. She gazed out of her window, watching the city awaken, its pace a mirror to the turmoil within her. A sense of irony struck her – here she was, seeking inner peace in a world that never paused, never quieted.

Emily's thoughts continued, a blend of self-criticism and determination. "Is this how it's supposed to be? Am I doing something wrong?" she pondered. The disappointment of not meeting her own expectations was exhausting.

Later that day, she shared her experience with Mrs. Kaur over a phone call. "It's like my mind has a mind of its own," Emily said, half-jokingly, yet revealing her inner turmoil.

Mrs. Kaur's voice, soothing and understanding, came through the phone. "What you're experiencing is completely normal, Emily. Meditation isn't about silencing your mind on the first try. It's about learning to observe without judgment, to be patient with yourself. The calm will come, give it time."

These words gave some relief to Emily's restless spirit. The realization that this was part of the process, that struggle was a steppingstone to mastery, rekindled her resolve.

Encouraged by Mrs. Kaur's reassurance, Emily continued her practice in the following days. Each session was a battle between expectation and experience, between her desire for instant peace and the reality of her untamed thoughts. Yet, with each attempt, she learned a little more about patience, about accepting her mind's wanderings as part of the journey.

In these early stages of her meditation practice, Emily learned lessons that transcended the act of meditation itself. She learned about the nuances of her mind, the importance of persistence, and the beauty of embracing imperfection. Each session, though fraught with challenge, was a step forward in her journey towards inner peace and self-understanding.

This journey, marked by initial struggles and eventual breakthroughs, reflected the very essence of personal growth – a path not of linear progression, but of falls and rises, of learning and unlearning. In the quiet corner of her room, within the chaos of her thoughts, Emily was not just meditating; she was evolving, one breath at a time.

"As morning light chases shadows, why does the mind's quest for quick calm stir deeper waves?"

As the days unfolded into weeks, Emily's journey into meditation and mindfulness was not marked by the serene progression she had envisioned, but by an internal struggle with her own impatience. Each session became a microcosm of this battle, a test of her resolve against the desire for immediate results.

The early morning light filtered softly through the curtains of her apartment, casting a gentle glow on the space where Emily sat in meditation. The tranquility of the scene belied the tumult within her as she attempted, once again, to still her restless mind.

"I should be better at this by now," Emily thought, her legs crossed and her hands resting lightly on her knees. The expectation of quick progress gnawed at her, feeding a growing sense of frustration. She inhaled deeply, trying to anchor herself to the present, but her mind rebelled, darting from one thought to another.

Her thoughts a constant commentary on her perceived lack of progress. "Why can't I do this? What am I missing?" The questions echoed in her mind, each one chipping away at her confidence. The calm and ease that Mrs. Kaur embodied during their sessions seemed like a distant reality, unattainable and elusive.

Later, while sharing her struggles with her friend Alex over coffee, Emily's words spilled out in a torrent of doubt and self-criticism. "I just can't seem to quiet my mind. Maybe this isn't for me," she confessed, her hands wrapped tightly around her cup.

Her friend offered a perspective that Emily hadn't considered. "Maybe it's not about mastering it quickly. Maybe it's more about the journey, about learning to be patient with yourself."

The words struck a chord in Emily. It dawned on her that her impatience reflected the very patterns of thought and behavior she was trying to understand and transform. She realized that the practice of meditation was not just about achieving a state of calm but also about confronting and understanding the layers of her psyche.

In her next session with Mrs. Kaur, Emily voiced her frustrations. Mrs. Kaur listened intently, a gentle smile playing on her lips. "Impatience is a common traveler on this path," she said. "But remember, the value of these practices lies in the journey, not just the destination. Each moment of struggle is as important as a moment of peace. It's all part of your growth."

Armed with this new understanding, Emily approached her meditation with a different mindset. She began to see each session not as a test of her ability to achieve tranquility but as an opportunity to observe and understand her mind's patterns. She learned to greet her thoughts and impatience with curiosity instead of judgment, observing them as they arose and gently guiding her focus back to her breath.

This shift in approach brought a subtle but significant change in Emily's practice. Though her mind still wandered, and moments of tranquility were fleeting, she found a new sense of peace in simply being present with whatever arose. The journey became less about reaching a state of perfect calm and more about embracing each moment, each breath, with mindfulness and patience.

In confronting her impatience, Emily discovered a profound lesson – that the path to inner peace was not linear, but a spiral journey of coming back to the present, again and again, each return deepening her understanding and acceptance. This realization marked a turning point in her journey, a step closer to the true essence of mindfulness and meditation.

"In the city's dance, where each step weaves the tapestry, can the seeker find stillness in motion?"

Emily faced the daunting task of weaving her newfound spiritual practices into the intricate tapestry of her daily routine. The days, brimming with the demands of her job and the whirl of social commitments, left her grappling with the challenge of carving out time for meditation and mindfulness.

Each morning, as the first rays of sunlight pierced through her bedroom window, Emily's alarm would beckon her to start her day. Lying in bed, she would mentally sift through the numerous tasks awaiting her – meetings, deadlines, emails, and social engagements. Within this mental checklist, she tried to slot in time for meditation, but the attempt often felt like trying to fit another piece into an already full puzzle.

At work, the constant buzz of activity and the pressure of expectations consumed her focus. The calm and clarity she sought through her spiritual practices seemed elusive in the face of relentless deadlines and the fast-paced rhythm of her professional environment.

Her lunch breaks were often spent in a flurry of activity, sometimes catching up on work or meeting friends. The moments she managed to steal for a brief meditation were frequently interrupted by the ping of a message or the buzz of her phone – reminders of the ever-present demands of her life.

In the evenings, Emily's social commitments – dinners with friends, family gatherings, or networking events – vied for her time. Though she cherished these moments, they left little room for the solitude and reflection her spiritual journey required.

The struggle to balance her responsibilities with her spiritual aspirations left Emily in a constant state of frustration. "How do I find balance? There's just not enough time," she would think, her mind racing as she lay awake in bed.

One evening, during a quiet dinner with her close friend Alex, Emily shared her struggles. "It feels like I'm trying to walk two paths at once," she said, her voice tinged with fatigue. "My job, my social life, my spiritual practice – I just can't seem to find the right balance."

Alex listened intently, then offered a perspective that struck a chord with Emily. "Maybe it's not about separating them. Perhaps it's about finding a way to integrate your practices into your daily life, making them a part of everything you do."

This conversation sparked a shift in Emily's approach. She began exploring ways to incorporate mindfulness into her everyday activities. Instead of viewing meditation as a separate task to be scheduled, she started using brief moments of her day for mindfulness – a few deep breaths before a meeting, a mindful walk during her lunch break, a moment of gratitude before meals.

She also started to set boundaries, prioritizing her need for personal time. Slowly, Emily found a rhythm that allowed her to blend her spiritual practices with her professional and social life. It wasn't a perfect balance, but it was a more harmonious integration of the different facets of her life.

There were days when her meditation was brief and unfocused, and moments when the pressures of work encroached upon her peace. But Emily persisted, driven by the belief that her spiritual journey was not just an escape from her daily life, but a means to live it more fully, more consciously.

Through this process of integration, Emily noticed subtle changes. She approached her work with greater calm and focus, her interactions became more mindful and present, and her appreciation for the small joys of life deepened.

In her quest to balance the various aspects of her life, Emily discovered that the essence of her spiritual journey was not in withdrawing from the world, but in engaging with it with a renewed sense of awareness and presence. This realization was just another step in her ongoing journey of growth and self-discovery.

"In the city's roar, where does the silent lotus bloom?"

Emily found herself yearning for quiet spaces – sanctuaries where she could reach deeper into her meditation practices uninterrupted. This quest for solitude became an essential part of her journey, a journey that was as much about finding inner peace as it was about navigating the challenges of her external environment.

The challenge was finding these moments of stillness within the relentless pace of her life. Her apartment, usually a refuge, was often filled with the sounds of the city - the distant hum of traffic, the occasional sirens, the chatter of neighbors. These were sounds she had grown accustomed to, yet now, as she sought to deepen her meditation practice, they felt like intrusions into her sacred space of peace.

Each time she sat down to meditate, she found her senses heightened, picking up every sound, every disturbance. The ring of her phone, the knock at the door, even the ticking of the clock seemed to pull her away from that elusive state of tranquility she so desperately sought.

This struggle for aloneness led Emily to explore new avenues. She began waking up earlier, hoping to find quiet in the early hours of the morning. But the demands of her body clock, accustomed to a different rhythm, made this quite a challenge. She would sit, bleary-eyed and yawning, trying to focus on her breath, only to find her mind wandering back to her bed.

Emily also sought solitude in parks and public gardens, places where the embrace of nature offered a semblance of peace. But here, too, she found distractions – the buzz of people, the playful shouts of children, the rhythmic thud of joggers' feet.

One evening, over dinner with her friend Alex, Emily voiced her frustrations. "I just can't seem to find a quiet place to meditate. It's like the world won't let me be still," she shared, her words tinged with a hint of despair.

Alex, leaning across the table, offered a perspective that Emily hadn't considered. "Maybe it's not about finding an external space of quiet, but about finding that quiet within you. Perhaps it's more about learning to be at peace within the noise."

This conversation sparked a new realization in Emily. She began to understand that seeking solitude wasn't just about finding a physical space of quiet; it was about cultivating an inner sanctuary, a place within herself where she could retreat, regardless of her external circumstances.

Armed with this new insight, Emily approached her meditation practice with a different mindset. She started to view the sounds and disturbances not as interruptions, but as part of the landscape of her practice. She learned to acknowledge them and then gently redirect her focus back to her breath, to the present moment.

This shift in approach brought a profound change in her practice. She found that she could access a sense of peace and stillness even in her noisy apartment or the background sounds of the park. The quest for external solitude transformed into an exploration of internal serenity.

In this process, Emily discovered a deeper truth about her spiritual journey. It was not about escaping from the world, it was about finding a way to coexist with it, to find harmony within the discord, peace within the turmoil. This realization marked another significant milestone in her journey, a step closer to the true essence of mindfulness and meditation – the ability to be at peace, anywhere, anytime, within oneself.

"In the city's rush, where does the quiet heart rest?"

As evening came, Emily sat in her apartment, the glow of the evening light spilling through her windows. In these moments of solitude, her mind often wandered into the realms of introspection and doubt. The journey she had embarked on, filled with the promise of inner peace and spiritual growth, now seemed to be riddled with more questions than answers.

Each attempt at meditation had become a reflection of her inner turmoil. The evenings quiet of her room, once a haven, now echoed with the discord of her doubts. "Is this really for me?" she pondered, staring at the flickering candle on her table, its flame dancing like the many thoughts in her mind. "Can I truly find balance and peace in my chaotic life?"

Her days were a whirlwind of activity – relentless work schedules, social commitments, the constant buzz of city life. Finding a consistent rhythm for her meditation practice amid this hustle felt like an uphill battle, a struggle that left her feeling more frazzled than centered.

In these moments of doubt, Emily's thoughts often drifted back to her conversations with Mrs. Kaur. She remembered Mrs. Kaur's words, "The path isn't easy, but it's worth every step." But in the thick of her daily grind, these words seemed like distant echoes, hard to grasp and even harder to live by.

During a lunch break at work, within the clatter of the office cafeteria, Emily confided in her closest friend and colleague, Alex. "I thought meditation would bring me peace, but all I feel is more unsettled. I'm not sure if I can integrate this spiritual path into my life."

Alex listened intently before replying, "Maybe it's not about fitting your life around meditation but finding a way for meditation to fit into your life. It doesn't have to be a long session; even a few minutes could make a difference."

The conversation with Alex gave her a new perspective. It wasn't about carving out a separate space for her spiritual practices; it was about integrating them into the fabric of her daily life, finding moments of mindfulness in the ordinary.

This approach led Emily to experiment with different methods. She started practicing mindful breathing during her commute, using the rhythmic movement of the train as a backdrop for her focus. She began to integrate short moments of contemplation throughout her day – a brief pause to center herself before a meeting, a mindful walk during her lunch hour.

Despite these adjustments, the doubts lingered. There were days when even a few minutes of meditation felt like an insurmountable task, when the pressures of life seemed to overshadow her quest for inner peace. On such days, Emily questioned the feasibility of her spiritual journey, the practicality of seeking tranquility in a world that seemed perpetually in motion.

But with each passing day, within the ebb and flow of confidence and doubt, Emily started to notice subtle shifts in her perspective. The moments of mindfulness began to thread through her days, bringing brief glimpses of calm. The realization that her journey should not be about achieving a perfect state of peace, but about embracing the imperfections of the process, began to take root.

In these moments of doubt and reflection, Emily was learning one of the most crucial lessons on her spiritual path – that the journey is not a linear trajectory towards enlightenment, but a winding path filled with highs and lows, clarity, and confusion. It was a journey that mirrored the very essence of life itself – unpredictable, challenging, but infinitely rewarding.

As she continued to navigate these moments of doubt, Emily found strength in the understanding that her journey was uniquely hers – a wealth of experiences that would eventually lead her to the inner peace she sought, one mindful step at a time.

"In the forest of change, who hears the silent footsteps of growth?"

During her transformative journey, Emily found herself at a crossroads in her relationships. The path of spirituality, once a solitary trail, now seemed to widen the chasm between her and some of her closest friends. Their gatherings, once filled with laughter and shared interests, had subtly shifted into arenas of disconnect.

It was during a Friday evening get-together at a bustling café, the air filled with the aroma of coffee and the murmur of conversations, that Emily felt this divide most acutely. Around her, her friends chatted animatedly about the latest fashion trends, office politics, and weekend plans. Emily, however, found her thoughts drifting away, no longer captivated by these discussions as she once was.

Her recent forays into meditation and mindfulness had altered her perspective, turning her gaze inward and toward more existential contemplations. The conversations around her, once engaging, now seemed superficial, lacking the depth that she yearned for. As her friends laughed over a shared joke, Emily's smile felt forced, her sense of belonging fading into a quiet sense of isolation.

Later that night, lying in her bed and staring at the ceiling, Emily's mind replayed the evening's events, a mixture of sadness and introspection. "Where do I fit in now?" she pondered. "My friends and I used to be so in sync, but now it feels like we're worlds apart."

This growing divide was not just about differing interests; it was a fundamental difference in outlook. Emily's friends, with their focus on material success and social pleasures, seemed to be on a different wavelength, one that Emily no longer resonated with. Her attempts to share her experiences and insights were often met with polite nods or changing the subject, a clear sign that her spiritual journey was a path they neither understood nor were interested in.

The following week, during a yoga session, Emily shared her feelings of disconnection with her instructor, a kind-hearted woman named Maya, who had become a confidante. "It's like I'm losing my friends," Emily confessed, her voice tinged with sorrow. "The more I walk this path, the lonelier it feels."

Maya, stretching out her mat, offered a gentle smile. "Spiritual growth often means outgrowing certain relationships," she said softly. "It's not about leaving people behind; it's about following your truth. Some will walk with you; others may take a different path. It's all part of the journey."

This conversation with Maya sparked a new realization in Emily. The path of spirituality, inherently personal and introspective, could indeed be lonely at times. But this solitude was not a sign of loss; it was an indication of her growth, to the evolution of her inner self.

Encouraged by this insight, Emily began to seek out like-minded individuals, joining spiritual groups and attending workshops. These new circles provided her with the connection and understanding she craved, filling the void left by her drifting friendships.

As she built these new relationships, Emily also learned to accept the changing dynamics with her old friends. She realized that each relationship had its place in her life, some serving as reminders of who she once was, others as examples of who she was becoming.

In this phase of disconnect, Emily discovered a deeper layer of connection – with herself and with those who shared her journey. It was a lesson in acceptance, in understanding the ebb and flow of relationships, and in finding comfort in the company of her own evolving spirit.

The journey of self-discovery, Emily learned, was about finding peace and balance within, along with navigating the complex web of human connections, learning to embrace both the solitude and the companionship that came with walking the spiritual path.

"In the dance of the solitary moon, who feels the echo of distant tides?"

In the quiet of her apartment, Emily found herself enveloped in a reflective solitude. The journey she had embarked upon had transformed her inner world and begun to reshape her external connections. Friends, who once stood as mainstays in her social life, now seemed like distant figures, silhouetted against the backdrop of her evolving spiritual path.

Each gathering with them had become a sad reminder of the growing chasm. The easy laughter and shared stories, which once flowed like a seamless river, now felt like trickling streams, struggling to find their course. It was not a rift borne out of conflict or resentment but a subtle drift, propelled by the currents of changing values and interests.

As she sat on her couch, wrapped in the soft folds of a throw blanket, Emily pondered over these shifts in her relationships. "We used to be so in sync," she mused, her mind replaying the recent gatherings – the dinner parties, the casual meetups at cafes, the birthday celebrations. Each event, though outwardly like the ones in the past, now left her with a lingering sense of being out of place, like a puzzle piece that no longer fit.

Her journey into spirituality, introspection, and mindfulness had subtly but irrevocably altered her perspective on life. Conversations about workplace drama, shopping sprees, and the latest TV shows no longer held the same appeal. Instead, she craved discussions about personal growth, philosophical musings, and the deeper meanings behind life's experiences.

This change in her interests was a profound shift in her identity. The realization that her friendships were evolving, some growing distant while others deepened, brought with it a mix of sadness and acceptance. "People change, and so do relationships," she whispered to herself, a truth she was beginning to understand and embrace.

Emily recalled a conversation with Mrs. Kaur, where she had expressed her feelings of disconnection. Mrs. Kaur had listened with her characteristic empathy before offering words of wisdom. "Relationships are like gardens," she had said. "Some plants thrive, while others wither away. It's the natural cycle of life. Cherish the memories and allow new flowers to bloom."

Armed with this insight, Emily began to look at her friendships through a lens of gratitude and understanding. She cherished the shared memories, the bonds that had once been strong. Yet, she also acknowledged that as she grew, it was natural for some relationships to fade, making room for new ones that resonated with her current self.

This period of reflection brought a sense of clarity and peace. Emily understood that her path was hers alone to walk, and it was okay for others to tread a different one. She began to embrace the idea of forming new connections with those who shared her values and interests, people who understood and supported her journey.

The process of reevaluating her relationships was not without its pangs of loneliness and nostalgia for what once was. It also opened her heart to the possibility of new, meaningful connections – relationships grounded in mutual understanding and shared growth.

In this introspective phase, Emily learned an invaluable lesson about the fluid nature of relationships. They were ever-changing, evolving as people grew and changed. This realization marked a new chapter in her journey, one where she could embrace both the joy of new connections and the bittersweet beauty of letting go.

Revelation
"Seeing the Ox"

"In the dance of the wind-blown leaves, where does the stillness reside?"

The crisp autumn air brushed against Emily's cheeks as she stepped out of her car, her gaze lifting to the sprawling meditation center nestled in the heart of the mountains. The serene beauty of the setting, with towering pines whispering secrets to the sky, seemed like a world away from the city she had left behind. As Emily walked towards the center, the gravel crunched under her feet, echoing her mix of anticipation and apprehension.

The center, a harmonious blend of modern architecture and natural aesthetics, stood as a testament to mindful living. Its walls, adorned with hues of earthy browns and calming greens, merged seamlessly with the surrounding wilderness. Emily's heart fluttered with a blend of excitement and nervousness as she crossed the threshold.

Inside, she was greeted by the warm smile of Mrs. Kaur, a woman whose wisdom had become a guiding light in Emily's journey of self-discovery. "Welcome, Emily. I'm so glad you could join us," Mrs. Kaur said, her voice a soothing melody.

As Emily was led through the halls, adorned with paintings and tapestries that spoke of inner peace and enlightenment, she felt a subtle shift within her. The walls seemed to echo with the silent stories of those who had walked this path before her, each seeking something, perhaps answers, perhaps peace.

Her room was a nest of tranquility, simple yet elegant. A large window framed a view of the mountains, their peaks standing tall against the canvas of the sky. Emily took a deep breath, the scent of pine and earth filling her lungs, grounding her in the moment.

At dinner, she found herself seated among strangers, yet there was a sense of camaraderie in the air. Conversations flowed like gentle streams, touching upon life, love, and the pursuit of tranquility. Emily listened, occasionally contributing, her mind and spirit soaring through the words and experiences shared at the table.

Later that evening, the group gathered in the main hall for a session of guided meditation. The hall, with its high ceilings and soft lighting, held a sacred aura. As Mrs. Kaur's voice led them through the meditation, Emily felt layers of tension she didn't know she carried begin to unravel. Her thoughts, which often raced like an insistent river, slowed to a gentle trickle.

In this space of stillness, Emily's mind wandered back to her recent interactions with her friends. She recalled the look of skepticism in their eyes, the subtle jabs, and the widening gap of understanding. A pang of loneliness tugged at her heart, but it was quickly enveloped by a wave of acceptance. Here, in this hall, surrounded by souls on similar journeys, she didn't feel the need to explain or justify her path.

As the weekend unfolded, Emily found herself immersed in deep philosophical discussions, often led by Mrs. Kaur. They spoke of the nature of reality, the pursuit of happiness, and the illusion of separateness. These dialogues, rich with introspection and wisdom, opened new doors of perception for Emily.

One afternoon, while walking along a forest trail, Emily encountered Mark, a fellow attendee with a kind smile and eyes that held a story of their own. Their conversation flowed effortlessly, touching upon their journeys, their struggles, and their aspirations. In Mark, Emily found a kindred spirit, someone who understood the language of her soul.

The retreat was a journey into the realms of meditation and mindfulness, as well as the depths of human connection. Emily found herself forming bonds with people who were once strangers, their stories and experiences weaving into the tapestry of her own.

As the day ended, Emily stood on the balcony of her room, gazing at the starlit sky. The mountains stood as silent guardians, their presence a reminder of the vastness of the world and the many paths that wound through it. Emily felt a profound sense of gratitude and a newfound strength to continue her journey, wherever it may lead.

In her heart, she carried the lessons of the day and a promise of new friendships, the warmth of shared understanding, and the courage to embrace her path with conviction. The retreat had become a turning point, a moment of transformation that would resonate with her forever.

"In the silence of the mountains, a mind whirls like a storm. Can the wind dance with the stillness of the peaks?"

As Emily stepped into the serenity of the meditation center, her mind was a whirlpool of thoughts, mirroring the chaotic city life she had momentarily left behind. The retreat, with its promise of tranquility and self-discovery, stood in stark contrast to the familiar rhythms of her daily life. The crisp mountain air whispered promises of peace, yet Emily's internal world buzzed with the relentless energy of a mind unaccustomed to stillness.

The next morning dawned with a golden hue, painting the center in a light that seemed to breathe life into its very walls. Breakfast was a quiet affair, the soft clinking of cutlery against plates mingling with the gentle murmur of fellow attendees. Emily's attempts at conversation were tentative, her words tiptoeing around the edges of deeper connections.

As the day unfolded, Emily found herself in a series of guided sessions, each designed to peel back the layers of noise and distraction that cluttered the mind. In a session of mindful walking, as her feet pressed against the dew-kissed grass, Emily's thoughts began to unspool, slowly and reluctantly. The natural rhythm of her steps became a gentle metronome, coaxing her thoughts away from their incessant whirl.

The true challenge, however, came during the meditation sessions. Seated on a cushion, along with the others in a similar quest for inner peace, Emily felt the full weight of her restless mind. Thoughts of work, lingering arguments, and trivial concerns jostled for attention, as evidence of the untrained nature of her focus. It was during these moments of struggle that Mrs. Kaur's gentle guidance proved invaluable. Her voice, seasoned with wisdom and compassion, was a light in the fog of Emily's thoughts, guiding her back to the present moment.

As the days passed, the serene environment of the center began to work its subtle magic on Emily. The high ceilings and soft lighting of the meditation hall, the verdant beauty of the surrounding forest, and the rhythmic chanting of mantras created a cocoon of calm, slowly seeping into the crevices of her busy mind.

In the evenings, Emily engaged in philosophical discussions with other attendees, their conversations meandering through topics of consciousness, reality, and the nature of happiness. These dialogues, steeped in introspection and curiosity, were soothing her long-standing yearning for deeper understanding.

In this journey of self-discovery, Emily formed a bond with Mark, a fellow attendee whose quiet strength and thoughtful insights resonated with her own quest. Their conversations, often laced with laughter and shared experiences, became a source of comfort and connection.

Emily grappled with moments of doubt, her skeptical mind occasionally piercing the veil of newfound beliefs and practices. In these moments, she turned to the mountains, their unchanging presence a reminder of the endurance of nature and the potential for stillness within her.

Emily found herself on the cusp of a transformation. The initial resistance and turmoil had given way to a burgeoning sense of clarity and calm. Her thoughts, once a raging river, now flowed like a gentle stream, guided by the banks of mindfulness and introspection.

Standing on the balcony of her room gazing at the star-studded sky, Emily felt a profound shift within. The retreat had planted seeds of tranquility and understanding in her heart. She realized that the journey was not about escaping the chaos of life, but about finding stillness within it.

"Is the mind the sky or a cloud passing through it?"

Mrs. Kaur, whose presence was as calming as the mountain air, guided Emily with a gentle yet firm hand. Her words, steeped in wisdom and compassion, guided her through the turbulent waters of her mind. "Let your thoughts come and go like clouds in a vast sky," she would say, her voice soothing Emily's restless spirit.

In these deepening meditation sessions, Emily learned to observe her thoughts without attachment, a skill that at first seemed as elusive as a mirage. The practice, initially a battle against her own mind, gradually became an act of surrender, a gentle letting go. The intrusive thoughts that once seemed like unrelenting waves crashing against her consciousness began to soften, turning into ripples on the surface of a deep, tranquil ocean.

As she progressed, Emily's thoughts took on a philosophical nature, probing questions about existence, the self, and the nature of consciousness. These were not discussions of words, but of silence, an exploration in the quiet recesses of her mind. The moments of stillness brought flashes of insight, fleeting yet profound, like glimpses of a distant shore.

Emily found Marks presence at the retreat a source of both comfort and intrigue. Their conversations, often held in the serene backdrop of the center's gardens, were an intricate dance of words and silences. Mark, with his thoughtful demeanor and insightful observations, provided a mirror for Emily's own thoughts and feelings, deepening her understanding of herself and her path.

Their bond, forged in the shared crucible of self-discovery, was tinged with the unspoken undercurrents of a budding romance. Yet, it was a connection that transcended mere words, rooted in the profound experience of exploring the innermost depths of their beings.

There were times when the walls of the meditation hall seemed to close in on her, and the silence felt oppressive, a stark reminder of the solitude of her path.

In these moments Emily turned to the teachings of Mrs. Kaur and the wisdom imparted in the meditation sessions. She learned to embrace the discomfort, understanding that growth often lay on the other side of struggle. The conflict within her became a catalyst for deeper exploration, a diving board into the unknown waters of her soul.

Over time Emily's meditation practice deepened, each session a step further into the heart of her being. The initial struggles with quieting her mind evolved into a graceful dance with her thoughts, a harmonious coexistence with the ebb and flow of her consciousness.

Standing on the threshold of newfound understanding, Emily gazed out at the mountains surrounding the center. She realized that the mountains, like her journey, held mysteries yet to be uncovered, paths yet to be trodden. Her journey interwoven with the timeless pursuit of self-discovery and inner peace, had found its rhythm in the silence of meditation, a practice enriched with layers of introspection, conflict, and the promising blooms of love.

"Can the heart's whisper be heard in the symphony of the universe?"

In the heart of one meditation session Emily found herself on the brink of a profound revelation. Surrounded by the whispers of fellow meditators, she sat, her posture a blend of grace and stillness, her breath a bridge to deeper realms of consciousness.

As the meditation deepened, the lines between Emily and the world around her began to blur. The walls of the hall, once solid and defined, seemed to dissolve into a blur of light and shadow. The sounds of nature outside – the breath of the wind, the distant call of a bird – merged with the rhythm of her heartbeat, creating a symphony of existence that resonated within her very core.

In this moment, Emily experienced an epiphany, a sense of interconnectedness so profound that it transcended language. It was as if she had tapped into a universal current, a flow of energy that connected her to every living thing, every star in the sky, every grain of sand. The sensation was both exhilarating and humbling, a reminder of her smallness in the vastness of the universe and yet her undeniable part in it.

This feeling of unity brought with it a flood of emotions – awe, gratitude, an overwhelming sense of love. Tears formed in Emily's eyes from the sheer beauty of the connection she felt. It was as though she had glimpsed the very essence of life itself, a truth so simple yet so profound that it could only be felt, not articulated.

As the meditation ended, and the participants slowly emerged from their journey inward, Emily sat in silence, savoring the remnants of this profound experience. The room gradually filled with the soft sounds of movement and quiet conversation, but for Emily, the echoes of her revelation lingered, a powerful presence in her heart.

Later, under the starlit sky, Emily shared her experience with Mark. They sat on a bench in the garden, the air cool and fragrant with the scent of night-blooming flowers. Mark listened intently, his eyes reflecting the stars above, as Emily described the sensation of oneness she had felt.

"That's the essence of meditation," Mark said thoughtfully. "To realize that we are not separate from the universe, but a part of it. Your experience... it's a beautiful insight into the nature of existence."

Their conversation meandered into the realms of philosophy and spirituality, exploring ideas of consciousness, the self, and the universe. Emily felt a deep sense of spiritual connection with Mark. Their dialogue was a shared journey into the mysteries of life.

This moment of connection with the universe and with another soul marked another turning point in Emily's spiritual journey. It was as if she had been given a glimpse behind the veil of the mundane, into a world of infinite possibilities and profound truths. This experience became a touchstone for her, a source of strength and inspiration as she navigated the complexities of her path.

As the night deepened, Emily lay in her room, the events of the day replaying in her mind. She realized that her journey of self-discovery was about understanding her place in the grand scheme of things. The sense of interconnectedness she had felt was a reminder that every step she took on her path was a part of a larger dance, a cosmic ballet in which she was both a participant and a spectator.

This revelation filled her with a sense of purpose and a deep sense of peace. As she drifted off to sleep, Emily felt a profound gratitude for this moment of connection, a precious gift that would continue to illuminate her path.

"How can one walk in a world where every step dissolves the path?"

In the quiet aftermath of her profound meditation experience, Emily found herself grappling with a reality that seemed at once both vividly clear and mystifyingly abstract. The retreat center, with its tranquil gardens and softly lit hallways, felt like a different world, one where the usual boundaries of time and space blurred into insignificance.

Emily walked along a stone path, lined with delicately swaying flowers, each step a dance with the newfound understanding that had enveloped her. She felt a deep sense of awe at the beauty of the world around her, seeing it as if for the first time. The vibrant colors of the petals, the intricate patterns of the leaves, even the tiny insects buzzing around – everything seemed imbued with a profound significance.

This sensation was exhilarating, a rush of freedom and connection, but it also left her slightly unsettled. Her usual perception of reality, grounded in logic and language, struggled to make sense of what she had experienced. How could she describe something that defied words? How could she explain a feeling that transcended the very concept of self?

As she sat on a bench, gazing at the setting sun, Emily's mind wandered through a maze of thoughts and feelings. She realized that what she had experienced, that moment of spiritual insight, was a fundamental shift in her understanding of existence.

Later, Emily joined a small group of fellow retreat-goers for dinner. The conversation flowed around her, but she felt somewhat detached, lost in her own reflections. A part of her longed to share her experience, to put into words the indescribable, yet another part of her hesitated, fearing misunderstanding or skepticism.

It was then that Mrs. Kaur, her mentor, and guide throughout this journey, joined her. Sensing Emily's inner turmoil, she asked, "How are you feeling after your meditation today?"

Emily looked into Mrs. Kaur's wise, knowing eyes and attempted to articulate her experience. "It was beyond words," she began, her voice hesitant. "I felt connected to everything, as if the boundaries between me and the universe dissolved. But now, I'm struggling to reconcile that with the world I've always known."

Mrs. Kaur nodded, her expression one of empathy and understanding. "What you've experienced is the essence of spiritual awakening. It's natural to feel unsettled. The mind tries to fit new experiences into old frameworks, but some experiences are too vast for those constraints."

Their conversation dove deeper into the nature of reality, perception, and the limitations of language. Mrs. Kaur shared stories of ancient mystics and philosophers who had similar experiences, drawing parallels between Emily's journey and those who had walked this path before.

As Emily listened, she felt a growing sense of comfort and validation. She wasn't alone in this experience; it was a part of a larger human quest for understanding and connection. The discussion shifted to the concept of non-duality, the idea that the separation between self and other is an illusion, a construct of the mind.

This idea resonated with Emily, aligning with the sense of oneness she had experienced. It was both a challenge and an invitation to explore a new way of seeing the world, one that transcended the limitations of conventional perception.

Later that night, as Emily lay in bed, she reflected on the day's events. The experience of deep connection and the subsequent philosophical discussions had opened a door to a new realm of understanding. She realized that her journey of personal growth was about exploring the very nature of reality itself.

She felt a mixture of excitement and apprehension about what lay ahead. There was so much to learn, so many possibilities to explore. But one thing was clear – her experience had changed her in a fundamental way, and there was no going back to the person she was before.

"Can one hear the song of a dawn that has never been silent?"

In the early dawn, Emily sat alone on the edge of a wooden dock, her legs dangling over the serene lake that mirrored the pastel sky. The retreat center, nestled in the heart of nature, seemed to be awakening with her, birds chirping in a harmonious symphony. This moment of solitude allowed her thoughts to meander through the maze of her recent experiences.

She pondered over the profound meditation session that had shattered her conventional understanding of reality. It was as if she had been living her life viewing the world through a frosted glass, seeing shapes and colors but missing the intricate details. Now, the glass was wiped clean, revealing a clarity and depth that both astonished and overwhelmed her.

As she reflected, Emily realized that her previous understanding of the world was akin to skimming the surface of a vast ocean without diving into its depths. The realization that a deeper reality underlay her everyday experiences was both enlightening and disconcerting. This newfound perspective was not just an expansion of her consciousness; it felt like an awakening to a truth that had always been there, hidden in plain sight.

The air around her felt charged with a subtle energy, as if the very atoms were alive with a secret dance of existence. The rustling leaves, the ripples on the lake, even the distant mountains, all seemed to be part of a grand, interconnected web. Emily sensed an underlying unity, a thread that wove through everything, binding it in silent harmony.

This deeper layer of reality was not something she could easily articulate. It was more than an intellectual understanding; it was a visceral, almost cellular recognition of the interconnectedness of all things. It was as if she had tapped into a universal rhythm, a cosmic heartbeat that pulsed through her very being.

As these thoughts swirled in her mind, Emily remembered a conversation she had with an elderly monk who visited the retreat. He had spoken of the illusion of separation, how humans construct walls of identity and difference, forgetting their inherent unity with the universe. His words now resonated with her deeply, casting a new light on her experience.

The realization that her previous perspective was limited was not a cause for regret but an invitation to explore this deeper reality. It was like discovering a hidden path in a familiar forest, a path that promised to lead her to uncharted territories of understanding and insight.

Emily's mind then drifted to the people in her life, her family, friends, and even strangers she encountered daily. She wondered how this new understanding would affect her relationships. Would she be able to convey this sense of oneness to others, or would it widen the gap of misunderstanding?

Her reverie was interrupted by the gentle voice of Mrs. Kaur, who had approached quietly. "You seem deep in thought, Emily. What are you contemplating?"

Emily turned, her eyes reflecting the calmness of the lake. "I'm realizing how limited my view of the world has been," she confessed. "It's like I've been asleep, and now I'm slowly waking up to a deeper reality, one that's both beautiful and complex."

Mrs. Kaur smiled warmly. "That's a significant realization, Emily. It's the first step towards true wisdom. The deeper reality you're beginning to perceive is the essence of all spiritual paths. It's the understanding that beneath the surface of our perceived separateness lies a profound unity."

Their conversation wove through the realms of philosophy and spirituality, exploring concepts of non-duality, the nature of consciousness, and the illusion of the ego. Emily listened intently, absorbing each word, each idea, like a parched land soaking up the rain.

As the sun rose higher, casting a golden glow over the lake, Emily felt a sense of peace and purpose. She knew her journey was just beginning, that there were layers upon layers of understanding to unravel. But for the first time, she felt equipped and eager to embark on this journey, to explore the depths of this deeper reality and find her place within it.

With a renewed sense of clarity and determination, Emily stood up, ready to face the day, ready to embrace whatever lessons and experiences lay ahead. The path before her was uncharted, but she was no longer afraid. She was stepping into a larger world, a world where every moment held the promise of discovery, and every encounter was a step closer to the ultimate truth.

"Is the reflection in the still lake the face of the water or the face of the sky?"

As the retreat continued, the days unfolded like the petals of a blooming lotus, each one revealing new layers of understanding and awareness for Emily. The once crisp boundaries of her inner world began to blur and merge with the vastness she had recently discovered. This phase of the retreat became less about seeking and more about integrating the profound experience she had encountered.

The mornings were filled with a gentle light that spilled across the tranquil grounds. Emily would often start her day sitting by the lake, the stillness of the water reflecting her own journey towards inner calm. These moments of solitude were vital for her to process the enormity of her experience.

During the day, the retreat offered various workshops and group sessions, where Emily found herself more open and engaged than ever before. She participated in discussions that ranged from the metaphysical to the practical aspects of spiritual practice. The conversations were both exchanges of ideas and gateways to deeper connections with fellow seekers.

One particularly impactful session was led by a visiting philosopher, whose discourse on the nature of consciousness resonated deeply with Emily. He spoke of the mind as a vast ocean, with thoughts and experiences being like waves that rise and fall. He suggested that beneath these waves lay a deeper stillness, an unchanging reality that was the essence of all existence. Emily listened, captivated, finding parallels between his words and her own experiences.

As days passed, Emily found herself engaging in heartfelt conversations with other participants. There was John, a middle-aged businessman who had come to the retreat seeking relief from his hectic life. He shared his struggles with finding balance and his desire to discover a deeper purpose. Emily found herself empathizing with his journey, realizing that despite their different paths, they were both seeking the same truth.

Then there was Aisha, a young artist with a vibrant spirit, who spoke passionately about using her art as a means to express and explore her spirituality. Emily was fascinated by Aisha's perspective, seeing in her a reflection of her own quest for expression and understanding.

Each encounter, each shared story, helped Emily to articulate her feelings and insights. She realized that this process of sharing and listening was not about finding the right words, it was about connecting at a deeper, more intuitive level. These interactions were like pieces of a puzzle, helping her to form a clearer picture of her own experience.

In the evenings, the retreat would often organize group meditations. It was during these sessions that Emily felt the most profound sense of integration. As she sat in silence, surrounded by fellow meditators, she could feel the collective energy of their presence. It was as if they were all tapping into the same source, a shared wellspring of peace and understanding.

These group meditations were also a time for Emily to reflect on her journey. She would often find herself revisiting her moment of profound interconnectedness, each time gleaning new insights and revelations. It was as though the experience had opened a door within her that led to an infinite corridor of wisdom and understanding.

The retreat had become a crucible for transformation. The Emily that had arrived at the retreat was not the same person who was now preparing to leave. She felt more grounded, more connected, both to herself and to the world around her.

As the final day of the retreat dawned, Emily sat by the lake, her heart filled with a mixture of gratitude and anticipation. She knew that integrating this experience into her daily life would be a challenge, but she felt ready. The retreat had given her the tools, the insights, and most importantly, the confidence to continue her journey.

She had come seeking tranquility and had found so much more. She had discovered a deeper reality, a truth that was ancient yet ever new. As she packed her bags, ready to step back into the world, she carried with her both memories and a new way of being, a new lens through which to view the world.

Emily's journey at the retreat was a reminder that sometimes, to move forward, one must pause, reflect, and connect – not just with the self, but with the world at large.

"In the garden of awakening, where the dew reflects the dawn, who walks the path - the person or the journey itself?"

Emily stood at the threshold of a profound

transformation. The world outside the serene confines of the retreat center beckoned her back, a world she now viewed through a lens altered by profound insight and a deepened understanding of interconnectedness. The once familiar landscape of her daily life awaited her return, but it was as if she was about to tread upon it for the first time.

She realized that the retreat had not just changed her; it had redefined her entire perception of reality. Where once she saw separation, she now saw unity; where once there was isolation, now there was a sense of oneness with all things. The chirping of the birds, the rustling of the leaves, the distant sound of a flowing stream – all these felt like different notes of the same symphony, the symphony of life itself.

The retreat had been a cocoon, nurturing her transformation, but now she faced the challenge of carrying this newfound perspective into her everyday life. How would her relationships change? How would her priorities shift? The questions fluttered in her mind like butterflies, each one opening new possibilities.

The journey home was a contemplative one. Emily found herself observing the world around her with a sense of wonder and curiosity that she hadn't felt since she was a child. The vibrant colors, the diverse faces of the people, the intricate patterns of life playing out around her – everything seemed imbued with a deeper significance.

Back home, the familiar surroundings of her apartment took on a new dimension. Each object, each space, held memories and meanings that were now seen through the prism of her expanded consciousness. It was as if she was rediscovering her own life, piece by piece.

As days passed, Emily's transformed perspective began to subtly influence her interactions. Conversations with friends and family revealed new depths. Her listening became more attentive, her responses more thoughtful. She found herself more patient, more compassionate, understanding that everyone was on their own journey, just as she was on hers.

At work, Emily's approach to challenges and conflicts underwent a change. She found herself less reactive, more centered. Her colleagues noticed a newfound calmness in her demeanor, a quiet strength that seemed to emanate from within.

But perhaps the most significant change was in her spiritual practice. Meditation, once a structured part of her routine, now became a living, breathing part of her existence. She found moments of mindfulness in everyday activities – in the act of preparing a meal, in the simple act of breathing, in the quiet moments before sleep.

As weeks turned into months, Emily's journey continued to unfold in beautiful and unexpected ways. She began exploring various spiritual texts and philosophies, each one adding layers to her understanding. Her conversations became deeper, often touching upon themes of existence, consciousness, and the nature of reality.

One evening, during a particularly reflective meditation, Emily experienced a flashback to her moment of profound interconnectedness at the retreat. It was a vivid, almost visceral memory that filled her with a sense of awe and gratitude. In that moment, she realized that her experience was not a fleeting epiphany but a pivotal point in her spiritual journey, a touchstone she could return to whenever she felt lost or disconnected.

Emily's transformation was not only a shift in perspective; it was a rebirth of her entire being. She now walked through life with a sense of purpose and a deep connection to the world around her. The journey was ongoing, the path endless, but Emily embraced it with an open heart and a soul awakened to the infinite possibilities of existence.

Perception

As Emily stepped out of the taxi and onto the familiar pavement of her busy city street, the world around her seemed to pulse with a new vibrancy. The retreat, nestled in the tranquility of the mountains, had recalibrated her senses, making the ordinary seem extraordinary. The metropolis she called home, once a blur of grey and noise, now danced with color and rhythm.

The early morning sun cast long shadows on the sidewalk, turning ordinary objects into artworks of light and shape. The chatter of passersby, the distant honking of cars, even the rhythmic tapping of her own shoes on the pavement, resonated with her in a way they never had before. She was the same person, yet everything felt different – as if she had been given a new lens through which to view the world.

As she walked, Emily's mind wandered back to the retreat. The serene environment, the deep meditations, and the philosophical discussions had opened doors within her that she hadn't known existed. Now, back in her daily routine, she wondered how to integrate these newfound insights into her everyday life.

At work, the change in Emily was subtle but noticeable. Where once she would react quickly to stress or conflict, she now found herself pausing, taking a breath, and responding with a calmness that surprised even her. Her colleagues took note, some curious, others skeptical of this new, serene Emily.

Her lunch breaks became moments of mindfulness. Instead of scrolling through her phone or rushing through her meal, she took the time to savor her food, to really taste and appreciate the flavors. She began spending these breaks walking in the nearby park, attuning herself to the beauty of nature amidst the urban sprawl.

Even her small, cluttered apartment, which she had always viewed as a mere stopping point in her busy life, took on new significance. She began to declutter, to create a space that reflected her inner transformation. Each object was considered for its purpose and beauty, turning her home into a sanctuary that mirrored the peace she had found within.

Her relationships, too, underwent a transformation. Conversations with friends and family became more meaningful. She listened more intently, not just to respond but to truly understand. Her empathy and compassion grew, changing the dynamics of these interactions in subtle but profound ways.

One weekend, Emily met with her friend Sarah for coffee. Sarah noticed the change immediately. "You seem different, more... centered," she remarked, stirring her coffee.

Emily smiled, her eyes reflecting a depth that wasn't there before. "I think I am," she replied. "The retreat helped me see things differently. There's beauty and value in every moment, even the small ones we usually overlook."

Sarah looked at her thoughtfully. "Sounds enlightening, but how do you keep that perspective in a place like this?" she gestured to the lively coffee shop.

"It's a practice," Emily explained. "Every day, every moment, is an opportunity to be present, to appreciate life as it is."

Their conversation drifted into discussions about mindfulness, purpose, and the complexities of modern life. Emily shared her experiences and insights, her words infused with a sincerity and conviction that came from deep within.

In the weeks that followed, Emily continued to navigate her transformed reality. She joined a local meditation group, finding comfort and connection with others on similar paths. She also started exploring various spiritual texts, each one adding a new layer to her understanding.

Yet, amid this evolution, there were moments of doubt and struggle. Integrating her spiritual insights into the practicalities of daily life had many challenges. Balancing her career, social life, and inner growth required a delicate dance, one that she was still learning the steps to.

But through it all, Emily held onto the essence of her experience – the realization that life, in all its chaos and simplicity, was a beautiful, interconnected dance. She had once felt like an observer, watching life unfold from a distance. Now, she felt like a participant, fully engaged in the rhythm of existence.

Her journey was an ever-unfolding path, leading her to new realizations and experiences. The retreat had been a turning point, a catalyst for a deeper exploration of life and her place within it. As Emily continued along this path, she did so with an open heart and a curious mind, ready to embrace whatever came her way, one mindful step at a time.

"Can the echo of a mountain's silence be heard in the city's roar?"

The transformation Emily underwent at the retreat had seeped into the very fabric of her interactions with the world. Gone were the days of passive listening and surface-level engagements. Now, each conversation, each encounter, resonated with a newfound depth and presence.

Walking down the busy streets of the city, Emily found herself more attuned to the lives unfolding around her. The hurried steps of a businessman, the tired smile of a waitress at a street café, the exuberant laughter of children playing in a nearby park – these were no longer mere background noise to her own life. They were vivid strokes in the intricate painting of human existence.

At work, Emily's approach to her colleagues and her tasks reflected this shift. She listened to her team not only to respond, but to understand, to really hear what was being said beyond the words. Her colleagues began to seek her out, finding comfort in her calm demeanor and thoughtful responses.

In meetings, where once she would zone out, she now found herself actively participating, offering insights that were both intuitive and pragmatic. Her boss, Mr. Andersson, a stern man of few words, remarked one day, "Emily, your perspective has been particularly insightful lately. Keep it up."

Her social interactions took on a new dimension. Dinners with friends, once dominated by small talk and gossip, now turned into meaningful discussions about life, dreams, and the complexities of human emotions. Her friends noticed the change too. "You're really present with us, Em. It's like you're seeing us for the first time," her friend Zoe commented one evening.

One such interaction stood out distinctly. It was a rainy Saturday afternoon, and Emily found herself in a cozy corner of a local bookstore, lost in the pages of a book on Eastern philosophy. A man in his late thirties, with curious eyes and a thoughtful expression, approached her. "That's a great read," he said, pointing to her book.

This stranger, introduced himself as Liam, sparked a conversation that effortlessly wove through topics of spirituality, literature, and personal growth. Emily found herself opening up about her experiences at the retreat, her journey of self-discovery, and the changes she was trying to integrate into her life. Liam listened, genuinely interested, sharing snippets of his own quest for meaning.

Their conversation felt like a dance of minds, each thought leading to another, a seamless flow of ideas and reflections. As they parted ways, Liam said, "It was refreshing to have such a profound conversation with a stranger. Perhaps we'll cross paths again."

At home, Emily found herself reflecting on this encounter, realizing that such depth in interactions was what she had been yearning for all along – connections that transcended the mundane, reaching into the essence of what it means to truly interact and understand another human being.

Emily's journey of integrating her retreat experience into her daily life continued. The world around her seemed richer, more vibrant. She found joy in small things – the way sunlight filtered through her window, the aroma of her morning coffee, the texture of her favorite book.

There were days when the weight of the world seemed too much, when her attempts to connect deeply were met with indifference or confusion. On such days, Emily would turn to her meditation practice, finding comfort in the stillness, reminding herself of the interconnectedness of all things.

Emily's inward journey impacted those around her, a ripple effect of her own transformation. She had become a catalyst for deeper understanding and presence, changing her own narrative as well as subtly influencing the narratives of those she interacted with.

As she lay in bed one night, Emily thought about the myriad ways her life had changed. She realized that this was just the beginning. There were still many layers to uncover, many lessons to learn. But one thing was clear – she was on a path that felt more authentic, more aligned with who she truly was and who she wanted to become.

"Does the leaf know it nurtures the tree as it falls to the ground?"

The subtle yet profound shift in Emily's perception had deepened her interactions and cultivated a blossoming garden of compassion within her. This new-found empathy was a transformation, reshaping her understanding of the world and her place within it.

On a crisp autumn morning, Emily found herself in the familiar embrace of the city park. The golden hues of falling leaves created a warmth against the cool, blue sky. As she walked, she noticed an elderly man sitting alone on a bench, his eyes reflecting a depth of unspoken stories. In the past, she might have walked by without a second thought. But now, something within her paused, a gentle nudge of empathy urging her to approach him.

"Beautiful day, isn't it?" she remarked, sitting beside him.

The man looked up, a flicker of surprise in his eyes before it settled into a quiet acceptance. "It is indeed," he replied, his voice carrying the weight of years.

They talked, their conversation meandering through various topics - the changing seasons, the busy city life, and eventually, the man's own life journey. He spoke of his youth, the dreams he had, and the harsh realities that often clouded them. Emily listened, both with her ears and with her heart, understanding that this conversation was a sharing of life itself.

As she walked away from the park, Emily realized how much this encounter had affected her. She felt a profound connection to the man's story, understanding that everyone she met was fighting their own battles, harboring their own dreams and disappointments.

This growth in compassion was not limited to strangers. At work, she became more patient with her colleagues, understanding that behind every terse email or stressed demeanor was a person trying their best to navigate through their own challenges. She became a confidante to many, her office turning into a sanctuary where her colleagues felt heard and understood.

Even in her personal life, this change was evident. Her relationship with her family deepened, especially with her younger sister, Lily. They had always been close, but now there was an added layer of empathy and understanding. Emily found herself more patient, more willing to listen to Lily's concerns about college and the future. Their conversations, once filled with casual chatter, now delved into deeper, more meaningful topics.

One evening, as they sat sharing a cup of tea, Lily opened up about her fears and anxieties regarding her career choices. Emily, instead of offering immediate advice, simply listened, allowing her sister to express herself fully. It was a small change, but it made all the difference to Lily, who felt truly supported and understood for the first time.

As days turned into weeks, Emily's compassion continued to grow, touching the lives of those around her in subtle yet significant ways. It was as if she had developed a new lens through which to view the world, one that allowed her to see the interconnectedness of all beings and the shared journey of the human experience.

This shift in perception had tangible effects on the world around her. She became involved in community service, volunteering at local shelters, and participating in charity events. Her empathy extended beyond her immediate circle, reaching out to those in need, offering a listening ear, a helping hand.

There were moments when the weight of this empathy felt overwhelming, when the pain and struggles of others seemed too much to bear. During these times, Emily turned to her meditation practice, reminding herself of the need for self-care and boundaries.

One evening, reflecting on the changes in her life, she realized that this growth in compassion was a fundamental part of who she was becoming - a more empathetic, understanding, and compassionate human being.

"Is the echo aware of the sound that birthed it? In the dance of the falling leaf, the wind finds its purpose."

Since her return from the retreat, Emily noticed a profound shift in her demeanor, particularly in the realm of patience. This was a deep-seated transformation that altered the very core of her being.

Emily now found a rhythm, a sort of harmonious flow. She began to see the city, with its myriad of personalities and stories, as a mosaic of individual journeys, each piece significant and deserving of patience.

This newfound patience was most evident in her daily commute. Where once the slightest delay in her train would set her teeth on edge, Emily now used these moments to observe, to reflect. The woman absorbed in her book, the child gazing wide-eyed at the world passing by, the couple sharing a quiet conversation - they were no longer mere background characters in Emily's life, but fellow travelers, each with their own unique story.

One afternoon, her patience was put to the test during a particularly challenging project meeting. As voices rose and tensions mounted, Emily remained tranquil. She gently steered the conversation, allowing each member to voice their concerns, acknowledging their frustrations, and gradually guiding them towards a consensus. It was a small victory, but one that left a lasting impact on the team dynamics.

Perhaps the most significant change was in how Emily viewed herself. She began to approach her own growth and mistakes with the same patience she extended to others. The inner critic, once quick to chastise her for every misstep, now spoke in kinder, more forgiving tones. She understood that her journey was a meandering path, with its own set of twists and turns.

During quiet evenings at home, Emily would often reflect on this shift. She pondered over the philosophical implications of patience, of how it was intrinsically linked to understanding and empathy. In these moments of introspection, she realized that patience was not a passive act of waiting, it was an active process of engagement with the present moment.

This realization came to a head one weekend as she engaged in a heartfelt conversation with her neighbor, Mr. Jensen, a widower who often shared stories of his late wife. In the past, Emily would listen politely, even though a part of her mind was already racing towards the next task. Now, she was fully present, truly absorbing the tales of love, loss, and the passage of time. Mr. Jensen, sensing this change, opened even more than ever before, revealing layers of his life that he had seldom shared. It was a poignant connection, one that left Emily humbled.

There were moments of frustration, times when her old, impulsive self-threatened to resurface. But these were quickly quelled by a deep, calming breath, a reminder of the peace and understanding that patience brought.

She found that this virtue subtly influenced her interactions with others, and her entire outlook on life. She became more tolerant of the uncertainties of the future, more accepting of the ebbs and flows of existence. Her life, once a frantic race against time, had transformed into a graceful dance with each step evidence of the power of patience.

"Does the shadow know it dances because of the light? In the silence of the seed, a forest dreams."

Emily's return from the meditation retreat was characterized by a heightened sense of awareness and introspection. The city that had once overwhelmed her with its relentless pace now seemed like a playground for her to practice the art of mindfulness and reflection. Each day, she found herself pausing, considering the ripple effects of her actions and words in the interconnected web of life that surrounded her.

In her compact apartment, adorned with mementos of her journey and potted plants that thrived in the sunlit corners, Emily began each morning with a moment of contemplation. As she brewed her tea, she pondered the origins of the leaves, the hands that had harvested them, and the journey they had taken to reach her. This simple act, once performed mechanically, had transformed into a ritual that connected her to the larger story of the world.

Her job, a demanding position, presented daily opportunities for Emily to practice her newfound approach. Where she once prioritized efficiency over everything, she now took a more holistic view. She considered the impact of her work on society and the environment. She found herself in discussions with her team, advocating for ethical practices and sustainable choices, her voice a gentle yet firm call for change.

Her colleagues saw a new depth in her, a thoughtfulness that was both intriguing and inspiring. Conversations with her became more than mere exchanges of ideas; they were explorations into the impact of their work and their responsibilities as global citizens.

One significant test of Emily's reflective approach came during a project that involved a major client. The client's request for a high-impact campaign was at odds with the sustainable practices Emily now championed. She found herself at a crossroads, torn between the demands of her job and her personal convictions.

In a meeting that would decide the direction of the campaign, Emily voiced her concerns with a calm confidence that silenced the room. "What we create here," she said, "echoes beyond these walls. We have the power to influence, and with that comes the responsibility to do so mindfully." Her words, steeped in sincerity, sparked a dialogue that eventually led to a more conscious approach to the project.

Outside of work, Emily's interactions with friends and family mirrored this shift in perspective. Conversations were no longer just about catching up; they were opportunities for meaningful connections. She listened more attentively, responded more thoughtfully, and often steered discussions towards topics that considered the well-being of others and the planet.

One weekend, while visiting her parents, Emily engaged in a deep conversation with her father about his business practices. Her father, a long-time entrepreneur, listened as Emily spoke passionately about sustainable business models. It was a dialogue that bridged generations and ideologies, ending with her father's thoughtful nod and a promise to reconsider his approach.

In her neighborhood, Emily became more involved, participating in community initiatives that focused on environmental conservation and social welfare. She organized clean-up drives, joined local forums on sustainability, and volunteered at community centers. Each action, each choice, reflected her commitment to making a positive impact.

Each evening, Emily's mind often wandered through the events of the day. She reflected on her interactions, the decisions she made, and their potential impact. This period of reflection was about understanding the intricate law of cause and effect.

There were moments of doubt, times when the weight of her choices felt overwhelming. But these were also moments of growth, opportunities to learn and to reaffirm her commitment to living a life that was both mindful and impactful.

"Where does the wind rest when the city sleeps?"

On late afternoon, Emily sat at her desk, her eyes wandering past the confines of her office to the busy streets below. The city, once a symbol of her aspirations, now echoed with questions that resonated deep within her. Amid the clatter of keyboards and the murmur of her colleagues, Emily found herself in a sea of introspection, questioning the path she had so diligently trodden.

Her job had been a source of pride and identity. Yet now, it felt like an ill-fitting garment, constrictive and strangely foreign. As she sifted through emails and reports, her mind wandered to the philosophical teachings from the retreat. "Do our actions align with our true purpose?" The question, posed by the serene instructor, now echoed in her heart with increasing urgency.

In the solitude of her apartment, Emily found comfort in her journal, pouring her thoughts onto paper. She wrote about her day, the campaigns she worked on, and how they made her feel. She realized that the excitement she once felt for developing advanced programs had waned, replaced by a longing for something more meaningful, more aligned with her new values.

Her evenings were spent in quiet reflection, accompanied by the soft strumming of her guitar, an old hobby she had recently revisited. Music became her refuge, a place where she could express her inner turmoil and hopes. The melodies she created were tinged with a sense of searching, of yearning for a path that resonated with her soul.

The weekends brought opportunities for deeper exploration. Emily attended workshops and seminars, delving into topics of sustainability, social entrepreneurship, and mindful living. She met individuals who had dared to step off the well-trodden path, carving their own way in pursuit of their passions and values. Their stories stirred something within her, a desire to align her career with her newfound perspectives.

Emily's conversations with her friend, Maya, became a source of comfort and inspiration. Maya, both a social worker and Yoga instructor, shared her experiences of working in communities, of the challenges and the profound fulfillment it brought. Their dialogues often meandered into philosophical realms, discussing the essence of meaningful work and the impact of societal structures on individual choices.

One evening, as they sat in a quaint café, the air filled with the aroma of freshly brewed coffee and the soft hum of conversation, Maya posed a question that struck a chord in Emily. "What would you do if you weren't afraid of failure or judgment?" The question lingered in the air, and in Emily's mind, long after their meeting.

At work, Emily found herself increasingly disengaged, her tasks feeling more like obligatory chores than fulfilling endeavors. She observed her colleagues, wondering if they too harbored similar doubts, or if they found genuine satisfaction in their work. She yearned for a connection, for a sense of purpose that transcended profit margins and market shares.

Her interactions with her boss, Mr. Henderson, became moments of silent rebellion. His focus on deadlines, once a driving force for Emily, now seemed shallow and unfulfilling. During meetings, she found herself voicing suggestions for more socially responsible products, only to be met with polite nods and non-committal responses.

The dissonance between her inner world and her external reality grew more pronounced, leading Emily to a pivotal moment of decision. One quiet Sunday morning, with the sun casting gentle patterns through her curtains, Emily sat with her journal, her thoughts, and her doubts. The decision she was about to make was about aligning her life's work with her deepest convictions.

She contemplated the risks, the uncertainty of stepping into the unknown. But more importantly, she contemplated the cost of staying on a path that no longer felt authentic. The decision was clear, yet daunting.

As Emily penned her resignation letter, she felt a mix of fear and exhilaration. She was stepping away from the security and prestige of her job, venturing into a realm of possibilities that aligned with her values and aspirations.

In the days that followed, Emily experienced a range of emotions - from liberating joy to unsettling doubt. But beneath it all lay a steady current of peace, a knowing that she was finally honoring her true self.

"Can the solitary tree hear its own leaves falling?"

The evening air was crisp, carrying the scent of autumn as Emily walked through the park, her thoughts as scattered as the golden leaves that crunched under her boots. The recent shifts in her life had altered her perspective on her career. Those shifts had also seeped into the very fabric of her relationships. As she walked, her mind replayed the recent interactions with friends and acquaintances, noticing a distinct change in her approach to these connections.

Gone were the days when Emily found comfort in the bustling nightlife, surrounded by laughter and chatter that, in retrospect, seemed to skim the surface of genuine interaction. She had always been the social butterfly, flitting from one group to another, her calendar a colorful mosaic of brunches, parties, and coffee dates. But now, these activities left her feeling hollow, craving something deeper, something more authentic.

Emily often found herself lost in thought, reflecting on the nature of her relationships. The realization dawned on her that many of her friendships were built on shared activities rather than shared values or emotional connection. She yearned for conversations that delved into the realms of philosophy, spirituality, and personal growth - conversations that lingered in her mind long after they ended.

This longing led Emily to seek out new avenues of connection. She joined book clubs, meditation groups, and attended lectures on topics that sparked her newfound interests. Here, she met individuals whose eyes shone with the light of similar quests, whose words resonated with depth and sincerity.

One such individual was Leo, a fellow member of a philosophy discussion group. Their first conversation had been an accidental encounter over a shared admiration for a quote by Rumi displayed in the bookstore. This encounter blossomed into a friendship marked by deep discussions about life, purpose, and the mysteries of the human experience.

As their friendship grew, so did Emily's understanding of what she truly sought in relationships. With Leo, she found a space where she could be her authentic self, where her thoughts and feelings were met with understanding and curiosity rather than judgment or indifference.

In her existing friendships, Emily noticed a shift as well. She became more selective, choosing to invest time in relationships that felt meaningful and enriching. Some friends, accustomed to the old Emily, struggled to understand her new approach, leading to moments of disconnect and, in some cases, distance.

But Emily remained steadfast in her journey, finding that the relationships that did withstand this shift grew stronger, more honest. Conversations with friends like Maya took on a new depth, exploring not just the events of their lives but the emotions, learnings, and reflections that these events evoked.

The change in Emily's approach to relationships was both a shift in her social life and a reflection of her inner transformation. She sought connections that mirrored her growth, that challenged her, that nurtured her spirit. This journey she embraced wholeheartedly, for it led her to a place where every interaction became an opportunity for deeper understanding and genuine connection.

"Does the reflection in the cup change the taste of the tea?"

The sun had barely risen, painting the sky in hues of orange and pink, as Emily sat by her bedroom window, a steaming cup of tea in hand. The events of the past few weeks had stirred something deep within her, like a dormant seed now sprouting in the fertile soil of introspection. She gazed out at the awakening cityscape, and the reflections shimmering within her.

These moments of solitude had become sacred to Emily, a time for her to delve into the depths of her being, to question and to understand. The profound experiences that had recently unfolded in her life had ignited a reevaluation of her core values and life goals. It was as though she was peeling back layers of herself, layers formed by years of societal expectations, familial pressures, and her own unexamined ambitions.

Her career, once a source of pride and identity, now seemed like a path chosen by a stranger. The long hours, the relentless pursuit of success, the accolades - they all felt hollow, echoes of a life that no longer resonated with her true self. Her relationships, too, were under scrutiny. The realization that she sought deeper, more meaningful connections had transformed her approach to friends, family, and love.

Emily pondered over what truly mattered to her. Was it the pursuit of wealth and recognition? Or was it something more intangible, like inner peace, fulfillment, and the joy of genuine connections? Her heart knew the answer, but her mind wrestled with the practicalities of such a shift.

She contemplated the idea of 'service' - how could she contribute to the world in a way that aligned with her values? Could her skills and passions be channeled towards a greater good? These questions swirled in her mind, each one opening doors to new possibilities and to uncertainties.

As she sipped her tea, Emily's thoughts wandered to a conversation she had had with her grandmother years ago. Her grandmother, a wise and gentle soul, had spoken of life as a tapestry of choices, each thread representing a decision, a chance to weave meaning and purpose into one's existence. Emily realized she was at a crossroads, holding the threads of her life in her hands, ready to weave a new pattern.

Her introspection was interrupted by the chirping of her phone - a reminder of a meeting with her mentor, Mrs. Kaur, who had been a guiding force in her life. Perhaps, she could offer perspective on her current crossroads.

Their meeting, set in the quaint ambiance of a local tea house, was a convergence of mentorship and friendship. As they talked, Emily found herself talking about her recent reflections and doubts. Mrs. Kaur listened intently, her eyes reflecting understanding and compassion.

She spoke of her own journey, how she had navigated similar crossroads, finding that sometimes, the most challenging paths led to the most fulfilling destinations. She urged Emily to listen to her inner voice, to trust that it would guide her towards her true purpose.

As they parted ways, Emily felt a sense of clarity and resolve. She knew the journey ahead would be fraught with challenges and uncertainties, but she also knew that she was ready to embark on it. Ready to redefine her life, to align it with her core values, to live a life that truly represented who she was and what she aspired to be.

The rest of the day passed in a blur of activity, but Emily's mind remained anchored in her newfound purpose. She knew that the path ahead would require courage, resilience, and faith, but she also knew that she was no longer the person who walked the well-trodden path without question. She was ready to create her own path, one that led to a life of meaning, fulfillment, and true joy.

"Can the wind in the leaves carry away yesterday's dust?"

As the first light of dawn crept through her curtains, casting a warm glow across her room, Emily lay in bed, her mind active with thoughts that had become her new companions. The journey of self-discovery she had embarked upon, an inward exploration was now urging her to reflect this transformation in her external world as well. Seeking alignment with her newfound beliefs, she pondered over the changes necessary in her lifestyle and habits.

Her room, once a haphazard collection of old furniture and random trinkets, had now transformed into a space that reflected her new values – simplicity, tranquility, and a touch of nature. Her wardrobe, also a reflection of her former life of fast fashion and impulsive shopping, was the next frontier. She sifted through her clothes, setting aside items for donation. Moving forward, she decided to adopt a more sustainable approach to fashion – choosing quality over quantity, and ethical brands that resonated with her values.

In the kitchen, Emily reviewed her eating habits. The shelves were stocked with processed foods, remnants of her busy, convenience-driven lifestyle. She made a mental note to start incorporating more whole, plant-based foods, aligning her diet with her growing consciousness about health and the environment.

The needed changes weren't just material. Emily realized that her daily routine also needed a shift. She decided to carve out more time each morning for meditation and reflection, to start her day grounded in her beliefs. She also committed to being more mindful in her interactions, ensuring her words and actions reflected kindness and empathy.

Her professional life, once a major part of her identity, was an area she approached with a mix of apprehension and hope. As she sat at her desk, surrounded by files and project plans, she contemplated how her work could better reflect her values. Could she volunteer her skills to a nonprofit? The possibilities seemed both daunting and exhilarating.

In her quest for alignment, Emily reached out to others who shared her journey. Conversations with friends, family, and even acquaintances took on a new depth. She found herself engaged in philosophical discussions about life, purpose, and the nature of happiness. Each interaction, each shared story, brought new insights and reinforced her commitment to her new path.

One evening, as she walked through the park, the setting sun casting long shadows on the path, Emily's thoughts turned introspective. She realized that this quest for alignment wasn't only about changing habits or routines; it was about redefining her identity. Each step, each decision, was a piece of the mosaic she was creating – a representation of her true self.

In a quiet moment of realization, while watching the dance of leaves in the gentle breeze, Emily understood that this journey was not a destination but a continuous process of growth and evolution. Her newfound beliefs were ideals to aspire to in her daily life.

"Is the flavor of coffee found in the bean or in the brewing?"

In the dimly lit corner of her favorite coffee shop, surrounded by muffled conversations and the occasional clink of cups, Emily found herself lost in yet another book about the profound mysteries of life. This period had become a time of enlightenment for her, a phase where every page turned, and every word absorbed brought her closer to a broader understanding of the world.

The coffee shop, with its rustic charm and walls adorned with local art, had become her refuge. Here, surrounded by the aroma of freshly brewed coffee and the comfort of her usual window seat, Emily explored the realms of philosophy and spirituality. Each author, each philosopher she encountered, from the ancient wisdom of Lao Tzu to the modern reflections of Thich Nhat Hanh, offered new perspectives, challenging, and expanding her views.

As winter turned to spring, the transformation in nature mirrored Emily's own internal metamorphosis. The once barren trees now burst with life, a vivid reminder of the cycles of growth and renewal. During her daily walks in the park, Emily contemplated these changes, often finding parallels between the natural world and her spiritual journey.

Her exploration was not confined to books and nature. Emily sought out conversations that could deepen her understanding. She found herself engaging more with Mr. Jensen, the elderly neighbor who spent his afternoons tending to his garden. His insights on life, drawn from years of experience, provided Emily with a unique perspective, often leading to discussions that lingered long in her mind.

In her pursuit of knowledge, Emily attended workshops and joined another local meditation group, where she practiced quieting her mind and listening to the subtle whispers of her inner self. These sessions were also opportunities to connect with like-minded individuals, each on their own journey of discovery.

Emily's world expanded beyond her immediate surroundings as she embraced different cultures and philosophies. She attended cultural events at the local community center, where she was introduced to diverse customs and traditions. Each experience added a new layer to her understanding, painting a more inclusive and enriched picture of the world.

Through books, nature, meditation, and meaningful interactions, Emily's view of the world transformed. She no longer saw life through a single lens, but through a kaleidoscope of cultures, philosophies, and experiences. Her journey of self-discovery had led her to a deeper, more profound understanding of the world and her place in it.

Emily realized that this journey was infinite. There was so much more to learn, so many more experiences to embrace. With a sense of awe and a heart full of gratitude, she closed her eyes, whispering a silent promise to continue this path of discovery, ever broadening her understanding of the world and the myriad mysteries it held.

Conflict

"In an office where ambition echoes and stillness whispers, where does true fulfillment reside?"

Emily had made the decision after much thought that rather than leave her company and pull away from the world she had known that she would stay and try to make positive changes where she could and learn to adapt to the profound growth she was experiencing.

The author W. Somerset Maugham said it best in his novel "The Razors Edge", it was easy to be a holy man up on the mountain. Emily would continue her journey not up on the mountain but in the boardrooms and offices she had relied on to provide the much needed finances to support her journey inward.

As Emily stepped into the office on a Monday morning, the familiar hum of workstations and the muted buzz of early conversations filled the air. The day promised the usual routine until she noticed a new face among the familiar crowd. Standing near the conference room was Michael, the new project manager. He was a tall figure with a commanding presence, his sharp suit and neatly groomed appearance speaking volumes of his professionalism.

Michael's introduction to the team was brief and to the point. He outlined his vision for efficiency, productivity, and success, his voice firm and confident. Emily listened, her thoughts a mix of curiosity and apprehension. His approach, emphasizing measurable results and aggressive timelines, was a stark contrast to the more reflective and mindful path she had been embracing.

In the days that followed, Michael's impact on the office environment became increasingly apparent. Meetings became more frequent and goal oriented. There was a palpable shift in the team's dynamics, a subtle undercurrent of stress replacing the previous ease. Deadlines were tighter, expectations higher, and the office buzzed with a new intensity.

Emily found herself grappling with this change. The focus on material success and the relentless pursuit of goals clashed with her new values of mindfulness and purpose. She felt a growing dissonance, a tension between her professional responsibilities and her personal beliefs.

One afternoon, during a project meeting, this tension came to a head. As Michael outlined a new strategy for maximizing profits, Emily hesitated before voicing her thoughts. "Have we considered the environmental impact of this approach?" she asked, her voice steady but unsure.

The room fell silent. Michael's eyes met hers, a flicker of surprise in his otherwise composed demeanor. "Our primary focus is on the bottom line," he responded, his tone polite but dismissive.

The meeting ended with a sense of unease for Emily. She sat at her desk afterward, her mind racing. This was more than just a professional challenge; it was a moral one. How could she reconcile her job with her evolving perspective?

In the following days, Emily sought counsel from her mentor, Mrs. Kaur. Over cups of steaming chai in their favorite Tea House, she shared her concerns. Mrs. Kaur listened, her expression thoughtful. "Remember, Emily," she said, "true change often comes from within. You have the power to influence your environment, but it requires patience, resilience, and sometimes, a bit of strategic thinking."

Emboldened by her words, Emily began to seek subtle ways to integrate her beliefs into her work. She proposed sustainable alternatives in meetings, initiated discussions on ethical practices, and advocated for community-oriented projects. Her efforts were met with mixed responses, but she persisted, believing in the power of small, incremental changes.

Her interactions with Michael, however, remained challenging. His results-driven mindset seemed unyielding, and Emily often felt like a lone voice advocating for a different approach. Yet, she did not relent, hoping to find a common ground where both perspectives could coexist.

Amid these professional challenges, Emily continued her journey of personal growth. She delved deeper into philosophical studies, attended meditation sessions, and nurtured her relationships with friends who shared her values. These activities became her refuge, a source of strength and clarity amid the tumult of her work life.

As weeks turned into months, Emily's resilience was tested time and again. But with each challenge, she grew stronger, more confident in her convictions. She realized that her journey wasn't only about transforming herself but also about inspiring transformation in others, even in small, subtle ways.

Michael, for all his focus on results, began to show signs of openness to Emily's ideas. He started asking questions, showing a flicker of interest in her proposals. It was a slow and uncertain process, but Emily saw it as a sign of progress, a glimmer of hope in aligning her work with her beliefs.

"Can the song of a soul harmonize with the orchestra of ambition?"

In the office, a new rhythm had begun to unfold, one that set the pace of Emily's days to a tune she was still learning to harmonize with. Michael, with his sharp, discerning eyes and a demeanor that exuded confidence, was the conductor of this new orchestra, one that played a melody vastly different from the one Emily had begun to cherish in her heart.

The next team meeting under Michael's leadership was a revelation of sorts for Emily. As she settled into the familiar embrace of her ergonomic chair, her notebook open to a fresh page, she observed Michael's manner of steering the discussion. It was methodical, precise, and focused singularly on targets and metrics. Profit margins, efficiency gains, and market dominance were the keywords that filled the air, creating an unmistakable feeling of ambition and drive.

Emily, whose recent journey into mindfulness and spirituality had opened her eyes to a different set of values, felt an immediate conflict. Her heart, now attuned to ideals of sustainability, community, and the intrinsic worth of individual contributions, struggled to resonate with the cold, hard numbers that Michael laid out with such conviction.

As the meeting progressed, Emily found herself increasingly at odds with the new narrative being spun around her. When Michael discussed streamlining operations by potentially downsizing, a wave of discomfort washed over her. She thought of her colleagues, not as numbers on a spreadsheet but as individuals with stories, dreams, and fears. The thought of them being reduced to mere variables in a business equation was jarring.

After the meeting, Emily retreated to her cubicle, her mind a whirlwind of conflicting emotions. She wrestled with the notion of speaking up, of sharing her perspective with Michael. Yet, the fear of being dismissed or misunderstood held her back. She questioned her place in this new order, wondering if her ideals had any room in a world driven by material success.

It was during a casual lunch break with her colleague and close friend, Sarah, that Emily found the courage to voice her concerns. Sarah, with her easy smile and a knack for listening, provided a comforting presence. As they sat in the sunlit corner of the cafeteria, Emily shared her apprehension about Michael's approach.

"You're not alone in this, Em," Sarah said, her voice laced with empathy. "It's hard, adjusting to such a drastic change. But maybe this is an opportunity for you to introduce your ideas. It's about finding a balance, right?"

Encouraged by Sarah's words, Emily began to contemplate ways to bridge the gap between her values and the demands of her role. She started to participate more actively in meetings, offering insights that gently nudged her team towards more ethical and sustainable practices. Her suggestions were met with varying degrees of reception, but she persisted, believing in the value of her contributions.

The true test came during a project meeting where environmental concerns were at stake. As the team discussed a new product launch, Emily seized the moment to highlight the potential environmental impact of their current approach. Her voice was calm but firm, her argument well-reasoned and compelling.

The room fell into a thoughtful silence following her speech. Emily could feel Michael's analytical gaze on her, evaluating, perhaps reassessing. He didn't immediately agree with her, but the seed of dialogue had been planted. It was a small victory, but a significant one for Emily.

Meanwhile, Emily continued to grapple with her inner turmoil. Nights of introspection and journaling helped her to process her thoughts and feelings, allowing her to approach each day with renewed purpose. She found consolation in her growing spiritual practice, which provided a counterbalance to the relentless pace of her professional life.

In her interactions with Michael, Emily maintained a respectful but assertive stance. She recognized the value in his results-driven approach but also believed in the importance of integrating ethical considerations into business decisions. Their exchanges, often charged with a subtle tension, became an intellectual battle of sorts, each trying to understand and navigate the other's worldview.

Through these experiences, Emily began to evolve, both professionally and personally. She learned the art of compromise and the power of standing up for her beliefs. Her inner journey was shaping up to be a complex puzzle of conflicts and resolutions, a chronicle that intertwined the material with the spiritual, the personal with the professional, and the ideal with the practical.

"Can the whisper of empathy echo in the corridors of efficiency?"

The office that once echoed with the sounds of collaboration and camaraderie was gradually morphing into a different world altogether, a world where the tick of the clock seemed louder, and the air carried a hint of urgency. Michael's arrival had ushered in a new era, one where efficiency and results were the twin pillars upholding every decision, every action.

Emily, with her newly awakened sense of spirituality and mindfulness, found herself increasingly at odds with this shifting environment. The office walls, once vibrant with the buzz of cooperative brainstorming, now seemed to close in on her, echoing the relentless demand for results and performance. She missed the days when colleagues would gather around a desk to solve a problem together, their discussions a blend of professional expertise and personal anecdotes.

The change was most evident in the team meetings. Where there used to be open discussions, there were now presentations focused solely on targets and forecasts. The faces around her, once relaxed and engaged, now seemed taut with the strain of meeting stringent deadlines and expectations.

As Emily navigated through this transformed landscape, she felt the strain of balancing her inner journey with the outer demands of her professional role. The pressure to conform to the new, more competitive atmosphere was at odds with her pursuit of harmony and understanding.

One particularly challenging day, as Emily sat at her desk, her eyes skimming over a project report that demanded her attention, she found her mind wandering. She thought of her conversations with Mr. Jensen, her elderly neighbor, whose wisdom had often provided her with a different perspective on life. She remembered his words, spoken during one of their leisurely afternoon chats in his garden, "Change, my dear, is the only constant. It's not the change itself, but how we respond to it, that defines us."

These words, simple yet profound, resonated with her now more than ever. She realized that she couldn't control the changes happening around her, but she could control how she responded to them.

With renewed determination, Emily began to seek ways to adapt to the new work dynamics while staying true to her principles. She started by initiating small, informal gatherings with her colleagues, creating spaces where they could share their challenges and support each other. These gatherings soon became a place where the competitive edge was softened by empathy and understanding.

In her interactions with Michael, Emily strived to find common ground. She began to frame her ideas and suggestions in a way that aligned with his results-driven approach while subtly infusing them with her values. It was a delicate balancing act, one that required her to be both assertive and tactful.

The conversations between Emily and Michael evolved into intellectual exchanges that, while often challenging, opened doors to new understandings for both. Emily introduced Michael to the concept of 'triple bottom line' - a business approach that encompassed profit, people, and the planet. To her surprise, he showed a keen interest, his analytical mind intrigued by the potential long-term benefits of such a holistic approach.

As weeks turned into months, the office atmosphere began to show subtle signs of change. The competitive edge remained, but there was a growing undercurrent of collaboration and mindfulness. Emily's efforts were slowly bearing fruit, creating a space where efficiency and empathy could coexist.

Emily continued to seek comfort in her spiritual practices. Her meditation sessions and philosophical readings were not just escapes from the demands of her professional life; they were sources of strength and clarity, helping her navigate the complex web of her day-to-day experiences.

The transformation in the office dynamics reflected a larger journey, one that Emily was undertaking both within and outside the confines of her workplace. It was a journey marked by challenges and triumphs, by conflicts and resolutions. In this journey, Emily was a catalyst, the bringer of change who was herself being transformed in the process.

"Can the seed of stillness flourish in the soil of relentless pursuit?"

The air in the office was charged with an unspoken tension, an undercurrent that rippled through the space, emanating from the growing rift between Emily and Michael. Michael, with his sharp business acumen and focus on tangible results, viewed Emily's evolving perspectives and practices with a skepticism that bordered on disdain. To him, her forays into meditation, mindfulness, and philosophical discussions were frivolous indulgences, distractions from the real work that needed to be done.

Emily, on the other hand, found these practices essential, not just for her personal growth, but as tools that enhanced her professional effectiveness. They helped her approach her work with clarity, creativity, and a sense of calm that was increasingly rare in their high-pressure environment.

The clash of their worldviews came to a head during a team meeting. As Emily proposed a new project approach that included a mindfulness exercise to enhance team cohesion and creativity, Michael's skepticism bubbled to the surface. "Let's keep our focus on the bottom line, shall we?" he interjected, his voice tinged with irritation. "We're here to work, not meditate."

The room fell silent, the team members exchanging uneasy glances. Emily, feeling a flush of embarrassment and frustration, struggled to maintain her composure. She believed in her approach but was unsure how to bridge the gap between her and Michael.

Later that day, as she sat in the park, the gentle rustling of leaves and the distant laughter of children playing provided a soothing backdrop to her tumultuous thoughts. She reflected on her journey, the insights she had gained, and the challenges she now faced. It was about integrating her beliefs into her professional life in a way that was productive and respectful of others' perspectives.

Determined to address the growing tension, Emily sought out Michael the next day. She found him in his office, surrounded by charts and reports. "Can we talk?" she asked, her voice steady.

Michael looked up; his expression guarded. "Sure, Emily. What's on your mind?"

Emily took a deep breath, choosing her words carefully. "I know we have different views on things like mindfulness and meditation. But I truly believe these practices can benefit our work. They aren't meant to be distractions. In fact, they can help us focus and think more creatively."

Michael listened, his expression softening slightly. "I'm all for creativity," he said, "but I fail to see how sitting quietly, doing nothing, helps our bottom line."

"It's more than just sitting quietly," Emily explained. "It's about training our minds to be present and focused. It can improve our decision-making and problem-solving abilities. I've experienced these benefits personally and I think our team could too."

Michael was silent for a moment, his gaze shifting to the window. "I'll be honest, Emily. I'm a results-driven person. This all sounds a bit too abstract for me. But I can see you're passionate about it."

"Would you be open to a compromise?" Emily suggested. "Maybe we can start with a short, guided session during a team break. It's a small step, but it could be a start."

Michael considered her proposal, the wheels of thought turning in his mind. "Alright," he finally said, "we can give it a try. But let's keep it brief and see if it actually makes a difference."

Emily smiled, relieved. "Thank you, Michael. I appreciate your openness to try something new."

As she left his office, Emily felt a glimmer of hope. The conversation had been difficult, but it was a step towards mutual understanding. She knew that change was a slow process, filled with setbacks and small victories. But she was ready to navigate this journey, armed with patience, empathy, and the conviction that even the smallest bridge of understanding could lead to meaningful change.

"Can the song of truth be heard in the silence of scrutiny?"

Emily could feel Michael's scrutinizing gaze on her like a physical weight, pressing down on her every time she presented a project or shared an idea. His critical eye, once merely a source of professional rigor, now seemed to pierce through her work, seeking flaws and questioning her contributions. This relentless scrutiny left Emily feeling stressed, her confidence wavering under the unyielding pressure of doubt and underappreciation.

The once vibrant and collaborative atmosphere of the office had become a landscape of quiet tension and unspoken apprehensions. Emily, who had always taken pride in her work, now found herself second-guessing every decision, every proposal she put forward. The constant questioning from Michael chipped away at her sense of worth, leaving her to wonder if her evolving perspectives were indeed a liability.

In a team meeting, as she presented her latest project, her voice wavered slightly under Michael's intense gaze. "Are you sure this approach is the most efficient?" he questioned; his tone sharp. "It seems like you're focusing more on theoretical benefits rather than practical results."

The room fell silent, the team members casting sympathetic glances toward Emily. She felt a flush of embarrassment, her mind racing to defend her approach, yet she struggled to find the words. The self-assured, innovative professional she once was seemed to be fading, leaving behind a shell of doubt and uncertainty.

Later, as Emily sat in her small apartment, she allowed herself a moment of introspection. Her heart was heavy with the burden of unspoken words and unacknowledged efforts. She pondered over the philosophical teachings she had recently embraced, seeking solace in their wisdom. Was it possible, she wondered, that her journey towards spiritual and personal growth was incompatible with her current professional environment?

Her thoughts were interrupted by a call from her friend, Laura, who had always been a sounding board for her ideas and emotions. "Emily, you sound drained. What's going on?"

Emily sighed; her voice tinged with frustration. "It's Michael. He questions everything I do. I feel like I'm constantly under a microscope, and it's exhausting."

Laura listened, her voice a comforting presence in the darkness of Emily's room. "Maybe it's time to have a heart-to-heart with Michael. He needs to understand how his actions are impacting you."

Emily considered Laura's advice. The thought of confronting Michael was daunting, yet she knew that communication was key to resolving this growing rift.

The next day, Emily requested a meeting with Michael. They sat in a small conference room, the morning light casting long shadows across the table. "Michael, I need to be honest with you," Emily began, her voice steady but laced with emotion. "Your constant scrutiny is really affecting me. I feel like my contributions are not valued."

Michael looked taken aback, his usual composed demeanor faltering. "Emily, I didn't realize my approach was having this effect on you. I'm just trying to ensure we maintain high standards."

"I understand that" Emily replied, "but there's a difference between maintaining standards and constantly questioning someone's ability. I need space to breathe, to be creative."

Michael nodded, a look of understanding crossing his features. "I'll try to give you that space. I appreciate your honesty, Emily. Let's work together to find a balance."

As Emily left the room, she felt a sense of relief wash over her. The conversation had been difficult, but it was a necessary step towards mutual understanding and respect. She knew that the road ahead would still have its challenges, but she felt a renewed sense of hope. With each small victory, she was learning that the journey of personal and professional growth was a path best navigated with open communication and the courage to stand up for oneself.

"In a forest of ambition, where shadows of doubt linger, a solitary flower blooms, untouched by the chaos. Can the flower sustain its fragrance amidst the storm, or does the storm itself nurture its essence?"

Emily's journey toward inner peace, once a path illuminated by the soft glow of tranquility, now seemed to be overshadowed by the looming presence of stress and tension from her workplace. The serene mindset she had so diligently cultivated through meditation and mindfulness began to fray at the edges, like a well-worn coat exposed to the harsh elements of a demanding environment.

Each day, as she stepped into the office, a wave of anxiety threatened to wash over her. The once inviting space now felt like an arena, where every word and action were scrutinized under the unyielding gaze of Michael. The incessant hum of computers and the staccato rhythm of keyboard taps seemed to sync with her racing heart, a constant reminder of the high-stakes environment she was navigating.

In team meetings, she found herself wrestling with an internal turmoil. Her mind, once a reserve of creative thought, was now a battleground where self-doubt clashed with the urge to prove herself. As Michael's piercing questions cut through the room, Emily felt her carefully maintained composure slipping. Her responses, usually eloquent and well-considered, now emerged as hesitant and unsure.

In these moments, she would often retreat into her own thoughts, seeking guidance from the philosophical teachings that had been her relief. She pondered on the words of ancient philosophers, who spoke of the impermanence of all things and the importance of maintaining inner balance amidst external chaos. Yet, these reflections, which once provided clarity, now seemed like distant echoes, muffled by the discord of her current predicaments.

The evenings were no longer a time of restful solitude but a period of introspection and self-doubt. As she sat in her apartment, the glow of the city lights casting a soft luminescence into her room, Emily grappled with a disquieting thought: was her pursuit of peace and balance an impractical ideal in a world driven by material success and relentless competition?

It was during one of these reflective evenings that Emily received a call from her mentor, Mrs. Kaur. Her voice, calm and reassuring, calmed her troubled spirit. "Emily, remember that true balance is not about eliminating challenges but learning to navigate them with grace and resilience," she advised.

Their conversation drifted towards the philosophical, exploring the concepts of duality and the middle way. Mrs. Kaur spoke of life as a balance of opposites – action and inaction, speaking and silence, giving and receiving – and the importance of finding harmony within these extremes.

Inspired by Mrs. Kaur's words, Emily began to view her situation through a different lens. She realized that her struggle at work was not just a challenge to her peace but an opportunity to practice it. She started to approach each day with a renewed sense of purpose, not to avoid stress and tension, but to embrace them as part of her journey towards growth and understanding.

Slowly, Emily began to reclaim her inner calm. She practiced mindfulness not just in the quiet of her apartment but within the commotion of her office. She found moments of peace in small things – a shared smile with a colleague, the satisfaction of a job well done, the serene beauty of the city skyline during her evening walks.

As she continued to navigate the challenging dynamics at work, Emily discovered that her sense of peace and balance was not a fragile state to be protected, but a resilient force that could adapt and thrive even in the most demanding environments. This realization was not the end of her struggles, but it marked a significant shift in her journey – a deeper understanding that peace is not just a destination to reach, but a path to walk, every day, with courage and mindfulness.

"In a forest of towering ambitions, a stream whispers of stillness. Can the song of the stream be heard over the rustling leaves, or does its melody become one with the wind?"

The conflict that simmered between Emily and Michael, once perceived as a personal skirmish, began to shift in Emily's understanding into something far more significant—a microcosm of a broader philosophical battle. It encapsulated a profound struggle between two worlds: the relentless, materialistic drive of the corporate landscape and the introspective, spiritual journey Emily found herself increasingly drawn to.

Emily's days in the office became a living theatre where this struggle played out. The sleek, glass-walled skyscraper, towering confidently over the city, was a monument to material success. Inside, the air was thick with ambition, every individual a cog in a machine that celebrated tangible achievements and measurable outcomes. Michael, with his sharp suits and sharper business acumen, was the embodiment of this world. His focus was laser-like, fixated on results, growth, and efficiency.

In contrast, Emily found herself drifting further from this paradigm. Her desk, nestled in the corner of the bustling office, became an island of introspection amid a stormy sea. The reports and spreadsheets that once seemed like gospel now appeared superficial in the light of her evolving perspective. She would often gaze out of the window, observing the rhythm of the city, and wonder about the countless stories and dreams hidden beneath the facade of urban efficiency.

Her philosophical explorations, once confined to the privacy of her home, began to seep more and more into her work life. In meetings, while others spoke of market trends and profit margins, her thoughts wandered to the teachings of Eastern philosophy, the ideas of mindfulness, and the quest for inner peace. She found herself questioning the relentless pursuit of material success, the constant need for more, which seemed to leave little room for spiritual fulfillment.

In hushed conversations by the coffee machine and in the reflective surface of the elevator, they exchanged curious glances and whispered speculations. Emily, once a rising star in the firm, was now an enigma, her changing attitudes, and behaviors a puzzle to many.

It was during a particularly tense project meeting that the conflict reached a crescendo. Michael, in his element, was outlining an aggressive strategy for the next quarter. His language was that of conquest and triumph. Emily, feeling increasingly alienated, yet again voiced her dissent. "Isn't there more to our work than just profits and targets?" she asked, her voice steady but her heart racing.

The room fell silent. Michael's eyes narrowed as he regarded her with a perplexing mix of intrigue and incredulity. "Emily, we're in a business, not a monastery," he said, his tone laced with sarcasm.

This exchange sparked a series of dialogues, both heated and enlightening. Emily and Michael found themselves engaged in unexpected philosophical debates, often drawing in other members of the team. Questions about the purpose of work, the definition of success, and the role of personal fulfillment in professional life became common topics in the office corridors and meeting rooms.

Through these discussions, Emily began to see her conflict with Michael in a new light. It was not a barrier to her journey but an integral part of it. Each debate, each challenging conversation was an opportunity to refine her beliefs, to articulate her evolving worldview, and to understand the perspectives of others.

Gradually the office transformed from a battleground of conflicting ideologies into a dynamic arena of ideas and beliefs. Intertwined with the lives of those around her, Emily became a witness to the possibility of harmony between the material and the spiritual, the corporate and the personal, external success and inner peace. It was a continuous process, a battle of opposing forces that, when embraced, led to a deeper understanding of the self and the world.

"Can the lotus of tranquility bloom in the concrete pond of commerce?"

As Emily wandered deeper into her spiritual journey, she found herself at a crossroads. The corporate world, with its relentless pace and material focus, seemed increasingly at odds with her inner transformation. Yet, she recognized the impracticality of abandoning her career altogether. The challenge, then, was to find a way to harmonize her spiritual growth with her professional responsibilities. It was a delicate balancing act, requiring both introspection and creativity.

Emily's office stood as a symbol of the modern corporate world. The building, a sleek edifice of glass and steel, reflected the bright city lights, embodying the quintessence of efficiency and success. Inside, the atmosphere was charged with ambition, the air humming with the sound of keystrokes and phone calls, a constant reminder of the unending pursuit of productivity.

Emily's workspace, however, began to transform subtly. Small changes appeared: a potted plant on her desk, a set of soothing, minimalist paintings on the wall, and a pair of noise-cancelling headphones to provide moments of relief from the constant buzz. These changes were symbolic of her attempt to create a sanctuary within the chaos, a physical manifestation of her desire to bring a sense of calm and mindfulness to her work environment.

Her approach to work continued to evolve. She started her day with a brief meditation session, finding a quiet corner in the office before the arrival of her colleagues. This practice helped her to center herself, to approach her tasks with a sense of calm and clarity. She also applied the principles of mindfulness to her work, focusing on one task at a time, fully immersing herself in it, and thereby enhancing both her efficiency and the quality of her output.

Emily's interactions with her colleagues also continued to change. Where she once engaged in conversations dominated by targets and deadlines, she now sought to bring more meaningful exchanges into her day. Lunch breaks became opportunities for deeper discussions, not just about work but about life, aspirations, and personal growth. She listened more intently, responded more thoughtfully, and gradually, her colleagues began to reciprocate, creating a more empathetic and supportive work environment.

The most significant shift, however, was in her meetings with Michael. Instead of approaching these interactions with apprehension, she saw them as opportunities to present a different perspective. She continued introducing her ideas into their discussions, not in a confrontational manner, but as gentle suggestions. She spoke of the benefits of a balanced approach to work, the importance of employee well-being, and the potential for mindful practices to enhance creativity and productivity.

Michael slowly began to show interest. The conversations between them grew more frequent and deeper, evolving from terse exchanges to engaging dialogues. They discussed the philosophy of work-life balance, the impact of corporate culture on individual creativity, and the possibility of integrating mindful practices into the workplace.

These discussions were not always smooth; there were moments of disagreement and frustration. But they were honest and thought-provoking, opening new avenues of understanding for both Emily and Michael. As they navigated these complex conversations, the office itself seemed to transform. A new energy began to permeate the space, one that balanced the pursuit of success with an awareness of the human element, the need for connection and fulfillment.

"Can the dance of the firefly illuminate the path in a forest of steel?"

Back at her apartment, Emily sat by the window. The city lights below danced like fireflies, each a story, a life, a struggle like her own. Her mind was a whirlpool of thoughts, seeking a resolution that would honor her integrity and newfound peace.

The room was filled with the soft, ambient glow of her table lamp, casting long, thoughtful shadows. She poured herself a cup of chamomile tea, the floral aroma gently wafting through the air, mingling with her thoughts. Sipping slowly, she contemplated the delicate balance she yearned to achieve between her inner growth and her professional responsibilities.

Emily's journey had always been underpinned by a strong sense of dedication and commitment to her job. Yet, the spiritual insights she had recently embraced were not just an escape from the stress but a profound part of who she was becoming. She pondered the philosophical implications of this duality – the material demands of her career versus the spiritual calling of her heart.

Her thoughts drifted to a conversation she once had with an old professor during her university days, a mentor who had always encouraged her to seek her own path. He had spoken of the ancient philosophy of 'Dharma', the importance of righteous living, and fulfilling one's duties while remaining true to oneself. His words now resonated more than ever, providing a glimmer of clarity in her quest for balance.

The next day at work, Emily approached her responsibilities with a renewed sense of purpose. She sought ways to integrate her inner growth into her daily tasks, even more to infuse mindfulness and compassion into every interaction and decision. She knew that her spiritual practices could coexist with her career, not as separate entities but as complementary facets of her life.

She pressed for more of her 'Mindfulness at Work' sessions, meetings where anyone could join to learn and practice mindfulness techniques. It was a small step, but it sparked curiosity and interest among her peers.

One evening, as she left the office, the sky was painted in brilliant hues of orange and purple, a canvas of nature's artistry. Emily stood for a moment, absorbing the beauty, a symbol of the harmony she sought. She realized that resolution did not mean a perfect balance, but the graceful dance of adapting and evolving, of being true to oneself while navigating the myriad roles and responsibilities life presents. In this dance, Emily found her rhythm, a harmonious blend of her professional aspirations and her spiritual journey.

Struggles and Efforts
"Catching the Ox"

"Can a single leaf retain its tranquility amidst the storm?"

As Emily returned to the hurried rhythm of her workplace each day she carried with her a fragile bubble of peace, a hard-won serenity that seemed at odds with the high-octane energy of the corporate world. The skyscrapers, towering like giants of ambition and success, loomed over her as she navigated the crowded streets, their shadows casting long, angular patterns on the pavement that mirrored the complexities of her inner journey.

The office, a hive of activity, buzzed with the sounds of ringing phones, clattering keyboards, and hurried footsteps. Her colleagues, absorbed in their own worlds of spreadsheets and sales targets, moved with a focused urgency that Emily once shared unquestioningly. Now, however, she felt like a visitor from a different realm, struggling to reconcile inner tranquility with the relentless pace of her professional life.

Her boss, Michael, noticed the ongoing shifts in Emily's demeanor. While he appreciated her previous drive and dedication, he couldn't help but wonder about the changes in her. He observed her taking brief moments to close her eyes and breathe deeply, a practice that seemed alien in the context of their busy office.

One afternoon Michael approached Emily's cubicle. "You seem different, Emily," he said, his tone a mixture of curiosity and concern. "Is everything alright?"

Emily looked up, her eyes reflecting a calm that felt contrasting in the surrounding chaos. "I'm fine, Michael," she replied. "Just trying to find a balance."

"A balance?" Michael echoed, his eyebrows arching slightly. "Between what exactly?"

"Between the demands of this job and the peace I seek," Emily said, her voice steady yet imbued with a hint of vulnerability.

Michael leaned against the partition, his gaze thoughtful. "I've always believed in the power of hard work and focus," he began. "But I've also seen people burn out. Is that what this is about?"

"Not burnout," Emily clarified. "It's about sustaining a sense of peace and interconnectedness in all aspects of my life, including work."

Michael nodded slowly, his expression softening. "I can't say I fully understand, but I'm willing to listen."

Their conversation unfolded slowly, threading through the afternoon. Emily spoke of her experiences at the retreat, the lessons in mindfulness, and her realization that personal well-being was intricately linked to professional effectiveness.

As the day waned, and the office lights dimmed, their dialogue ventured into realms of mental health, work-life balance, and the role of inner peace in fostering a healthy, productive workplace. Michael, a man of logic and results, found himself intrigued by Emily's perspective, considering the possibility of a more holistic approach to leadership.

Meanwhile, around them, the office continued its relentless pace, unaware of the seeds of change being planted in that quiet corner. Other colleagues, like Sarah from marketing and John from finance, also taking notice of Emily's calm demeanor and her small acts of mindfulness.

Intrigued, they approached her, seeking to better understand the changes they had been observing. Emily found herself in impromptu discussions about stress management, the benefits of meditation, and the importance of staying connected to one's inner self, even during a hectic workday.

These conversations, initially hesitant and filled with skepticism, gradually evolved into deeper exchanges. Emily's cubicle became a safe place where her colleagues could find a moment of peace and a listening ear. Her personal journey of finding balance began to ripple outward, touching the lives of those around her, creating a subtle but tangible shift in the office atmosphere.

As days turned into weeks, Emily's challenge to sustain her inner peace amid the demands of her job continued. There were moments of doubt, times when the stress and pressure threatened to overwhelm her newfound serenity. Yet, with each challenge, she found herself returning to the lessons of her retreat, drawing on the practices of mindfulness and meditation to anchor herself.

Her relationship with Michael also continued to evolve, moving from a purely professional interaction to a more nuanced connection, where ideas and philosophies were exchanged with mutual respect. He began to see the value in Emily's approach, considering ways to integrate mindfulness into the workplace, not just for increased productivity, but for the holistic well-being of his team.

As Emily left the office each evening, walking beneath the towering buildings that once seemed oppressive, she felt a renewed sense of purpose. The city, with its pulsating energy and endless possibilities, no longer felt like a battlefield but a canvas, upon which she could paint her journey of balance and growth.

She realized that the true test of her growth lay not in the quiet of a secluded sanctuary, but in the heart of the hurried city, where the dance of life was most vibrant.

"In a world of relentless ambition, can the soul's quiet song be heard?"

The noise of the office, ringing phones, clicking keyboards, and urgent voices, had once been the soundtrack to Emily's professional aspirations. Now, however, it clashed discordantly with the serene melodies of her spiritual awakening. The skyscraper that housed her office stood as a stark reminder of the corporate ambition that had defined her life. Yet, as she gazed out of her window at the sprawling city below, Emily couldn't help but feel a sense of disharmony between her inner world and the external realities of her job.

In her cubicle, Emily battled waves of doubt and frustration. Her fingers hovered over the keyboard as she tried to concentrate on a demanding project, but her mind wandered, pulled by the undercurrents of her internal struggle. The balance between her professional duties and her spiritual growth, once a source of pride, now felt like a tightrope walk over an abyss of uncertainty.

"Everything okay, Em?" Sarah asked one afternoon, her voice tinged with concern as she peered over the partition separating their workspaces.

Emily forced a smile, the corners of her lips betraying the effort. "Just a bit overwhelmed," she admitted, her voice barely rising above the hum of office activity.

Sarah nodded sympathetically. "I've noticed you've been... different. More introspective, maybe?" She ventured gently, her eyebrows knitting together in a frown of genuine concern.

Emily sighed, her gaze drifting to the small Zen Garden she had placed on her desk, its raked sand, and smooth stones a stark contrast to the clutter of reports and files. "I'm trying to hold onto the calm and insight I had gained but it's hard. This environment," she gestured vaguely around the office, "it's so... intense."

Sarah leaned closer, her voice dropping to a conspiratorial whisper. "Maybe you need to find a way to merge the two worlds? Bring some of that retreat calm here?"

Emily pondered Sarah's suggestion, her mind winding through the possibilities. Could she find a better way to integrate her spiritual insights into the relentless rhythm of corporate life?

Over the next few days, Emily experimented with small changes. She began each morning with a brief meditation in the quiet before her colleagues arrived, seeking to anchor herself in a place of calm. She introduced short, mindful pauses into her day, moments where she would simply stop, breathe, and center herself amidst the chaos.

These practices, though subtle, began to make a difference. Her responses to the pressures of work became more measured, her interactions with colleagues more thoughtful. Yet, the doubt lingered, a persistent shadow that trailed her efforts.

One particularly challenging day, as deadlines loomed and tensions in the team rose, Emily felt her hard-won serenity slipping away. The familiar tendrils of stress and anxiety wound their way through her thoughts, suffocating her attempts at mindfulness. In a moment of frustration, she escaped to the rooftop garden, a space where employees seldom ventured.

The garden, with its array of potted plants and a solitary bench, offered a panoramic view of the city. Emily sat there, the sounds of the city a distant murmur, and allowed herself to feel the full weight of her doubts and fears. She questioned the practicality of her spiritual journey, the feasibility of maintaining inner peace in a world that seemed to thrive on stress and competition.

As the sun dipped below the skyline, bathing the city in a soft, golden light, Emily's thoughts turned introspective. She recalled a conversation with her yoga instructor, a wise woman who had spoken of the ebb and flow of spiritual growth, how it was natural to feel out of sync at times. "It's in these moments of doubt," the instructor had said, "that we find our true strength and resilience."

Heartened by these memories, Emily realized that her journey was not just about achieving a constant state of calm. It was also about learning to navigate the storms with grace. She understood that her spiritual insights were not fragile blooms to be shielded from the harsh realities of the world but resilient forces that could adapt and grow in any environment.

"In the dance of day and night, can tranquility be a bird in flight, alighting briefly yet profoundly, in the world's unending round?"

Emily's alarm clock chimed softly, its melodious tone a gentle nudge from the realm of dreams to the reality of a new day. In the soft, early morning light filtering through her curtains, she sat up and rubbed the sleep from her eyes. Today, she reminded herself, she would start her day with meditation, a commitment she had made to integrate her spiritual practices into her daily life.

The tranquility of her small apartment, with its minimalist decor and soothing colors, offered a sanctuary from the rushing city outside. She unfurled her yoga mat with a sense of purpose, sitting cross-legged in the center. As she closed her eyes and began to focus on her breath, Emily sought to quiet the persistent thoughts about the day ahead - the meetings, deadlines, and the unending to-do list.

Despite her efforts, her mind raced, a relentless stream of consciousness that resisted her attempts at stillness. She found herself checking the clock every few minutes, her meditation disrupted by a growing sense of urgency.

The tranquility she sought seemed like a distant shore, unreachable amid the currents of her hectic schedule.

At work, Emily's resolve to maintain mindfulness throughout her day faced similar challenges. The office was a whirlwind of activity, a maelstrom of demands that pulled her in multiple directions. She tried to take short breaks, moments to breathe and center herself, but these were often interrupted or cut short by an urgent email or a colleague's query.

During lunch, she found comfort in a conversation with a co-worker who had expressed interest in her spiritual journey. They sat in the break room, their conversation a welcome break from the chaos outside.

"I've been trying to meditate in the mornings, but it's hard," Emily confessed, stirring her salad absentmindedly. "There's always so much to do, and my mind just won't settle."

"Maybe it's not about finding a perfect routine but about adapting your practice to fit your life as it is," he suggested. "Perhaps shorter, more frequent moments of mindfulness could work better than a rigid schedule."

Emily pondered this, the idea resonating with her own experiences. She realized that her pursuit of a strict routine might be another form of the perfectionism that drove her in her professional life. Maybe, she thought, there was a different way to approach this, a more flexible path that allowed for the ebb and flow of her daily realities.

Emily began experimenting with different approaches. She introduced brief moments of mindfulness during her day - a minute of deep breathing before a meeting, a moment of reflection while waiting for her coffee to brew, even a few seconds of gratitude before answering a phone call.

These small practices began to weave a thread of calm through the course of her day. They were not the extended periods of meditation she had initially envisioned, but they brought a sense of presence and awareness that was both refreshing and grounding.

One evening, as she walked home through the city park, Emily reflected on her journey. The path was illuminated by the soft glow of streetlights, casting long shadows on the pavement. She thought about her conversation with a co-worker and how it had opened her eyes to a new way of seeing her spiritual practice.

In the quiet of the park, with the distant hum of the city as her backdrop, Emily felt a sense of peace. It was not the outcome of a perfect routine or an uninterrupted meditation session. It was, she realized, the result of her willingness to adapt, to find spirituality in the imperfections and challenges of everyday life.

"In the symphony of life, where shadows meet light, can one walk the tightrope between worldly duty and inner sight, finding harmony in the dance of day and night?"

In the half-light of dawn, as the city still slumbered in a nest of shadows and whispers, Emily sat perched on the edge of her bed, her mind teetering on the brink of the day ahead. The serenity of her room, with its soft hues and gentle contours, stood in stark contrast to the relentless rhythm of her professional life—a life increasingly at odds with the spiritual journey she had embarked upon.

The delicate balance between her inner quest for enlightenment and the outer demands of her career was akin to walking a tightrope, each step a negotiation between the call of her soul and the clamor of her corporate responsibilities. As she sipped her morning tea, the warmth of the cup seeping into her palms, Emily's thoughts unfurled like the steam rising in delicate spirals above her. How could she maintain this precarious equilibrium?

The office loomed large in her mind even before she arrived. Its corridors echoed with the footsteps of ambition, its walls reverberated with the buzz of strategy and competition. Here, in this citadel of business and efficiency, Emily's newfound spiritual insights seemed like whispers drowned out by a roar—a roar composed of deadlines, meetings, and bottom lines.

As she traveled through her day, flitting from task to task like a leaf caught in a whirlwind, Emily's thoughts were a turbulent mix of philosophical musings and practical considerations. She mulled over the teachings of Thich Nhat Hanh, the poetry of Rumi, and the wisdom of the Bhagavad Gita, seeking guidance. Yet, these moments of reflection were often interrupted by the ping of a new email or the ring of a phone, each a reminder of the relentless pace of her professional world.

The contrast of her existence was most profound in her interactions with her colleagues. In meetings, while her peers discussed market trends and revenue forecasts with fervor, Emily's mind often wandered to more existential realms. She pondered on the nature of success, the meaning of fulfillment, and the pursuit of a purpose that transcended profit margins. These contemplations, though enriching, left her feeling increasingly alienated in a world where such thoughts were considered unnecessary.

Her closest ally on this journey was Mark, a colleague who had become a friend and confidant. Their conversations, often over lunch in a quiet corner of the noisy cafeteria, were escapes of understanding in a desert of disconnect. Mark, with his own budding interest in mindfulness, provided a sounding board for Emily's thoughts, a fellow traveler on the road less taken.

One day, as Emily wrestled with a complex project, her struggle reached a climax. The project, while critical to her career, seemed trivial when weighed against the existential questions that now occupied her mind. The conflict within her was a storm, her heart and mind in tumultuous debate.

Needing a break, Emily escaped to the park adjacent to her office. The green expanse, with its ancient trees and meandering paths, was a sanctuary. Here, within the rustling leaves and the soft whispers of nature, Emily found a semblance of peace. She sat on a bench, closed her eyes, and allowed the philosophical dialogues within her to unfold freely.

As she meditated on the teachings of the great mystics and philosophers, Emily realized that the struggle she faced was not unique. It was the eternal struggle of human existence—the quest to find meaning and purpose in the mundane, to reconcile the spiritual with the material. This realization brought a sense of comfort, a feeling of being part of a larger story that spanned centuries and cultures.

With renewed resolve, Emily returned to her office. She approached her work with a different perspective, seeing it not as a series of tasks to be completed, but as a part of her larger journey of growth and discovery. She began to find small ways to infuse her work with her spiritual insights, whether through mindful communication, ethical decision-making, or simply bringing a sense of presence to her interactions.

"In the office forest, can a mindful stream reshape the currents without losing its depth, finding harmony in the dance of stillness and speed?"

Emily's transformation, deeply personal and spiritual, did not occur in isolation. It rippled outward, touching the lives and routines of those around her in the office. The change in her demeanor – her newfound calmness, her deliberate way of speaking, her occasional pauses to collect her thoughts – was a stark contrast to the Emily her colleagues knew before: the fast-paced, efficiency-driven professional.

This shift unwittingly sowed seeds of conflict in her interactions. Her colleagues, accustomed to her brisk, no-nonsense approach, now found themselves navigating an unfamiliar terrain. In meetings, her thoughtful silences were often mistaken for disengagement, her measured responses perceived as reluctance. The very traits that grounded Emily in her spiritual journey were misinterpreted as a lack of enthusiasm or commitment to her work.

During a project planning session, Emily, adhering to her new practice of mindful communication, took a moment to reflect before responding to a question. This pause, however innocuous, was met with an impatient sigh from John, a team member known for his directness. "We don't have all day, Emily. What's your take?" he snapped; his tone laced with frustration.

The room tensed, the air thick with unspoken reprimands. Emily felt a familiar surge of defensiveness, a remnant of her old self, rise within her. But she suppressed it, recalling the teachings of her spiritual mentor about embracing challenges as opportunities for growth. With a composed demeanor, she replied, addressing not only the question at hand but also acknowledging John's frustration, trying to bridge the gap widened by misunderstanding.

Her response, though well-intentioned, only served to deepen John's annoyance. "We need clear, quick decisions, not philosophy," he retorted. The meeting ended with a tangible divide between Emily's new approach and the team's expectations.

The conflict with John was a sign of the larger challenge Emily faced. Her journey not just about her inner transformation was also about how this transformation interacted with her external world. It was a delicate balancing act, one that required her to be true to her spiritual self while also being cognizant of the dynamics of her workplace.

After the meeting, Emily sought refuge in a quiet corner of the office park. The lush greenery and the gentle whisper of the wind provided contrast to the sterile confines of the office. Here, in nature, she reflected on the incident. It was a moment of introspection, a chance to reassess her approach. She realized that while her spiritual journey was her own, its expression in a professional setting needed a language that resonated with her colleagues.

This realization was a pivotal moment for Emily. It marked a transition from a purely inward focus to an outward expression that considered the perspectives and comfort zones of those around her. She started to tailor her communication, blending her new-found mindfulness with the clarity and directness her team was accustomed to. Her efforts were subtle yet deliberate, aiming to build bridges rather than walls.

In the days that followed, Emily's colleagues noticed the change. She was still the reflective, serene presence she had become, but now her interactions were more attuned to the rhythm of the office. She learned to express her thoughts more promptly, without compromising her mindfulness, and to listen not just for understanding but also for alignment.

"Can you weave inner growth that harmonizes spirit and profession?"

One evening, Emily found herself seated in the comforting warmth of Mrs. Kaur's living room. The aroma of spiced tea mingled with the subtle scent of jasmine incense, creating an ambiance that was both soothing and inviting. Mrs. Kaur, her spiritual mentor, sat across from her, her eyes reflecting a depth of understanding and empathy.

Emily unfolded her tale of struggle, her voice tinged with frustration and vulnerability. She spoke of the challenge of integrating her spiritual practice into her professional life, of the misunderstandings with colleagues, and the internal turmoil it sparked. As she spoke, Mrs. Kaur listened intently, her presence a calming force in the storm of Emily's emotions.

When Emily paused, Mrs. Kaur gently offered her perspective. "The path of integration is like walking a tightrope," she began, her voice soft yet clear. "It requires balance, patience, and an understanding that not all environments will be conducive to your spiritual practice. The key is to adapt without losing the essence of your journey."

Their conversation wandered through the realms of philosophy and practicality, exploring strategies and mindsets that could help Emily navigate her workplace dynamics without compromising her spiritual growth. Mrs. Kaur emphasized the importance of empathy and effective communication, suggesting that Emily could be a conduit of peace and understanding, even in the most stressful situations.

Heartened but still somewhat uncertain, Emily later sought the company of her friends, hoping to gain more perspective. They gathered at their favorite coffee shop, a place that had become their retreat for sharing and bonding. The clatter of dishes and the murmur of conversations around them provided a backdrop to their discussion.

Her friends, each coming from diverse professional backgrounds, offered their insights. Some spoke of similar struggles, of trying to fit their personal growth into the rigid structures of their work lives. Others suggested practical tips – time management strategies, stress relief techniques, and ways to assertively communicate her needs and boundaries.

As the evening wore on, the conversation shifted from earnest advice to stories of their own experiences, laughter mingling with words of encouragement. Emily felt a sense of camaraderie and support, a reminder that she wasn't alone in her journey.

Yet, as she left the coffee shop, the night air crisp against her skin, Emily knew that the road ahead was still daunting. The advice from Mrs. Kaur and her friends was like a lantern in the dark, offering light but not clearing the path. The practical application of these insights in her day-to-day interactions at work remained a puzzle, each piece requiring careful placement.

She realized that this journey was about finding balance and resilience, about learning through trial and error. It was about adapting her spiritual practices in a way that they became seamless with her professional persona, not an added layer but an integrated part of her being.

As Emily walked home, her thoughts wandered to the days ahead. She envisioned herself at work, armed with new strategies and a renewed sense of purpose. There would be challenges, undoubtedly, but also opportunities for growth and understanding. Her journey of change about herself was also about influencing her environment in subtle, yet meaningful ways.

"In the quiet where dawn's light meets the ticking clock, can the heart of stillness transform the rhythm of a rushing world?"

In the stillness of her apartment, where the only sound was the soft ticking of a clock, Emily sat cross-legged on her floor cushion, her eyes closed in meditation. The early morning light filtered through the curtains, casting a serene glow that seemed to envelop her in a layer of tranquility. Here, in this sacred space, Emily sought refuge from the whirlwind of her professional life.

As she breathed in deeply, her mind gradually shed the layers of stress and anxiety, revealing a calm center within. It was in these moments of introspection that Emily sought counsel from her deepest self, from the well of wisdom that she had begun to tap into during her retreat. The teachings of mindfulness, the essence of interconnectedness, and the pursuit of inner peace - these were the beacons that guided her through the fog of daily challenges.

With each exhale, Emily visualized releasing the tensions that bound her to the relentless demands of her job. She imagined her worries and doubts rising like smoke, dissipating into the ether. This practice was a reconnection, a way to align her inner world with the external chaos that surrounded her.

Her mind wandered to the philosophical dialogues she had engaged in, the ancient texts she had poured over, seeking answers to the timeless questions of purpose and fulfillment. These teachings spoke of the importance of living authentically, of aligning one's actions with one's true nature. For Emily, this meant finding a way to infuse her work with the same sense of purpose and peace that her spiritual practices had brought her.

In the quiet of her room, Emily began to envision a new way of being. She saw herself as a corporate employee and as a conduit of positive change, bringing her insights into her workplace. She imagined integrating principles of mindfulness into her daily interactions, approaching each task with presence and intention, and fostering an environment of empathy and understanding.

As the sun rose higher, casting its rays into her room, Emily opened her eyes. She felt a renewed sense of purpose, a clarity that had been elusive amid the rush of her daily routine. With a deep breath, she embraced the day ahead, ready to start weaving the threads of her inner growth into the fabric of her external world.

"As dawn's breath whispers through the city's heart, can the stillness on a balcony bloom amidst the chaos of streets?"

The cool, early dawn air wafted through Emily's slightly ajar window, bringing with it the subtle scents of the waking city. She sat, legs folded beneath her, on the small balcony of her high-rise apartment, a sanctuary amidst the urban sprawl. This was her sacred time, a daily ritual of recommitment to her spiritual journey, a journey that, she knew, would be riddled with challenges and distractions.

As the city stirred below, Emily closed her eyes, feeling the vibrations of life around her. The distant hum of traffic, the sporadic chirping of birds, the faint sounds of life beginning anew - they were all reminders of the interconnected web of existence she was a part of. In this moment of stillness, she reflected on the recent obstacles that had seemed to derail her spiritual progress. The demanding job, the endless meetings, the constant pressure to perform - these were not just hurdles but also opportunities to practice her beliefs in the most testing of environments.

Her mind examined the teachings she had embraced, the philosophies that spoke of growth being a non-linear journey, often fraught with setbacks. These teachings urged resilience, an understanding that true growth often occurred in the face of adversity. With a deep, grounding breath, Emily felt a renewed sense of commitment wash over her. She would not let the chaos of her work life disrupt her spiritual path; instead, she would use it as a catalyst for deeper growth.

Clash with Ordinary Life

"Can a tree, rooted in familiar soil, stretch its branches to touch a distant sun?"

In the heart of her personal transformation, Emily found her social landscape shifting as dramatically as her inner world. The coffee shops and quaint bistros of the city, once venues for light-hearted banter with friends, now became stages for subtle misalignments and misunderstandings.

As Emily traveled deeper into her spiritual journey, her conversations took on new depths, her words infused with the insights and revelations that had begun to shape her life. But her friends, still anchored in the familiar rhythms of their everyday concerns, struggled to connect with her evolving perspective.

One crisp autumn evening, in a cozy café, Emily met with her close friends, Sarah and Mark. The air was scented with the rich aroma of coffee and baked treats, a comforting backdrop to their gatherings. However, this evening, the usual ease of their conversation was punctuated by a subtle tension, an undercurrent of disconnect.

Emily shared her experiences with meditation and mindfulness, her voice tinged with enthusiasm. She spoke of the tranquility she found in stillness, the clarity that came from introspection. But as she dove into the philosophical underpinnings of her practice, Sarah's eyes glazed over, and Mark fidgeted with his coffee cup, a sign of his growing impatience.

"It's great that you've found something that works for you, Emily," Sarah said, her tone polite yet distant. "But all this spiritual stuff isn't for everyone. I mean, we can't all just meditate our problems away, right?"

Mark chimed in; his words laced with skepticism. "Don't you think this is just a phase, Em? It's like when you went vegan for a month. Remember how that turned out?"

Emily felt a twinge of frustration, a sense of being unseen and misunderstood. She realized that her friends, so integral to her past, were not fully equipped to journey with her into this new phase of her life. Their responses, though not ill-intentioned, felt dismissive, reducing her profound experience to a mere whim.

The conversation shifted to safer, more familiar territories — work, movies, the latest city gossip. Emily participated, but a part of her remained silent, retreating into a cocoon of introspection. She pondered the nature of friendships, the ebb and flow of connections as people grow and change.

Later that night, in the solitude of her apartment, Emily reflected on the evening. She opened her journal, the pages a repository for her thoughts and emotions. She wrote about the challenge of maintaining friendships when paths diverge, the delicate balance between holding on and letting go. Her pen moved across the paper, tracing the contours of her inner dialogue.

In this introspective space, Emily realized that her journey about self-discovery was also about learning to navigate the complexities of relationships. She understood that growth often meant accepting that not everyone would understand or support her path, and that was okay. It was a lesson in embracing change, not just within herself but also in her external world.

The following weeks brought a subtle shift in Emily's social interactions. She sought out communities and groups aligned with her interests, finding pleasure and inspiration in the company of like-minded individuals. These new connections brought fresh perspectives and supportive conversations, a stark contrast to the misunderstandings with her old friends.

Yet, Emily did not sever ties with Sarah and Mark. She valued their shared history and the joy of their past camaraderie. She accepted that while their conversations might now skim the surface of her inner life, there was still comfort in their familiarity.

"In a home where traditions grow like ivy, how can one branch into unknown spiritual paths without breaking the bonds of family roots?"

In the heart of Emily's family home, a quaint, ivy-clad house nestled in the suburbs, a subtle transformation was unfolding. The house, with its familiar creaks and comforting aromas of home-cooked meals, had always been a refuge for Emily. Yet, as she embarked on her spiritual journey, the walls that once echoed with laughter and understanding began to resonate with a sense of disconnect.

Emily's parents, John, and Linda were the embodiment of traditional values and simple joys. John, now retired, found joy in his garden, tending to his roses with the same meticulous care he had once devoted to his professional life. Linda, a nurse, filled the house with warmth and nurturing, her hands skilled in both healing and culinary arts.

Their love for Emily was unwavering, a constant in here journey through life. However, as Emily traveled farther into her spiritual quest, exploring realms of meditation, mindfulness, and philosophical introspection, her parents struggled to keep pace. Their attempts to understand and connect with her new interests were sincere but often fell short.

Dinner conversations, once a time for sharing and laughter, now carried an undercurrent of unspoken confusion. John would often try to engage Emily in discussions about her meditation practices, his questions laced with a mix of curiosity and bewilderment. Linda, in her gentle way, would encourage Emily to join them in more conventional activities, hoping to bridge the gap that seemed to be widening.

Emily appreciated their efforts, touched by their intention to connect. Yet, each well-meaning question, each attempt to bring her back to the world they understood, only served to highlight the distance that had grown between them. It was not a gap of love, but of understanding, a silent acknowledgment that the path she walked was one they could not follow.

These interactions with her family were a representation of Emily's broader experience. Each member characterized a different response to change and growth — acceptance, confusion, effort, and understanding. This dynamic added layers to Emily's understanding, showcasing the multifaceted nature of personal transformation within the context of family relationships.

As Emily thought about these interactions with her family, she reflected on the nature of growth, both personal and relational. She pondered the delicate balance between staying true to oneself and maintaining connections with loved ones who may not fully comprehend her path.

Emily would sit by her bedroom window, gazing at the stars, her thoughts wandering to philosophical realms. She contemplated the interconnectedness of all beings, the universal quest for understanding and acceptance. These reflections were integral to her journey, shaping her responses and interactions with her family.

Emily's journey was now becoming a meditation on the universal themes of connection, understanding, and the courage to walk one's own path, even in the face of incomprehension.

"How can the bird of the soul soar into unseen skies without severing the ties that bind it to the earth?"

In the soft twilight of her childhood bedroom, Emily sat cross-legged on the bed, a journal open in front of her. The room, with its pastel walls and shelves lined with books from different phases of her life, felt both familiar and alien. It was a sanctuary where memories lingered in every corner, yet now it also harbored a sense of dissonance as Emily struggled to articulate her inner transformation.

Her family, just beyond these walls, moved in a world that seemed increasingly distant from hers. Emily's journey into the depths of her own consciousness had opened doors to insights and experiences that were profoundly personal and, at times, indescribable. The challenge of articulating these to her family felt akin to translating a complex, foreign language into simple, everyday terms.

The gap in communication was not for lack of trying. Emily's attempts to convey her experiences often resulted in conversations filled with metaphors and analogies, her words painting pictures that only seemed to obscure the view. Her parents were very patient, listening with a mix of concern and perplexity, their responses tinged with polite confusion.

She pondered the nature of language and its limitations, how words could both illuminate and obscure the essence of an experience. Her thoughts probed into the philosophical musings on the inadequacy of language to fully capture the depth of human experience, a theme that resonated with her more each day.

These reflections were interspersed with vivid descriptions of her spiritual experiences – moments of profound connection, of transcending the mundane, where time seemed to stand still, and she felt at one with the universe. Yet, when she tried to share these moments, her words felt hollow, a pale shadow of the reality.

To bridge this gap, Emily turned to other forms of expression. She began to sketch and paint, letting colors and shapes do the talking where words failed. Her family observed this new mode of communication with a mix of curiosity and encouragement, a silent acknowledgment that some experiences were too deep for words.

Emily's struggles with articulation were the reflection of a universal human experience – the quest to share one's deepest truths in a world where words are often inadequate messengers. Her exploration of the boundaries of language, the power of non-verbal communication, and the enduring quest for connection and understanding, were something new for her to meditate on.

"Can the bird that touches the sky still sing songs that resonate in the hearts of those who walk the earth?"

In the solitude of her small, softly lit apartment, Emily sat by the window, her gaze lost in the city lights. The world outside contrasted sharply with the stillness within her. These moments of solitude had become her refuge for self-reflection, a place where she could grapple with the doubts that continued to cloud her mind.

Her journey, once a source of profound joy and enlightenment, now bore the weight of isolation. The more she plunged into her inner world, the more she felt disconnected from the world around her.

Emily pondered the essence of her journey. She recalled the moments of epiphany, the feelings of interconnectedness with the universe, and the inner peace she had discovered. These experiences were real and transformative, yet conveying their depth seemed an insurmountable task. The more she tried to share her insights, the more they seemed to slip through the cracks of language and understanding.

Emily questioned the nature of growth – was it inherently solitary, or was there a way to grow alongside others? Her thoughts explored the philosophy of personal change, the nature of relationships, and the human yearning for connection.

As Emily grappled with these questions, flashbacks of her past interactions played in her mind. She remembered the warmth of shared laughter with her friends, the comfort of her family's unconditional love, and the excitement of shared experiences. These memories stood in stark contrast to her current reality, where her spiritual pursuits had unintentionally built walls between her and her loved ones.

Throughout this process, Emily evolved. Her moments of doubt and reflection deepened her understanding of herself and her journey. She began to realize that true growth was about learning to navigate the complex web of human relationships.

"Can one sail the virtual waves and still find the shore of true connection?"

In the dim, early hours of the morning, Emily sat wrapped in the peace of her apartment, her laptop's screen casting a soft glow in the otherwise dark room. The silence around her was a stark contrast to the noise of her thoughts, buzzing with the urgency of finding kindred spirits. Her recent journey of self-discovery and spiritual awakening had, paradoxically, led her into a tunnel of isolation. The more she ventured down this path, the more she felt alienated from her familiar social circles.

Determined to bridge this growing chasm, Emily turned to the vast expanse of the internet, a digital sea where she hoped to find islands of shared understanding and empathy. She began her quest by joining online forums and social media groups dedicated to spiritual growth, mindfulness, and personal transformation. These platforms became her new asylums, spaces where she could freely express her thoughts and connect with individuals who resonated with her experiences.

She engaged in philosophical discussions, absorbing the diverse perspectives and wisdom shared by others on similar paths. These dialogues, rich in introspection and insight, became a source of comfort and inspiration. She found herself eagerly participating in conversations about the balance between material pursuits and spiritual fulfillment, the challenges of maintaining mindfulness in a hectic world, and the beauty of personal growth.

As Emily explored deeper into these communities, she encountered a myriad of characters, each with their unique stories and insights. There was Jasmine, a yoga instructor whose posts about integrating spirituality into daily life were both practical and profound. Then there was Martin, a fellow corporate professional, who shared his struggles and successes in balancing a demanding career with his meditative practices. Through these interactions, Emily discovered not only camaraderie but also a wealth of knowledge and different perspectives that enriched her own understanding.

In a quaint bookstore with shelves overflowing with books on every conceivable aspect of spirituality, Emily met Nora, an elderly woman whose life experiences and spiritual depth added a new layer of wisdom to Emily's journey. Their conversation, rich with anecdotes and reflections, highlighted the timeless nature of the human quest for meaning and connection.

Through these meetings and online conversations Emily started learning the art of articulating her experiences in ways that resonate with others, and in doing so, she found her voice and a sense of belonging.

"Can the calm of the soul echo louder than the city's frenzy?"

Emily walked the streets with a mind teeming with thoughts that seemed out of step with her surroundings. The bright billboards, the constant stream of people, the blaring horns of traffic – all these external realities now contrasted sharply with the tranquility she sought within. This duality, the ever-widening gap between her internal metamorphosis and the external world, became the arena for her latest struggles.

Emily's days were a delicate balance of maintaining her relationships while honoring the profound changes within her. Each interaction with friends and family was laced with the silent question of how much of her new self to reveal. Conversations often felt like navigating a labyrinth; she longed to share her journey but feared the misunderstanding and judgment that might follow.

At a casual dinner with old friends, Emily found herself at odds with the conversation. Topics that once engaged her now seemed trivial. She attempted to steer the discussion towards her newfound interests in spirituality and personal growth, only to be met with polite nods or, worse, dismissive laughter. The chasm in understanding was tangible, and Emily left feeling more isolated than ever.

In her loneliness, Emily wrestled with the philosophical implications of her path. Her thoughts revealed questions on the nature of change, the essence of true connection, and the price of personal evolution. These thoughts were often interspersed with flashbacks to moments of her past, emphasizing how far she had come and how much she had left behind.

In this turmoil, Emily found peace in her quiet moments of meditation and reflection. In these periods of stillness, she contemplated the teachings of ancient philosophers and modern thinkers alike, drawing parallels between their insights and her experiences. These sessions were bridges to deeper understanding, helping her to reconcile her inner transformation with her outer life.

Emily learned to navigate her dual worlds with more grace. She started to accept that not everyone would understand her journey and that some relationships might fade as a result. But she also recognized the value of the connections that endured and the new ones that formed. This acceptance was not resignation but a profound understanding of the fluid nature of relationships and the necessity of personal growth.

Emily, in a state of quiet resilience had begun to master the art of living in two worlds, honoring both her external reality and her internal changes. She was now at a crossroads, poised between her old life and the new possibilities that lay ahead, symbolizing the universal human experience of growth, change, and the constant search for balance.

Developing Relationships

"In the silence between words, where understanding dawns, can the echo of a sage's wisdom calm the turbulent sea of a seeker's soul?"

The soft light of dawn gently illuminated Emily's room as she prepared for her visit to her mentor. Mrs. Kaur's presence had become a huge sense of comfort in Emily's turbulent world, a world where her personal and professional challenges seemed to intertwine in an intricate web.

Mrs. Kaur's home was a port of tranquility, its walls adorned with artifacts from her travels and shelves lined with ancient texts. The aroma of incense and the soothing sound of a distant chime welcomed Emily as she stepped inside. Mrs. Kaur greeted her with a warm smile, her eyes reflecting a depth of understanding.

As they sat in the cozy living room, the morning light casting a golden aura around them, Emily poured out her heart. She shared her struggles at work, where her newfound spiritual insights often clashed with the corporate ethos. She talked about the sense of alienation she felt, the loneliness that crept in despite being surrounded by people.

Mrs. Kaur listened intently, her nods and gentle hums reflecting her empathy. When Emily paused, the older woman spoke in a voice that was both soft and firm. "My dear, the path of enlightenment is often a solitary one. But remember, the lotus blooms in muddy waters. Your struggles are the very soil from which your spirit will grow."

"Life's journey is akin to sailing on a vast sea. The waters sometimes serene, sometimes turbulent, always in motion. Your struggles, dear Emily, are not blockades but waves. They may toss you, but they also propel you forward on your path."

"Remember, each challenge you face is a lesson in disguise," Mrs. Kaur continued, her gaze steady and reassuring. "The resistance you encounter is not there to defeat you, but to strengthen you. It's in these moments of struggle that your spirit is tested, and your true growth occurs."

Their conversation continued through realms of spirituality and practicality. Mrs. Kaur shared anecdotes from her life, each a lesson in resilience and faith. She spoke of times when she too had faced adversity, how her beliefs had been tested, and the strength she found in staying true to her path.

Emily's heart lightened as she listened. Mrs. Kaur's words were comforting to her soul. She realized that her journey of seeking peace was also about learning to thrive amid chaos. It was about finding harmony within herself, which could then radiate out into her interactions, both personal and professional.

As the hours passed, the conversation took a philosophical turn. Mrs. Kaur spoke of ancient teachings, of the delicate balance between doing and being, action and introspection. She talked about the duality of life, the coexistence of light and shadow, and the importance of embracing both.

As the night deepened, Mrs. Kaur's advice became more pragmatic. She suggested specific practices for Emily to integrate her spiritual journey with her professional life, emphasizing mindfulness and compassion. "See your workplace as a garden," she said. "Each interaction, each task, is a chance to plant seeds of positivity and growth, not just for you but for those around you as well."

Emily felt a profound shift within her. Mrs. Kaur's insights provided a new lens through which to view her challenges. She left their meeting feeling empowered, armed with a deeper understanding and a renewed sense of purpose. Her steps were lighter, her heart more at peace as she made her way back through the busy city streets.

"Can the flicker of inner peace in one spark a flame of curiosity in another, illuminating the unseen path that winds through the forest of logic?"

After her enlightening evening with Mrs. Kaur, Emily returned to work with a renewed sense of purpose and clarity. Her interaction with colleagues, once a source of stress, now became opportunities to practice mindfulness and patience.

Alex couldn't help but notice the subtle yet profound changes in Emily. There was a new calmness in her demeanor, a serenity in her voice that hadn't been there before. Her responses to workplace challenges were measured and thoughtful, exuding a confidence that was deeply rooted in tranquility rather than mere determination.

One late afternoon, as the office buzzed with the typical end-of-day frenzy, Alex found himself in Emily's office, supposedly to discuss a project deadline. But as they talked, his curiosity got the better of him. "Emily, I've noticed you've been... different lately," he began, hesitantly. "It's like you're seeing things from a new perspective. What's changed?"

Emily smiled, her eyes reflecting a deep inner peace. "I've been spending time with a mentor," she shared, "someone who's helping me see life and its challenges in a new light." She spoke of Mrs. Kaur and the lessons learned, her words painting a picture of her spiritual journey.

Alex listened with genuine interest. "So, you're saying that these changes are because of... what, philosophy? Spirituality?" His tone was one of intrigue rather than skepticism, a subtle shift that did not go unnoticed by Emily.

"Yes, in a way," Emily replied. "It's about finding balance, understanding that our professional and personal growth are deeply interconnected." She talked about the importance of inner harmony, how it influenced her interactions and decision-making at work.

The conversation gradually shifted to broader philosophical discussions. They explored topics like the nature of success, the pursuit of happiness, and the role of personal values in professional life. Alex, who had always valued empirical evidence and concrete results, found himself intrigued by these abstract concepts.

Emily shared anecdotes from her own life, explaining how her new outlook had altered her approach to everyday challenges. She talked about seeing conflict as an opportunity for growth and understanding, rather than as a hurdle.

Their dialogue continued, with the setting sun casting long shadows across the office. It was a conversation that marked a turning point in their friendship. For Alex, it was an eye-opener, a glimpse into a world of thought he had previously dismissed. For Emily, it was an affirmation of her journey, a chance to articulate and thereby solidify her own understanding.

As they wrapped up their discussion, there was a mutual acknowledgement that their dynamic had shifted. What had started as a professional relationship was evolving into a deeper connection, one that was now enriched by shared philosophical explorations.

"When the mind, like a relentless river, meets the serene waters of the spirit, does it reflect the sky above or discover its own depths?"

The newfound camaraderie between Emily and Alex, sparked by their recent philosophical discussion, began to evolve with a gentle, yet persistent curiosity. Alex, traditionally grounded in the tangible and practical, found himself increasingly intrigued by the subtle transformation in Emily. The once predominantly professional air of their interactions was now tinged with a burgeoning interest in the philosophical and spiritual underpinnings of her changed demeanor.

It was on a brisk, autumn morning when Alex initiated what would become a series of profound dialogues. The office was just stirring to life, the early rays of the sun casting a warm glow through the large windows. Emily, who had arrived early, was sipping her tea, lost in thought, when Alex walked in.

"Good morning, Emily. Do you have a moment?" Alex asked, his voice carrying a hint of earnestness that was relatively new.

"Of course, Alex. What's on your mind?" Emily replied, sensing the shift in his approach.

Alex hesitated, searching for the right words. "I've been thinking about our last conversation, about finding balance and purpose. I'm... curious about how you started on this path."

Emily smiled, recognizing the significance of his inquiry. She began to share her journey, intertwining personal anecdotes with the wisdom she had gleaned from Mrs. Kaur. Her words painted a vivid picture of self-discovery, replete with doubts, revelations, and moments of clarity.

Alex listened intently, "So, this journey of yours, it's not just about coping with work stress, is it? It's more holistic?" he asked, his tone reflecting a burgeoning openness to concepts beyond his usual realm.

"Exactly," Emily affirmed. "It's about integrating our personal values with our professional lives, finding harmony in all aspects of our existence."

Their conversation touching on topics like the nature of consciousness, the pursuit of happiness, and the concept of mindfulness. Emily spoke of the interconnectedness of all things, how her spiritual practice had brought a sense of unity to her life's experiences.

As they explored these ideas, the office around them buzzed with the typical morning activity, oblivious to the profound exchange taking place. Colleagues passed by, offering casual greetings, unaware of the significant shift occurring in the dynamic between Emily and Alex.

Throughout these discussions, Emily noticed a subtle change in Alex. His questions became more introspective, his responses more reflective. It was as if a door had opened within him, revealing a willingness to explore beyond the confines of his previously held beliefs.

In the days that followed, their conversations became a regular occurrence, a shared journey into philosophical exploration. Emily found herself looking forward to these discussions, not only as an opportunity to share her insights but also to learn from Alex's perspectives, which were rooted in logic yet increasingly open to the metaphysical.

"In the forest of the ordinary, can the whispers of wisdom be heard over the rustle of routine?"

As the days shortened and a crisp autumn chill permeated the air, the corridors of Emily's workplace, once merely a stage for professional pursuits, began to resonate with a newfound warmth and understanding. These changes were represented best by her evolving relationship with Alex. Once just a colleague, Alex was gradually becoming a confidant, a companion in the journey of philosophical inquiry and personal growth.

Emily's mornings at the office took on a new perspective. The exchange of friendly, casual greetings soon gave way to deeper, more reflective conversations. It wasn't just about deadlines and project updates anymore; their talks wandered through the realms of existential questions, personal beliefs, and the pursuit of meaning in the mundane.

One particularly brisk morning, as Emily wrapped her hands around a steaming cup of coffee in the break room, Alex joined her, his demeanor reflective. "You know, Emily," he began, his eyes searching hers, "I've been thinking a lot about our discussions. They've opened a new way of seeing things for me."

Emily, touched by his sincerity, felt a surge of gratitude. "I'm really glad to hear that, Alex. It means a lot to have someone to share these thoughts with."

Their dialogues, once limited to the confines of office breaks, began to spill over into collaborative work sessions, infusing a sense of purpose and mindfulness into their professional undertakings. The projects they worked on together seemed to thrive in this new dynamic, marked by mutual respect and a shared desire for deeper understanding.

Meanwhile, Emily's thoughts grew richer, more nuanced. She found herself reflecting on the nature of relationships, the interconnectedness of personal and professional lives, and the transformative power of open-minded dialogue. These reflections often took her back to her conversations with Mrs. Kaur, drawing parallels between her spiritual guidance and her burgeoning friendship with Alex.

Emily's colleagues started to take notice of the change. There was a substantial shift in the office atmosphere – a sense of camaraderie and openness that seemed to emanate from Emily and Alex's interactions. Emily, who pondered over it in her quieter moments, recognizing the ripple effect of personal change on a communal scale.

One afternoon, as they sat in a small, sunlit conference room, poring over a project, Alex paused and looked up at Emily. "You know, I never saw the value in looking beyond the surface of things, in questioning the why behind our actions. But these discussions, they've given me a new perspective."

Emily smiled, her heart light. "It's a journey, isn't it? Finding meaning, understanding ourselves and each other a bit better."

Alex became a cornerstone in Emily's life, a source of strength and comfort within the challenges of her professional role. His open-mindedness and genuine interest provided a safe space for her to express her thoughts and feelings, contributing significantly to her sense of belonging and well-being at work.

"When two winds collide, does the storm negate the journey, or define it?"

The workday dawned as the kind of morning where the sun seemed hesitant to assert its presence. As Emily walked down the familiar corridors of her office, she braced herself for another encounter with Michael, her project manager. There still was a tension between them because of their contrasting ideals and methodologies.

Michael, with his pragmatic and results-driven approach, often found himself at odds with Emily's more contemplative and process-oriented style. Their meetings occasionally were battlegrounds of differing philosophies.

As Emily entered the conference room, the air was thick with unspoken grievances. Michael, already seated, regarded her with a mix of impatience and begrudging respect. The room, usually a neutral space, felt charged with an invisible energy, a silent witness to their discord.

"Emily, we need to talk about the Henderson project," Michael began, his voice betraying a hint of frustration. "Your approach is too idealistic. We need practical, time-efficient solutions, not philosophical musings."

Emily, feeling a familiar surge of defensiveness, took a deep breath, searching for the right words. "Michael, I understand your concern, but I believe that a thoughtful, holistic approach will yield better long-term results. We can't just rush through without considering the broader implications."

Their exchange was a battle of opposing views, a delicate balance between assertiveness and diplomacy. Emily's recent personal growth had equipped her with a newfound patience, but it was constantly tested in these interactions. She could sense the strain not just in Michael's words, but in the subtle tension of his shoulders, the way his hands formed tight fists on the table.

As the meeting progressed, their conversation became a small-scale version of a larger philosophical debate. It was efficiency versus depth, immediacy versus sustainability. Emily, while holding firm to her beliefs, couldn't help but wonder about the root of their conflict. Was it merely a clash of work styles, or something deeper, a reflection of their intrinsic values and worldviews?

Outside the conference room, the tension between Emily and Michael was again becoming a topic of quiet speculation among their colleagues.

Whispers and exchanged glances in the break room hinted at a growing awareness of the rift, adding an undercurrent of unease to the office dynamics.

Emily sought advice from Alex on this ongoing tension with Michael. Their discussions, once a source of intellectual stimulation, now provided a much-needed emotional relief. She found herself increasingly grateful for his open-mindedness and support.

As the day wound down, Emily sat alone in her office, the glow of her computer screen casting a soft light in the dimming room. She pondered over the day's events, her thoughts a whirlpool of frustration, introspection, and a flickering hope for resolution.

"In the meeting of light and shadow, where does understanding dwell?"

The morning light streamed through the blinds of Emily's office, slicing the room into alternating bands of light and shadow. It was a visual metaphor for her current predicament with Michael, a juxtaposition of clarity and obscurity. As she sat at her desk, her mind was a whirlwind of conflicting emotions, each thought a fragile leaf caught in a tempest of professional and personal turmoil.

Today, she had resolved to apply her newfound personal insights to the ongoing conflict with Michael. It was a conscious attempt to transform her perspective, to see the situation not just as a source of stress, but as an opportunity for growth and understanding.

Emily's recent forays into spirituality had provided her with a sense of inner calm, a well of patience she could draw from in times of turmoil. She had learned to observe her emotions without being overwhelmed by them, to acknowledge her reactions without letting them dictate her actions. This inner work had been a solitary journey, but now it faced the ultimate test in the real world.

As she prepared for another meeting with Michael, Emily focused on her breathing, feeling the steady rhythm anchoring her in the building storm of anxiety. She visualized the meeting as a space for dialogue and mutual respect. It was a challenging shift in perspective, especially given the history of their interactions.

The meeting began with the usual formalities, a thin veneer of civility masking the underlying tension. Michael was his usual self, efficient and direct, his words sharp like arrows aimed at the heart of the matter. Emily listened, her mind a quiet observer, noting the rise and fall of her own reactions.

"Emily, we can't afford to delay this project with unnecessary complexities," Michael stated, his tone laced with impatience.

Instead of responding with immediate defensiveness, Emily paused, allowing a moment of silence to permeate the room. When she spoke, her voice was calm, yet firm. "I understand your concern, Michael. However, I believe that addressing these complexities now will lead to a more sustainable outcome in the long run."

Emily's words were reflections of her inner transformation. She was no longer reacting; she was responding with intention.

The discussion continued, a slow and deliberate exchange of viewpoints. Emily found herself tapping into a well of compassion, trying to see the situation from Michael's perspective. It was a challenging exercise in empathy, an attempt to bridge the gap between their contrasting approaches.

As the meeting ended, Emily felt a small shift in the dynamics of their interaction. There was no miraculous resolution, no sudden alignment of their perspectives, but there was a sense of mutual acknowledgment, a begrudging respect for each other's stance.

Back in her office, Emily reflected on the meeting. It had been a test of her patience and compassion, a real-world application of her spiritual practices. The conflict with Michael was far from resolved, but she had taken a significant step in navigating it with a newfound sense of maturity and understanding.

"Is it the whisper of the wind that bends the tree, or the tree that captures the wind's song?"

In the dim glow of her computer screen, long after her colleagues had left, Emily sat alone in her office. The muffled sounds of the city outside barely penetrated the thick glass windows, creating a bubble of seclusion around her. Here, in the quiet aftermath of another challenging day, Emily found herself wrestling with an internal storm that seemed to grow more turbulent by the hour.

The day had been a relentless test of her patience, each interaction with Michael chipping away at her resolve. His critical, materialistic approach to their project clashed jarringly with the values she was striving to cultivate. Where Emily saw potential for innovation and depth, Michael saw unnecessary complications, his focus fixated on deadlines and bottom lines.

As she replayed the day's events in her mind, Emily felt a familiar surge of frustration. It was a visceral reaction, a tidal wave of emotion that threatened to sweep away her hard-won serenity. She had embarked on a journey of spiritual growth, seeking to infuse her life with patience, understanding, and empathy. But in the face of Michael's relentless pragmatism, these qualities felt like fragile boats in a storm.

She remembered a particular moment in a meeting, when Michael had dismissed one of her suggestions with a curt, "Let's stick to what's practical, Emily." The words had stung, not just for their dismissive tone, but for the underlying implication that her ideas were somehow detached from reality.

In that moment, Emily had felt a rush of indignation, a desire to assert herself and defend her perspective. But she had swallowed the retort that sprang to her lips, choosing instead to nod and redirect the conversation. It was a choice that left her feeling both proud and hollow, a paradox of assertiveness and submission.

Now, in the quiet of her office, Emily allowed herself to feel the full weight of her emotions. She felt the heat of anger, the sting of frustration, the heavy cloak of disappointment. These were not emotions she wanted to suppress or deny; they were signposts on her journey, indicators of the deep internal work she still needed to do.

As she leaned back in her chair, Emily's gaze drifted to the small potted plant on her desk, its leaves a vibrant green against the stark office backdrop. She thought of the patience required to nurture a plant, the understanding that growth was a slow, incremental process, often invisible to the naked eye.

This thought brought a measure of calm to Emily's turbulent mind. Her journey, like the growth of the plant, was not something that could be rushed. It required patience, not just with others, but with herself. She was learning, evolving, and with each challenge, she was given an opportunity to practice the very qualities she sought to embody.

With a deep breath, Emily turned off her computer and gathered her belongings. As she stepped out into the cool night air, she felt a renewed sense of determination. Tomorrow, she would face Michael and the challenges of her job with a renewed perspective. She would strive to balance assertiveness with patience, to stand firm in her values while remaining open to compromise.

"Can the light of inner peace shine through the shadows of a relentless career?"

Emily's world, once marked by a clear delineation between her personal and professional life, now shimmered with the delicate interplay of her spiritual journey and career challenges. The stark fluorescent lights of her office seemed to flicker in rhythm with her internal struggles, casting long shadows over her efforts to maintain equilibrium.

Her desk, a landscape of scattered reports and blinking electronic devices, stood as evidence to the relentless pace of her work. Yet in all this chaos, Emily sought refuge in moments of mindfulness and meditation. These practices had become her anchor, a lifeline in the stormy seas of corporate life.

Each morning, before the rush of meetings and deadlines, Emily carved out a sacred space of tranquility. Seated at her desk, she would close her eyes, allowing the hum of the air conditioning and distant chatter to fade into a gentle murmur. In these moments of stillness, she focused on her breath, feeling the rise and fall of her chest, the air cool against her nostrils, a rhythmic dance of life pulsing within her.

This daily ritual had become more than a practice; it was a shelter where Emily reconnected with her inner self. Here, she found the strength to face the day, to approach each challenge with a sense of calm and balance. The world around her remained the same, but her perception of it had shifted.

She was learning to observe her reactions, to understand that her peace did not have to be contingent on external circumstances.

However, finding harmony in her interactions, especially with Michael, was a more complex melody. The tension between them was a substantial force, an undercurrent that threatened to disrupt even the most mundane conversations.

One afternoon, as she prepared for a project meeting, Emily paused to ground herself. She envisioned a serene lake, its surface a perfect mirror, undisturbed by the winds of conflict. This image brought a sense of composure, a reminder that beneath the surface turmoil, there was a depth of calm available to her.

As she entered the meeting room, Emily carried this sense of serenity with her. She greeted Michael with a nod, her demeanor composed yet open. Throughout the meeting, she practiced active listening, giving space to his viewpoints while gently offering her own perspectives. It was a delicate balancing act, blending assertiveness with empathy.

At one point, when Michael's tone grew sharp over a scheduling conflict, Emily felt the familiar stirrings of frustration. But instead of reacting, she paused, took a breath, and responded with a measured calmness. The tension did not dissipate entirely, but it did not escalate either. It was a small victory, a step towards harmony.

"In every challenge, a lesson lurks. Can the storm of conflict water the seeds of wisdom?"

In the heart of Emily's journey, nestled between the relentless ebb and flow of her daily routines, lay an unexpected gift – the conflict with Michael. To an onlooker, their interactions might have seemed fraught with tension, a standard clash of personalities in the workplace. Yet, for Emily, this was a crucible for profound transformation.

Each encounter with Michael was like a new scene set upon a stage of fluorescent lights and sterile office walls, a place where the drama of human interaction unfolded in real time. Emily, once a mere participant in this play, now observed each act with a philosopher's gaze, seeking wisdom amid strife.

The conflict, though unnerving, was a sign calling her to deeper understanding. It was a test of her resolve to live by her spiritual principles in the face of adversity. Each sharp word from Michael was like a bell tolling, reminding her to return to these principles.

In these moments, Emily often found herself retreating into the sanctum of her mind, seeking counsel from her inner sage. Here, in her thoughts, she unraveled the threads of each confrontation, examining them with a blend of curiosity and detachment. These were not mere musings but vibrant, living dialogues with her deeper self, each one revealing layers of understanding about patience, compassion, and the nature of conflict.

"Conflict is not just an obstacle," she would remind herself, "It's a teacher, showing me where I hold resistance, where I need to grow."

In seeking to navigate these choppy waters while holding onto her spiritual beliefs, Emily often recalled a conversation with her mentor, a scene that played out in her memory like a cherished flashback. Under the warm glow of a coffee shop's pendant lights, her mentor had shared a vital insight: "True spiritual practice is not about avoiding conflict but learning to move through it with grace and awareness."

This wisdom was a lighthouse guiding Emily as she charted her course through each interaction with Michael. She started to view their disagreements as opportunities to practice assertiveness tempered with empathy. When Michael's materialistic approach clashed with her values, she sought to understand his perspective, to see the world through his lens, however briefly. This did not mean she diluted her principles; rather, she learned the art of holding her ground without losing her peace.

Their discussions, once a battleground of egos, slowly transformed into a duel of differing viewpoints. Emily learned to listen deeply, to respond rather than react, and to express her views with clarity and respect.

Integrating Spiritual Insights into Daily Life
"Taming the Ox"

"How can one bloom in stillness when surrounded by the relentless dance of progress?"

As the first light of dawn stretched across the city, Emily stood by her apartment window, her eyes tracing the silhouette of the awakening metropolis. Today, she resolved, would be different. She breathed in deeply, drawing in the crisp morning air and the promise of a new beginning. Today she would try very hard to integrate her practice of mindfulness into her work life.

The office, when she arrived, was a hive of activity. The clatter of keyboards, the hum of conversation, and the incessant ringing of phones created quite the racket. Emily paused at her desk, taking a moment to anchor herself in the here and now. She observed her surroundings with a heightened sense of awareness, each detail sharp and clear.

As she began her day, Emily consciously immersed herself in each task. When reviewing reports, she did so with meticulous attention, letting no detail escape her notice. During team meetings, she listened intently, her mind fully present in each discussion. This mindful approach lent her a calm, focused demeanor.

Alex, a team member with a keen interest in Emily's spiritual journey, approached her during lunch. "I've noticed a change in you today," he said, his curiosity piqued. "There's a sense of calm about you, even more than you've had before."

Emily smiled, welcoming the opportunity to share her experiences. "I've been working very hard on my mindfulness," she explained. "Especially at work in this type of difficult environment."

Their conversation continued to explore the philosophies and practices of mindfulness. Emily spoke of her struggles finding peace during the turmoil. Alex listened, fascinated, as he too was trying to figure out a way to remain calm and focused at work.

Rumors of a looming merger with another company had sparked a wave of anxiety among the staff. Uncertainty hung in the air like a dense fog, affecting morale and productivity.

In times like this, Emily would turn inward remembering that "Mindfulness is not about eliminating stress or conflict; it's about learning how to navigate them with a calm mind and an open heart."

"Can a single voice harmonize the chorus, or does the melody emerge from the silence of listening?"

Emily contemplated the transformation unfolding within her. Gone were the days of solitary striving; now, she envisioned a path lit by the spirit of collaboration. Her heart was set on fostering a culture of unity and shared purpose in her workplace.

As Emily walked through the office, the familiar sounds and sights of her daily environment took on a new significance. She saw a group of individuals who were a collective, a team with untapped potential for synergy and cooperation. Today, she would pivot from the conventional culture of competition to one of collaborative success.

Her first meeting of the day was a project brainstorming session. Traditionally, these meetings had been battlegrounds of egos, each participant vying to have their voice heard, their ideas validated. Emily entered the conference room with a different agenda. She took a deep breath, centering herself in the principles of mindfulness and collaboration she had recently embraced.

As the meeting commenced, Emily listened attentively to her colleagues, her gaze steady, her mind open. She encouraged quieter members to share their thoughts, weaving their contributions into the conversation. When Richard, known for his assertive demeanor, dominated the conversation, Emily gently steered the discussion to include others, balancing the scales of participation.

In this new atmosphere, ideas flowed freely, blending, and building upon each other. The team, once fragmented by internal competition, began to find a rhythm of collective creativity. Emily's heart swelled with pride as she witnessed the birth of a more inclusive, supportive dynamic.

Later, at her desk, Emily reflected on this shift. She recalled a dialogue with her mentor, an exchange that had sparked her transformation. In her mind's eye, she revisited that peaceful park bench where they had sat, surrounded by the gentle rustle of leaves and the distant chatter of city life. "True strength," her mentor had said, "lies in unity, in the ability to bring diverse minds together towards a common goal."

This philosophy became Emily's mantra, illuminating her approach to collaboration. She sought not only to participate but to connect, to understand, and to unify. Her interactions were no longer transactions but opportunities for building relationships and fostering a sense of belonging.

The project meetings, once a noise of discordant voices, slowly transformed into symphonies of collaborative effort. Emily's ability to listen, integrate, and harmonize diverse viewpoints became the cornerstone of this transformation.

In these moments of teamwork, Emily found profound fulfillment. She realized that collaboration was a strategy and a way of being, of giving and taking that enriched both the individual and the group. It was a revelation that resonated deeply with her spirit, a realization that we are all interconnected parts of a larger whole.

The team gathered to celebrate the successful completion of the cross-departmental project basking in the glow of their shared achievement. Emily looked around at the faces of her colleagues, now allies and friends, and felt a deep sense of gratitude. Not only was this a professional victory; it was a testament to the power of collaboration, and hope for a more united, empathetic world.

As she left the office that evening, Emily walked with a light step, her heart full. She not only had changed the way she worked but had also sparked a change in those around her. Armed with the knowledge that together, we can achieve far more than we ever could alone, she was ready for whatever challenges lay ahead.

"In the forest of voices, one leaf falls silently – does its presence alter the grove?"

The office, a mosaic of diverse personalities and talents, buzzed with the usual morning activity as Emily arrived. Her recent journey into mindfulness and compassion had transformed her inner landscape and delicately altered her interactions with her colleagues. Today, she felt a gentle yet compelling urge to share her insights, to offer a glimmer of her newfound understanding to those around her.

Emily's transformation was evident in her demeanor; a calmness enveloped her, a stark contrast to the frenetic pace of the corporate world. As she made her way to her desk, her colleagues couldn't help but notice the serene aura that she carried.

It was during a casual coffee break that Emily found her opportunity. Gathered around the break room, a few colleagues discussed the challenges of balancing work and personal life. Emily listened; her heart empathetic to their struggles. When a pause in the conversation presented itself, she shared a piece of her journey.

"As many of you know I've been exploring mindfulness for a while now.," Emily began, her tone light, conversational. "It's really helped me find a bit of calm in the day-to-day hustle. Just a few minutes of being present can make a big difference."

Her words were met with a mix of curiosity and skepticism. Mark raised an eyebrow, "Sounds a bit too Zen for this place, doesn't it?"

Emily smiled gently. "Maybe, but it's more practical than you might think. It's about being fully present in the moment, which can actually improve our focus and efficiency."

The conversation that followed was a slew of ideas and perspectives. Emily sharing her insights while remaining open to the views of her colleagues. She avoided any tone of preachiness, instead adopting a stance of sharing and exploration. Her words were like seeds, planted in the fertile soil of open minds, watered by sincere intention.

As the days progressed, Emily's subtle influence began to ripple through the office. Conversations around mindfulness and compassion became more frequent, and some colleagues even approached her for tips on incorporating these practices into their daily lives.

Meanwhile, Emily continued to deepen her own understanding. She often found comfort in philosophical dialogues with her mentor, looking into the nuances of mindfulness and its application in the modern world. These discussions were spiritual nourishment, feeding her soul and sharpening her mind.

One particularly poignant dialogue explored the balance between personal growth and the influence one can have on others. "Change begins within," her mentor noted, "but its true power is realized when it extends beyond ourselves, touching the lives of others."

This insight resonated with Emily, fueling her desire to share her journey while respecting the unique paths of those around her. She became more attentive to the subtle dynamics of her workplace, recognizing moments where a word of kindness or a gesture of understanding could make a difference.

One of her colleagues Linda, struggling with stress management, she found support in the mindfulness techniques Emily shared. Then there was young Alex, curious and open-minded, who became a kind of protégé, eagerly absorbing the wisdom Emily imparted.

Slowly the office transformed, subtly yet significantly, into a more compassionate and mindful environment. The changes were not complex but rather small shifts in attitudes and behaviors, like the gentle turning of a flower towards the sun.

There were still days of doubt and moments of misunderstanding. Yet, through each obstacle, Emily found a deeper sense of purpose and clarity. Her growth was proof of the transformative power of mindfulness and compassion, hope in a world often clouded by haste and indifference.

Emily was discovering the delicate art of sharing insights tactfully. She was learning that true wisdom is not about imposing one's views. True wisdom is about inviting others to explore new possibilities with you.

"In a forest of solitude, a single tree whispers. Do the others learn its language?"

In the evolving terrain of the office, Emily's journey of mindfulness and compassion began to bear fruit. As she navigated her workdays with an open heart and a non-judgmental mind, her interactions with her colleagues started to transform. The air around her seemed to hum with the potential of deeper connections, as if her newfound perspective had unlocked a hidden level of communication.

The once routine coffee breaks and corridor conversations began to evolve into more meaningful exchanges. Emily's colleagues, who had initially been curious about her calm demeanor, now sought her out, drawn by her genuine interest and empathetic listening. Her desk, nestled in the corner of the office, became a small oasis of peace where open, honest dialogues unfolded.

One particularly memorable conversation took place on a rainy Tuesday afternoon. The raindrops, like tiny percussionists, beat a rhythmic pattern on the windows, providing a soothing backdrop to the day's work. Emily was joined by Sarah, a colleague usually reserved and private, who seemed to carry an invisible shield around her.

"I keep seeing a change in you, Emily," Sarah began, her voice hesitant. "There's a sense of peace about you. How do you manage that in this craziness?"

Emily smiled, her eyes reflecting the soft glow of the computer screen. "It's been a long and hard journey," she replied. "I've been really focused on my mindfulness and trying to be present in each moment, no matter how chaotic it seems."

As they spoke, Sarah's initial reserve melted away, revealing her struggles with anxiety and the constant pressure to perform. Emily listened intently, offering insights from her own experience but never overstepping the delicate line of personal boundaries. Their conversation meandered from work stress to personal aspirations, from fears to small triumphs.

This deepening connection with Sarah was not an isolated event. Emily found that her openness and non-judgmental attitude acted as a catalyst, encouraging others to share their experiences and perspectives. The office, once a place of superficial interactions, began to reveal a richness of human stories and emotions.

Emily's interactions with Mark, who had once skeptically raised an eyebrow at her mindfulness practices, now took on a new dimension. Their discussions ventured beyond the pragmatics of work, touching on topics like work-life balance and personal fulfillment. Mark, who had seemed perpetually guarded, shared his passion for landscape photography, a hobby that brought him immense joy yet remained unseen by his colleagues.

As these connections deepened, Emily's thoughts became more reflective. She pondered the nature of human connection, the invisible threads that bind us in shared experiences and mutual understanding. Her conversations with her mentor took on new depths, exploring the concept of interconnectedness and the role of empathy in forging meaningful relationships.

These philosophical explorations were not just theoretical musings; they were lived experiences, playing out in the world of her workplace. Emily began to see her colleagues not as co-workers but as fellow travelers, each with their unique struggles and stories.

In this atmosphere of openness and connection, even the most mundane tasks took on new significance. Emily found joy in the small moments, whether it was a shared laugh over a coffee break or a supportive word during a challenging task. The office, once a battleground of egos and competition, was transforming into a community of collaboration and mutual support.

"In the stillness of dawn, a single leaf flutters. Does the wind shape its dance?"

As Emily's journey of self-discovery and mindfulness unfolded within the confines of her office, its ripples extended beyond the work environment, seeping into the very fabric of her daily life. Her newfound awareness was not just a tool for managing workplace dynamics but a transformative force reshaping her entire lifestyle.

The once unexamined routines of her life were now under the scrutiny of her evolving values. Each day, as the sun spilled its first light through her apartment window, Emily found herself pausing, reflecting on the choices that structured her life. The morning, once a frantic race against the clock, became a time of contemplation and intention setting.

She began with her diet, an area she'd always approached with a mix of convenience and indulgence. The colorful array of processed foods that filled her pantry now seemed at odds with her quest for mindfulness and wellbeing. With a thoughtful yet determined spirit, Emily embarked on a journey of culinary exploration, one that favored whole, unprocessed foods. The act of cooking transformed from a mere necessity to a meditative practice, where each chop and stir was a celebration of the present moment.

Exercise, which had always been a sporadic and half-hearted endeavor, took on a new meaning. Emily dived even deeper into her yoga, finding in its fluid movements and mindful breathing a perfect harmony of body and mind. The yoga studio, with its soothing ambiance and the gentle guidance of her instructor, became a sacred space where she nurtured her physical health and inner calm.

These changes in her lifestyle were not just physical, they were deeply philosophical. Emily found herself researching literature that explored themes of minimalism, sustainability, and wellness. Her evenings were no longer spent mindlessly scrolling through social media or binging on TV shows. Instead, they were dedicated to reading, reflecting, and sometimes, writing in her journal.

Through these writings, she engaged in dialogues with herself, questioning the very essence of happiness, success, and fulfillment. She pondered the societal constructs that had shaped her earlier choices and how her new perspectives were diverging from those paths.

Her relationships, too, were reevaluated in this new light. Conversations with friends and family took on a deeper dimension as Emily sought connections that were nurturing and authentic. Some relationships strengthened, enriched by mutual understanding and respect, while others, built on superficial foundations, naturally fell away.

In her professional sphere, this reassessment led to a greater alignment of her work with her values. Projects that once seemed purely transactional were now opportunities for meaningful contribution. Emily found herself advocating for initiatives that promoted wellbeing, sustainability, and community engagement within her company.

"In the market of endless choices, a mindful step echoes. Does the echo shape the path, or does the path shape the echo?"

In Emily's evolving life, a new thread was emerging, vibrant and significant – the thread of conscious consumption. This shift in her lifestyle was an alteration of habits, a profound manifestation of her deepening respect for the environment and a growing awareness of her role in the global ecosystem.

The transformation began subtly. Emily's mornings, once a flurry of hastily consumed coffee and convenient breakfast options, now dawned with mindfulness. The aroma of fair-trade coffee filled her kitchen, a deliberate choice reflecting her commitment to ethical sourcing. Each sip became a moment of gratitude, an acknowledgment of the journey from distant farms to her cup.

Her wardrobe, a colorful array of fabrics and styles, underwent a thoughtful scrutiny. The fast-fashion items, once an indication of her trendy lifestyle, now seemed conflicting with her values. In their place, Emily curated a collection of clothing that spoke of sustainability and ethical labor practices. Each garment she chose was not just a piece of fabric but a chronicle of responsible creation – organic cottons, recycled materials, and artisanal craftsmanship.

Even her shopping habits were changing. The bustling malls and online marketplaces, with their endless array of products, no longer held the same allure. Emily sought out local markets and eco-friendly stores, places where each purchase supported small businesses and sustainable practices. The act of shopping transformed from a passive consumption to an active contribution to the kind of world she wished to see.

In her home, every object began to tell a story of mindful selection. Single-use plastics gave way to reusable alternatives, cleaning products were eco-friendly, and even her furniture bore the marks of sustainable sourcing. Emily's living space became a tribute to her environmental consciousness, each item a deliberate choice echoing her respect for the planet.

Her dietary choices, already leaning towards health and mindfulness, took on an additional layer of consciousness. Plant-based meals became more frequent, a decision rooted not only in health benefits but also in a consideration for animal welfare and environmental impact. The colorful array of fruits, vegetables, and grains on her plate was a mosaic of her commitment to living in harmony with nature.

Emily found herself engaging in deeper conversations with her peers, particularly with Michael. Their dialogues, once confined to the realms of work and personal growth, now ventured into discussions about environmental sustainability and ethical living. Michael, initially skeptical, found himself intrigued by Emily's perspective, leading to debates and exchanges that enriched their understanding of these complex issues.

These conversations served as a gateway to broader philosophical discussions, exploring themes of consumerism, ecological responsibility, and the interconnection of all life.

"In a garden of shared toil, hands nurture more than soil. Does the seed of community blossom in the heart or in the earth?

Emily's foray into volunteering began on a crisp Saturday morning, the city still basking in the gentle golden tint of dawn. She walked towards the local community center, her heart aflutter with a blend of excitement and nervousness. The center, a humble building with walls echoing stories of countless community gatherings, stood as an example of hope and support in the neighborhood.

Her decision to volunteer was a thoughtful one. She had sifted through various causes and organizations, seeking alignments with her beliefs and values. Her choice finally settled on a program dedicated to environmental education and community gardening – a perfect harmony of her passion for sustainability and her desire to foster connection and growth within her community.

As she engaged in the activities, Emily found herself immersed in a world vastly different from her corporate environment. Here, within the lush greens of community gardens and the eager faces of local residents, her role transcended professional expertise. She was a learner, a teacher, and a fellow community member, all at once.

The garden was a collaboration. Every plant, from the vegetables to the delicate herbs, told a story of collective effort and care. Emily's hands, once accustomed to keyboards and screens, now dug into the earth, planting, nurturing, and connecting with the cycle of life. The physical work, though tiring, brought a unique sense of fulfillment and grounding.

Her interactions with fellow volunteers and community members were enriching. Conversations flowed effortlessly, ranging from casual discussions about plant care to deeper dialogues about environmental conservation and community welfare. In these exchanges, Emily found herself both sharing her insights and absorbing new perspectives, a mutual exchange of wisdom and experience.

These volunteering days became a cherished part of Emily's life. They offered a balance to her professional endeavors, a grounding connection to the immediate tangible world. Through this engagement, Emily discovered a new aspect of her identity –she was now a contributor, a caretaker of her community and environment.

"In stillness, a mind wanders through a forest of thoughts. Can the tree of self-understanding grow in the soil of silence?"

Emily's decision to carve out these moments of solitude was a thoughtful response to the whirlwind of changes and growth she was experiencing. It was her acknowledgment that amid the hustle of her professional life, the joy of volunteering, and her pursuit of personal development, there needed to be a sanctuary of stillness for her inner self.

She chose the early hours of the morning for this practice, a time when the world around her was still asleep, and the first light of dawn was just beginning to paint the sky. In these tranquil moments, her apartment, usually buzzing with the energy of her active life, transformed into a refuge of serenity.

With a steaming cup of herbal tea in hand, Emily would sit by her window, gazing out at the awakening cityscape. The rising sun brought with it a palette of soft oranges and pinks, casting a gentle glow over the world. This setting was a gateway to her inner world.

During these reflective sessions, Emily engaged in a blend of meditation, journaling, and silent contemplation. She found meditation to be a grounding exercise, a way to center her thoughts and emotions. Journaling, on the other hand, allowed her to articulate her reflections, to give form and structure to the whirlwind of thoughts and feelings swirling within her.

These moments of introspection were not always easy. They often led her down paths of uncomfortable truths and unexplored emotions. Yet, Emily found value in these challenges. They were opportunities for growth, for understanding herself and her place in the world more profoundly.

The impact of this practice on Emily's life was multifold. It kept her grounded and balanced, providing a foundation of inner peace that she carried into her daily interactions. It also influenced her decisions and actions, making them more aligned with her true self and values.

The effects of these reflective practices began to subtly permeate other aspects of Emily's life. They influenced her conversations, her approach to work and volunteering, and even her relationships.

"In a forest of solitude, one tree reaches out, seeking others. Can a single seed of connection grow a grove of understanding?"

Emily's journey, the creation of a supportive community wove together individuals who shared her burgeoning values of mindfulness and compassion. This step was a natural progression from her personal exploration into a collective experience, reflecting her desire to connect with others on a similar path.

Emily's initiative to build this community was a deliberate one, born from her realization that the journey of self-discovery and personal growth was not just an inward journey, but one that thrived in the presence of shared experiences and mutual support. She began by reaching out to a few colleagues and friends who had shown an interest in her transformation and the principles she was now embracing.

The first meeting was held in a cozy corner of a local café, known for its serene ambiance and a beautiful view of the city park. The setting was carefully chosen, a reflection of the harmony and peace that Emily wanted to foster within the group. The café, with its warm lighting, soft music, and the gentle tone of quiet conversations, provided a comfortable and inviting space for open, heartfelt discussions.

As the group members gathered, there was a real sense of curiosity and anticipation. This was a new role for Emily, that of a facilitator and connector, and she hoped to create a space that was both nurturing and empowering.

The conversations began with introductions and sharing of personal journeys. Each story was unique, yet there was a common thread – a desire for deeper meaning, understanding, and connection with oneself and others. Emily listened, occasionally guiding the discussion, but mostly allowing the natural flow of dialogue.

As the meeting progressed, the atmosphere in the group transformed from one of polite interest to genuine connection. People shared their successes along with their struggles and vulnerabilities. It was this sharing of authentic experiences that forged a bond among the members.

In subsequent meetings, the community evolved, becoming more than just a space for sharing. Workshops, meditation sessions, and group activities were introduced, each designed to deepen the understanding and practice of mindfulness and compassion. Emily found herself growing with the group, her role expanding from a participant to a leader.

As the community grew, it began to have a ripple effect. Members carried the insights and experiences from the group into their own lives, impacting their workplaces, families, and wider circles. Emily's vision of a supportive network was materializing as a sanctuary for like-minded individuals, and as a catalyst for broader change.

This development of a supportive community was a witness to the power of collective wisdom and the human need for connection and belonging. Emily's transformation was a renaissance that touched every corner of her life. As she navigated her days, the lines between her spiritual journey and her everyday world began to blur, each influencing and enriching the other. The integration of her values into all aspects of her existence had become a necessity, a way of life that brought her a profound sense of harmony and fulfillment.

Her interactions with colleagues, too, had transformed. Meetings, once straightforward discussions of business strategies, now often began or ended with brief moments of shared mindfulness. Emily's openness and authenticity invited deeper connections. She listened more to the emotions and stories behind them. Her office became a refuge, a place where her colleagues felt comfortable sharing their own journeys.

Family dinners, once tedious routines, turned into gatherings of shared experiences and meaningful conversations. Her relationship with her friends deepened, moving beyond the superficial to explore questions of purpose, happiness, and the interconnectedness of life.

Integrating her spiritual beliefs with the demands of a modern professional life brought its own set of conflicts. Skepticism from some peers, the balancing act between career ambitions and personal values, and the weight of traditional family expectations added complexity to her life.

It soon became evident that her personal transformation was inspiring change in others. Her journey had a ripple effect, slowly creating a community of like-minded individuals drawn together by shared values of mindfulness and compassion. This emerging network provided mutual support and encouragement, symbolizing the power of individual change to inspire collective evolution.

Emily's transformation was a reawakening that touched every corner of her life. As she navigated her days, the lines between her spiritual journey and her everyday world began to blur, each influencing and enriching the other. The integration of her values into all aspects of her existence had become a necessity, a way of life that brought her a profound sense of harmony and fulfillment.

Turning Point in Gaining Control Over Internal Struggles

"Can the stillness of one heart quell the storm of many?"

Emily's office building towered like a silent observer, its glass facade reflecting the relentless pace of the world outside. Inside the labyrinth of cubicles and conference rooms, a critical situation was unfolding that would test the very essence of Emily's spiritual and professional journey.

The project that Emily and Michael were spearheading, once a signal of innovation and collaboration, had hit unforeseen obstacles. Deadlines loomed like storm clouds, and the team's morale was eroding under the weight of mounting pressure. The challenge was a test of resilience, patience, and leadership.

Emily, her mind a whirlwind of strategies and solutions, tried to maintain her composure. She remembered the mornings spent in meditation, the calming rhythm of her breath, and the serene stillness she had cultivated. But in the eye of this storm, her inner peace was faltering.

Michael's approach to the crisis was starkly different. His pragmatism, usually an asset, now seemed to clash with the need for creative problem-solving. Their discussions, once a dynamic exchange of ideas, had become tense standoffs. Emily could sense the frustration in Michael's terse emails and curt conversations, mirroring her own internal struggle.

One evening, as the office emptied, and the city's lights twinkled to life, Emily and Michael found themselves in an impromptu meeting. The room was suffused with the glow of the setting sun, casting long shadows that echoed their dilemma.

"Emily, we need to rethink our strategy," Michael said, his voice taut with urgency. "Aside from meeting these deadlines; it's about our credibility, our careers."

Emily took a deep breath, searching for the balance between her mindfulness practices and the realities of their situation. "I understand the stakes, Michael," she replied, her voice steady. "But we can't let fear dictate our actions. Let's approach this with a clear mind and maybe, find a solution we haven't seen yet."

Their conversation unfolded, a puzzle of conflict and collaboration. Emily's suggestions were met with skepticism, but she persisted, her words infused with the wisdom of her spiritual journey. She spoke of viewing challenges as opportunities for growth, of leading with empathy and understanding.

Emily shared a personal anecdote, a story of overcoming a significant challenge in her past. It was a tale of resilience, a reminder that obstacles were not dead ends but detours on the path to success.

The resolution to their crisis came unexpectedly. A brainstorming session, fueled by Emily's holistic approach and Michael's pragmatic insights, led to a breakthrough. The solution was unconventional, a blend of creativity and practicality that saved the project and, perhaps, their careers.

This major conflict became a pivotal moment in Emily's journey. It was proof of her growth, a demonstration of how her spiritual insights could influence and improve her professional life. The experience deepened her relationship with Michael, turning a challenging work dynamic into a partnership built on respect and mutual growth.

"In a forest of diverse trees, each branch tells its tale to the wind. Can the chorus of leaves sing a harmony that reaches the sky?"

The office of 'Shiyuantech Solutions' stood as an example of progress and ambition. Inside, the clatter of keyboards and the murmur of focused conversations, Emily navigated the maze of cubicles with a sense of purpose. Today, more than ever, she was determined to infuse her team with the spirit of collaboration and mindfulness she had been cultivating.

The project they were working on was a tribute to their collective ingenuity and resilience. Recently the team had hit a snag. The challenge was complex, involving intricate technology and tight deadlines. Tensions were high, and the usual energy of the office had taken on an edge of apprehension.

Emily, stepping into her role as the project leader, called for a meeting. The conference room, usually a place of straightforward discussions and PowerPoint presentations, was transformed under her guidance. She began with a moment of collective mindfulness. "Let's take a minute to center ourselves," she suggested, her voice calm yet commanding attention. The team, initially surprised, followed her lead, closing their eyes and taking deep, intentional breaths.

As they reopened their eyes, the atmosphere had subtly shifted. The air was charged with a newfound focus, and the team members looked at each other with a sense of renewed purpose. Emily seized this moment to foster open dialogue. "Let's approach our challenge today as an opportunity to innovate and grow together," she proposed.

The discussions that followed were markedly different from previous meetings. Emily actively encouraged each team member to voice their ideas and concerns. Even the quieter members found themselves contributing, their suggestions met with encouragement and constructive feedback.

Mark, a software engineer known for his brilliant but often solitary working style, surprised everyone with a novel approach to the technical problem they were facing. Emily listened attentively, building on his idea, and weaving it with others' suggestions. It was a blend of thoughts and perspectives, each member bringing their unique strengths to the table.

Sarah, talented but shy, had often found herself overshadowed in such settings. However, Emily's inclusive approach allowed her to step forward. Her insight into user experience brought a crucial element to the discussion, changing the course of their strategy.

As the meeting progressed, Emily's role as a leader shone. She had become a catalyst for unity and innovation. Her ability to listen deeply, to synthesize diverse ideas, and to maintain a harmonious environment was evident. The team, under her guidance, began to view the project to be completed as a journey they were on together.

This approach had a ripple effect beyond the conference room. Conversations around the office became more open, more cooperative. The competitive undercurrent that had once defined their work culture was giving way to a more collaborative character.

Emily reflected on this shift. Her thoughts were rich with introspection on leadership, teamwork, and the delicate balance between guiding and empowering. Her focus was to transform the way they worked as a team, about creating a space where innovation could thrive in an atmosphere of mutual respect and support.

"In a forest where two trees stand firm, their roots entangled beneath the soil. Can the wind of conflict teach them to move together?"

Within the walls of Shiyuantech Solutions, Emily, with her newfound resolve, continued to face one of her greatest challenges - navigating the ongoing conflict with Michael, her project manager. This situation, always fraught with tension, tested her professional skills along with the mindfulness and compassion she had been nurturing.

This new conflict centered around a key project that Emily and Michael were co-leading. Their approaches, as different as night and day, had led to a series of misunderstandings and frustrations. Michael, with his laser focus on deadlines and results, clashed with Emily's more holistic, process-oriented style. This project was a crucible in which their professional relationship was being reforged.

Emily's first step in addressing the conflict was to request a private meeting with Michael. The meeting room, usually a neutral space for formal discussions, took on a new significance. It became the arena where their differences were to be confronted and, hopefully, reconciled.

As they sat across from each other, the tension was palpable. Michael's initial stance was defensive, his words sharp with frustration. Emily, drawing upon her inner reserves of patience and understanding, listened intently. She acknowledged his concerns, validating his perspective before gently presenting her own.

Their conversation, initially a volley of differing viewpoints, gradually transformed into a dialogue of mutual exploration. Emily guided the discussion towards their common goal - the success of the project and the team. She emphasized the value of their diverse strengths and how, when combined, they could lead to innovative solutions.

Throughout the meeting, Emily's approach was a delicate balancing act. She remained assertive yet empathetic, firm in her convictions yet open to compromise. Her ability to maintain composure under pressure and to communicate effectively became the key to turning the tide of the conversation.

Emily and Michael began to find common ground. They agreed on a plan that incorporated both their strategies, blending Michael's emphasis on efficiency with Emily's focus on a thoughtful, inclusive approach. This compromise was a tribute to their shared commitment to the project's success.

The atmosphere in the office shifted from one of underlying tension to one of renewed enthusiasm and cooperation. Emily's role in navigating this challenging situation earned her the respect of her colleagues, and her relationship with Michael evolved into one of mutual respect and collaboration.

Emily reflected on this experience. Her meditations rich with introspective insights, revealed her thoughts on conflict, leadership, and the power of empathy. She pondered the delicate interplay of assertiveness and understanding, and how true leadership was about guiding teams through storms, not just calm waters.

As Emily left the office that evening, the city lights shimmered against the darkening sky, reflecting her own inner light - a light of resilience, compassion, and the unyielding pursuit of balance and harmony in both her personal and professional life.

"In a garden of diverse flowers, each unique, can the gardener's gentle touch unify their fragrances into a single breeze of harmony?"

The final phase of the project was a whirlwind of activity. Deadlines loomed, and the pressure was mounting. Within this chaos, Emily stood as a pillar of calm and focus. Her desk, usually an organized array of documents and digital screens, had become the command center for the project's final push.

Emily's leadership style, infused with mindfulness and empathy, had gradually seeped into the fabric of the team. The once fragmented group, riddled with conflicts and competing agendas, had transformed into a cohesive unit, united in their pursuit of a common goal. Emily's influence was profound; her calm demeanor, her inclusive approach to problem-solving, and her unwavering commitment to the project's vision had inspired her team to rise above their individual limitations.

The days leading up to the project deadline were a symphony of collaboration. The team worked in unison, their skills and strengths harmonizing to overcome each obstacle. Emily's role as a leader wove together the diverse talents and perspectives into a collage of collective effort.

Late-night brainstorming sessions, fueled by coffee and determination, took place in the glow of fluorescent lights. Moments of tension and breakthroughs were interspersed with light-hearted banter, creating an atmosphere of camaraderie and shared purpose.

When the project was finally completed, the sense of achievement was overwhelming. The team gathered in the conference room, a space that had witnessed their journey from discord to unity. The presentation of their work was a showcase of their professional skills and as a celebration of their journey together.

Emily pondered the intersection of her spiritual journey with her professional role, the balance between leading and learning, and the profound impact of empathy and mindfulness in a corporate setting.

The project's success reverberated beyond the team. Upper management recognized the successful outcome but more importantly the manner in which it was achieved. Emily's approach, once viewed with skepticism, was now seen as a model for leadership and team dynamics.

The success of the project had opened new doors for her, both within the company and in her personal growth. Her journey had become an inspiration to others, as evidence of the power of integrating one's inner values with their outer world and to find harmony between the spiritual and the mundane, the personal and the professional.

"In a world where silence speaks and action whispers, can one dance to the rhythm of the heart and still lead the ballet of progress?"

In the aftermath of the project's success, Emily found herself in a reflective state, her office now a crucible of newfound recognition and self-affirmation. The walls, adorned with charts and timelines of the recently completed project, seemed to echo back to her a story of triumph both in professional terms and in personal growth as.

The early morning light filtered through her office window, casting a gentle glow on her workspace. Emily sat there, sipping her green tea, allowing herself a moment of quiet introspection. Her mind replayed the project's journey, each challenge and resolution a tribute to the practical application of her spiritual beliefs.

She realized how her mindfulness practices, once confined to her personal life, had seamlessly integrated into her professional world. She thought about the countless decisions, the stress-laden moments, and the high-stake meetings, all of which were navigated with a calmness and clarity born from her spiritual discipline.

Emily's mind wandered to a recent philosophical dialogue with her mentor. In their favorite café, over the aroma of roasted coffee beans, they had discussed the intersection of spiritual practice and practical life. "The true measure of your practice is not how you soar in solitude but how you navigate the storm," her mentor had said. These words now resonated with her more than ever.

In the office, the atmosphere was marked with a sense of camaraderie and respect. Her colleagues, who were once skeptical of her methods, now approached her with a mixture of admiration and curiosity. Conversations at the snack machines and during lunch breaks often steered towards inquiries about mindfulness and balancing stress.

Among these colleagues, Michael's transformation was the most notable. The project had started with friction and skepticism between them but had evolved into a relationship marked by mutual respect and understanding. Their interactions now carried an undercurrent of shared experience, a bond forged in the fires of a challenging project.

Emily's relationship with other team members like Alex and Linda also deepened. Their interactions were enriched by Emily's approach to teamwork and communication, fostering a workplace culture that valued empathy and cooperation. Alex, inspired by Emily, initiated a mindfulness group within the office, extending the influence of her beliefs.

The success of the project had not only reaffirmed her beliefs but had also elevated her status within the company. There were whispers of potential promotions and new opportunities, each a doorway to greater challenges and wider influence.

Emily's journal entries became more introspective, reflecting on her journey and the impact she was making. These moments of self-reflection were a conscious weaving of her experiences into the larger story of her life.

How Transformation Influences Those Around You

"Can the song of the cicada and the hum of the computer harmonize in the dance of growth?"

The morning sun streamed through the expansive windows of Shiyuantech Solutions. In this dynamic environment, where ambition and technology merged, Emily had become an undeniable influence. It wasn't just her recent professional success that drew the eyes and minds of her colleagues; it was the profound transformation within her that piqued their curiosity.

Among them was Alex, a colleague who had worked closely with Emily. He had observed the changes in her – the serene confidence, the depth of her insights, and her newfound balance between assertiveness and empathy. These changes, initially a source of intrigue, had now sparked a flame of inspiration within him.

Alex, known for his analytical prowess and detail-oriented approach, had always prioritized logic over introspection. Yet, witnessing Emily's journey, he found himself at a crossroads, pondering his path. In the modern, sleek confines of the office, among the hum of computers and the constant flow of data, Alex's journey of self-discovery began.

His conversations with Emily, once strictly professional, started to explore the realms of philosophy and personal growth. Emily shared her experiences with mindfulness and self-awareness, her words weaving a fabric of transformation that resonated with Alex. Their dialogues, often held over cups of steaming coffee in a quiet corner of the office cafeteria, became a convergence of minds exploring the intersections of personal development and professional fulfillment.

Alex grappled with skepticism and his ingrained preference for tangible, empirical evidence. Yet, the more he engaged with Emily, the more he began to question his long-held beliefs. His thoughts, once dominated by logistical and practical concerns, now swarmed with questions about purpose, fulfillment, and the essence of true happiness.

Emily's reflections on Alex's journey provided her with insight as she saw a bit of her past self in him – the initial hesitation, the struggle to align inner truths with external realities. Her mentorship of Alex was about learning from his unique perspectives, a reciprocal exchange of insights that enriched both their paths.

Alex found himself at a small park near the office during a lunch break, a place Emily had often mentioned as her sanctuary for reflection. Sitting on a bench, surrounded by the gentle rustle of leaves and the distant hum of the city, Alex contemplated his future. He realized that his journey, inspired by Emily's transformation, was about finding a deeper sense of purpose and fulfillment.

"Amidst the glow of monitors, can the rhythm of a healthy heart echo through the halls of thought?"

The Shiyuantech Solutions office, a hub of innovation and ambition, witnessed the unfolding of a new chapter in Alex's life. His decision to embark on a journey of physical wellness and psychological self-help, influenced yet distinct from Emily's spiritually oriented path, marked a significant shift in his approach to personal growth.

Alex's day began earlier than usual, the first rays of dawn accompanying his morning jog. The city, with its towering skyscrapers and sprawling parks, offered a backdrop that mirrored his internal transformation. Each stride was a step towards greater physical health, a commitment to a routine that balanced the demands of his high-stress job.

From the disciplined art of yoga, with its promise of strength and flexibility, to the high-energy rush of spin classes, each new activity brought a sense of discovery and accomplishment. His physical transformation was profound, not just in the newfound energy that coursed through his veins but in the way his colleagues began to perceive him.

Nutrition, once an afterthought in Alex's busy schedule, now took center stage. The office cafeteria, a place of hurried lunches and vending machine snacks, became the background for his dietary experiments. Armed with nutrition plans and a newfound interest in culinary arts, Alex explored a world of balanced diets and mindful eating. His lunchbox, filled with vibrant salads and nutrient-rich meals, often sparked conversations among his colleagues, inspiring some to reconsider their own dietary choices.

His nights, previously occupied by endless scrolling through social media or mindless television watching, were now dedicated to reading about psychological wellness, meditation, and mindfulness. His apartment, a reflection of his changing lifestyle, gradually transformed into a sanctuary of tranquility, with books on mental well-being gracing his shelves and meditation apps on his phone.

Balancing a demanding career with a rigorous fitness regimen and a quest for mental well-being required discipline and time management, skills that Alex had to develop along the way. His reflections, previously dominated by work-related stress, now juggled thoughts of workout schedules, meal preps, and self-help techniques.

Linda and Michael began to take notice of Alex's transformation. Linda, intrigued by his dietary changes, engaged him in discussions about nutrition and its impact on overall health. Michael, observing Alex's increased energy and focus, started to show interest in his fitness routines.

His story, though different from Emily's, was a demonstration to the diverse paths individuals can take towards personal growth and the impact such transformations can have on one's life and the lives of those around them.

"In a room filled with whispers of ink and paper, can a mind navigate the labyrinth of words to find the essence of self?"

Alex's quest for self-improvement led him to the rich and varied world of self-help literature. Nestled in his cozy apartment, surrounded by the soft glow of the evening lights, he researched books that promised insights into the human psyche and strategies for personal growth.

Each book he opened was a portal into new ways of thinking. He absorbed the teachings of positive psychology, marveling at the concepts that wove happiness and fulfillment into a science. The pages brought forth ideas of gratitude, resilience, and the power of a positive mindset, each concept a building block in his quest for a better self.

Mindfulness, a theme that resonated deeply with Alex, became a subject of intense study. He pored over texts that unraveled the intricacies of being present in the moment, of acknowledging thoughts and feelings without judgment. These readings complemented his fledgling meditation practice, providing a theoretical foundation to the experiences he encountered on the mat.

The world of personal effectiveness was another topic that captivated him. Books on time management, goal setting, and productivity offered practical advice that he eagerly applied to his daily life. The once cluttered and chaotic spaces of his work and home transformed into organized environments that reflected his new-found understanding of efficiency.

Evenings in Alex's apartment turned into introspective sessions, where he reflected on the day's learnings. The quiet space became a sanctuary where he journaled his thoughts, connecting the dots between the theories in his books and his personal experiences.

At work, the influence of his readings started to show. Meetings with Emily and other colleagues were now punctuated with references to his latest insights. His contributions became more thoughtful, reflecting a depth of understanding that went beyond the surface. Conversations with friends revealed a new Alex, one who spoke of concepts like emotional intelligence and the growth mindset with ease and enthusiasm.

"In a world where paths diverge and converge, can two travelers share their maps and still find their unique destinations?"

Emily and Alex, both embarking on their unique paths of personal growth, found in each other an invaluable source of support and learning. Their friendship, once confined to the realms of work-related discussions, now blossomed into a rich exchange of experiences and insights. Their conversations examined the depths of their individual journeys. Emily, with a calm and thoughtful demeanor, shared the nuances of her spiritual path.

She spoke of her meditation practices, the moments of profound peace she encountered, and how these experiences transformed her perspective on life and work.

Alex, his eyes alight with curiosity, listened intently. He shared his own adventures in the world of physical wellness and psychology. He talked about the exhilaration of his new fitness regimen, the clarity he found in meditation, and the fascinating concepts he was discovering in his self-help books.

Their dialogues were a blend of philosophical musings and practical discussions. Emily's insights into mindfulness and compassion provided a spiritual dimension to Alex's more physical and psychological focus. In turn, Alex's enthusiasm about his newfound knowledge of mental health and fitness offered Emily a different perspective on holistic well-being.

"In a cafe where two roads meet, can the traveler of the mind and the seeker of the body share a cup without drinking from the same well?"

Emily and Alex's paths, divergent in their nature, converged in their morning meetings, creating a mosaic of insights and experiences. A small neighborhood diner provided a serene backdrop to their deepening bond and mutual exploration.

As they settled into their usual spot by the window, looking out at the city's busy streets, their dialogues took on a new depth. Emily shared the latest revelations from her meditation and mindfulness practices. She spoke of the subtleties of her introspective journey, how it led her to profound realizations about her inner self, and its impact on her professional life.

Alex, energized and enthusiastic, contrasted her reflections with his own experiences. He spoke about the physical exhilaration he found in his new fitness regime, the mental clarity from his meditation sessions, and the practical wisdom he gleaned from self-help literature. His approach, more tangible and immediate, offered a different perspective on personal development.

Their discussions, rich with philosophical underpinnings, explored the intersections and divergences of their paths. They debated and dissected ideas, finding joy in the intellectual and emotional exchange. Emily's spiritual insights provided a deeper, more reflective angle to Alex's practical strategies, suggesting a holistic approach to well-being.

In the office, the influence of their shared learnings began to manifest. Their interactions with colleagues were marked by a blend of Emily's empathetic listening and Alex's pragmatic problem-solving. This fusion created a dynamic work environment, where team members felt both understood and efficiently guided.

"In the dance of mind and muscle, where does the spirit rest?"

One crisp morning, as the first rays of sun pierced through the urban landscape, Emily found herself reflecting on Alex's recent foray into physical wellness. His enthusiasm for fitness and mental health strategies had sparked a new awareness in her. She realized that while she had been focusing on her spiritual and emotional well-being, she had somewhat neglected her physical health. Inspired by Alex, Emily decided to integrate more physical activities into her routine. She started with morning yoga sessions, feeling the synergy between her meditative practices and the physical movements.

Alex, for his part, found himself intrigued by the depth of Emily's spiritual insights. Their conversations often explored topics beyond the physical aspects of well-being. Emily spoke of the interconnectedness of mind, body, and spirit, and how neglecting one could affect the others. This perspective opened a new dimension in Alex's understanding of wellness. He began to incorporate mindfulness into his daily routine, seeking to balance his physical activities with mental and emotional introspection.

Their mutual influence was evident in the office as well. Emily's approach to her work began to change subtly. She took short breaks throughout the day to stretch and walk, often inviting Alex and other colleagues to join her. These moments of physical activity became a source of rejuvenation and camaraderie among the team.

Alex, meanwhile, started to approach his tasks with a newfound calmness. He found that his mindfulness practice helped him to manage stress better and enhance his focus. His productivity and creativity flourished, earning him accolades from his peers and superiors.

"In a garden of diverse blooms, can the oak and the rose speak the same language of growth?"

Emily's workspace, once a symbol of conventional efficiency, now exuded a sense of balance and serenity. Her colleagues, initially curious about the subtle changes in her demeanor and approach, began to engage in deeper conversations with her. They noticed her calmness in high-pressure situations, her thoughtful responses to complex problems, and her ability to inspire collaboration within the team. These observations sparked discussions around mindfulness and the integration of personal values into professional life.

Alex's transformation, too, was hard to miss. His colleagues observed a newfound vitality in his steps and a clarity in his communication. The once reserved software engineer now shared his experiences with fitness regimes and mental health strategies, enthusiastically advocating for a balanced lifestyle. His desk, adorned with books on psychology and wellness, became a hub for discussions on physical and mental well-being.

Their individual journeys, though distinct, intersected in ways that enriched the office culture. Lunch breaks and casual gatherings turned into impromptu forums for sharing experiences and insights. Emily and Alex, often seen deep in conversation, became the catalysts for a broader discourse on personal development.

"In a garden of diverse blooms, can the orchid of serenity and the oak of strength grow side by side?"

In the vibrant ecosystem of Shiyuantech Solutions, the contrasting yet complementary journeys of Emily and Alex served as a demonstration to the diversity of paths in personal growth and well-being.

Emily's office, adorned with symbols of her journey – a small Buddha statue, an array of meditation books, and soothing plants – reflected her inner tranquility. Her approach to challenges and interactions was deeply rooted in her mindfulness practices, influencing her decision-making and leadership style.

In contrast, Alex's journey took a more physical and psychological route. His workspace, once nondescript, now featured a vision board with goals for fitness achievements, mental health milestones, and quotes from self-help gurus. He had embraced a regimen of early morning runs and gym sessions, complemented by evenings spent exploring the depths of positive psychology and self-improvement literature.

Their differing paths sparked rich dialogues among colleagues, igniting curiosity and opening doors to new perspectives on personal development. Lunch breaks often turned into impromptu discussion forums, where Emily shared insights on meditation and spiritual alignment, while Alex talked about the latest in wellness trends and mental resilience strategies.

This diversity in approaches to personal growth extended beyond the confines of their office. Friends and family members of Emily and Alex noticed the positive changes in their lives, leading to broader conversations about the varied paths to self-improvement. Emily's sister started exploring yoga, inspired by Emily's calmness, while Alex's best friend took up journaling and mindfulness to emulate his newfound mental clarity.

Some colleagues found it hard to relate to Emily's spiritual practices, viewing them as too esoteric for the workplace. Others were skeptical of Alex's enthusiastic adoption of physical and mental wellness regimes, dismissing them as mere trends. These conflicts showcased the hurdles in embracing personal growth in a diverse environment.

However, the overarching impact of their journeys was one of positive influence and acceptance. Personal growth is not a linear or uniform process but a multifaceted journey unique to each individual, underscoring the importance of respecting and learning from different approaches to self-discovery and well-being.

Achieving Balance Between Spiritual and Worldly Lives

"Riding the Ox Home"

"Can the silence of the mind echo in the rhythm of keyboards?"

The morning sun streamed into Emily's office, casting a warm, golden light over her desk. It was a special day for her, one where she would extend the tranquility, she found in her personal meditation practices to her colleagues at Shiyuantech Solutions. With a calm determination, Emily prepared the conference room for the first session of the meditation group she had initiated.

She arranged the chairs in a semi-circle, creating an inviting and open space. In the center, she placed a few candles and a small bowl of fresh flowers, their gentle fragrance subtly filling the room. On each chair, she laid out a pamphlet that she had prepared, outlining the basics of meditation and its benefits for mental well-being.

As her colleagues began to arrive, there was a mix of curiosity and intrigue in their expressions. Emily greeted each person with a warm smile, guiding them to their seats. She could sense a blend of skepticism and openness among the group, a natural response to something new and unfamiliar in a corporate setting.

Once everyone was settled, Emily began the session with a brief introduction. She spoke softly but confidently, sharing her journey with meditation and how it had transformed her approach to work and life. Her words were inviting, encouraging her colleagues to explore this practice with an open mind.

She then guided them through a basic meditation exercise. Her instructions were clear and simple, focusing on mindful breathing and awareness of the present moment. The room, usually buzzing with the energy of corporate discussions, was now enveloped in a tranquil silence.

As the session progressed, Emily observed the gradual relaxation in her colleagues' postures. Some closed their eyes, while others kept a soft gaze, but all seemed to be engaging with the practice in their way.

The meditation lasted for about fifteen minutes, but the impact was profound. As the group slowly emerged from their state of relaxation, there were gentle stretches and soft sighs of contentment. Emily encouraged everyone to share their experience, and while some expressed difficulty in quieting their minds, others spoke of a surprising sense of calm and clarity.

The session ended with Emily expressing gratitude to her colleagues for their participation and openness. She announced that the meditation group would be a regular weekly event, an oasis of calm in their busy work schedule.

As the group dispersed, returning to their desks, the atmosphere in the office seemed subtly different. There was a sense of shared experience, a small but significant shift towards incorporating mindfulness into their corporate lives.

In the days that followed, Emily's meditation group began to gain momentum. More colleagues joined, intrigued by the initial participants' positive feedback. The sessions became a cherished break from the demands of work, a time for collective relaxation and mental rejuvenation.

This initiative by Emily was a manifestation of her commitment to sharing the benefits of her practices with those around her. It was a step towards creating a more mindful and compassionate work environment, reflecting Emily's belief in the power of inner peace to positively impact one's outer world.

"Does the tree of insight bloom in the garden of shared stories?"

One evening, as the city lights began to flicker on, Emily set up her living room for the first of her informal discussion groups. She arranged the furniture to create a cozy circle, a space that felt both welcoming and intimate. Cushions were strewn across the floor, and a few chairs were pulled up to accommodate her friends.

Emily had carefully chosen a blend of soothing music to play in the background, setting a calm and reflective mood for the evening. On a small table, she placed an assortment of herbal teas and healthy snacks, anticipating that the discussions might stretch into the night.

As her friends began to arrive, there was an air of excitement mixed with curiosity. They were a diverse group – some were colleagues from work, others were old friends, and a few were acquaintances who had expressed interest in Emily's journey.

Once everyone had settled in with their cups of tea, Emily opened the discussion. She shared her experiences with mindfulness and how it had positively impacted her life, both personally and professionally. Her words were genuine and heartfelt, inviting her friends to explore these concepts in their own lives.

The topic for the evening was 'The Role of Mindfulness in Personal Growth.' Emily facilitated the discussion, encouraging everyone to share their thoughts and experiences. The conversation flowed naturally, with each person bringing their unique perspective to the table.

One friend, a graphic designer, spoke about the creative blocks she faced and how mindfulness techniques could help in overcoming them. Another, a teacher, shared how he used mindfulness to deal with the stress of his job. The stories were varied, but the underlying theme was the same – the desire for a more balanced and fulfilling life.

Throughout the evening, Emily listened attentively, offering insights, and gently steering the conversation when it veered off course. She had a natural ability to make everyone feel heard and valued, fostering a sense of community among the group.

As the discussion wound down, the group reflected on the insights they had gained. They agreed to make these gatherings a regular event, each time focusing on a different aspect of personal growth and well-being.

After everyone had left, Emily sat alone in her living room, a sense of contentment washing over her. She felt grateful for the opportunity to share her journey with others and to learn from their experiences. The discussion group, though a small initiative, was a step towards building a supportive community, a space where people could come together to explore and grow.

Emily looked forward to future gatherings, to the deepening of friendships and the sharing of wisdom. She saw these discussions as an extension of her own journey, a way to not only enrich her life but also to positively impact the lives of those around her.

"Can a single candle ignite a hall of mirrors?"

Emily's initiative to cultivate a community of like-minded individuals began to bear fruit. The venue for their gatherings varied, sometimes in the calm of a local library's meeting room, other times in the comfort of her own living room, transformed into a cozy, inviting space for deep conversations and shared experiences.

The group, initially small, began to grow as word spread. Each session was structured yet fluid, allowing for the organic flow of dialogue and exchange of ideas. Emily, with her innate ability to connect and empathize, facilitated discussions that ranged from personal growth and mindfulness to the challenges of integrating these practices into daily life.

On one evening, the group met at a community center, a place that resonated with a sense of purpose and openness. As the meeting commenced, Emily introduced a topic that had been on her mind: the balance between personal growth and societal responsibilities. This sparked a vibrant discussion, with each member contributing their perspectives. There was John, a teacher, who spoke about applying mindfulness in his classroom, and Sarah, a nurse, who shared how compassion fatigue affected her work and how mindfulness practices helped her cope.

The diversity of experiences enriched the conversation, providing a backdrop of real-life applications of the principles they all were exploring. Emily listened intently, interjecting with thoughtful questions or insights that deepened the understanding of the topic. Her ability to guide the discussion, while allowing each member to have their voice heard, was a tribute to her growth as a leader and facilitator.

As the evening progressed, a new member, David, shared his skepticism about integrating such practices into his high-pressure corporate job. This led to a spontaneous and insightful dialogue about practical mindfulness in the workplace. Emily shared her experiences, detailing how she navigated her professional environment with a mindful approach. Her stories resonated with David, offering him a new perspective on how these practices could be relevant in his own life.

Towards the end of the session, the group engaged in a brief guided meditation led by Emily. The room fell into a serene silence, each member turning inward, reflecting on the evening's discussions. The meditation served as a grounding exercise, bringing a sense of peace and closure to the gathering.

As the members began to depart, there was a deep sense of community and shared purpose. They left with new insights and a feeling of being understood and supported. The group had become a haven for those seeking to navigate the complexities of life with a mindful approach.

Emily stayed back, tidying up the space, her heart full of gratitude for the community that was forming. She realized that what had started as an extension of her journey was now evolving into a collective exploration of life's deeper questions.

In the quiet of the night, as she locked the community center's door, Emily felt a deep connection to this group and a sense of responsibility towards nurturing it. The experience left a sense of anticipation about how this community would evolve and the impact it would have on its members' lives.

"Does the unspoken word in a room of talk change the conversation?"

Emily's initiative to introduce meditation breaks at her workplace began to bear fruit. Initially met with curiosity and mild skepticism, these short sessions gradually became a valued part of the office routine for many of her colleagues.

On a typical workday, just after the mid-morning rush of meetings and emails, Emily would send out a gentle reminder through the office communication channel: "Meditation break in 10 minutes in the conference room. All are welcome!" Gradually, what began as a small group of participants started growing, as word spread about the benefits of these mindfulness pauses.

In these sessions, Emily guided her colleagues through various simple but effective meditation techniques. Sometimes it involved focusing on the breath, other times it involved a guided visualization to release stress. Each session, lasting about 10 to 15 minutes, provided a much-needed break from the day's demands.

The effects of these meditation breaks were noticeable. Colleagues who participated regularly reported feeling more relaxed and focused throughout the day. Conversations around the snack machines or during lunch breaks often included positive remarks about the meditation sessions. "It's just a few minutes, but it makes such a difference," one colleague would say. "I feel less frazzled and more centered," another would add.

The changes were not just confined to the personal experiences of her colleagues. The overall atmosphere in the office started to shift. There was a noticeable decrease in the levels of stress and tension. Meetings became more productive, with participants appearing more centered and thoughtful in their responses.

Even those who were initially hesitant began to show interest. Emily's boss, who had observed the positive changes, approached her one day. "I was skeptical at first, but I've noticed a real difference in the team. I'm thinking we should make these meditation breaks an official part of our wellness program," he suggested, much to Emily's delight.

This newfound acceptance and appreciation of mindfulness practices in the workplace was a significant milestone in Emily's journey. It validated her belief in the positive impact of spiritual practices in professional settings. This really highlighted the gradual but impactful transformation within the office, proof of the power of one individual's initiative to bring about positive change in a collective environment.

"Can a single seed of calm bloom a garden in the office?"

Encouraged by the success of her meditation breaks at work, Emily began to contemplate the next step in her journey to bring wellness into the workplace. She recognized the potential to expand her impact beyond the brief sessions she had been conducting. With the growing interest among her colleagues, she saw an opportunity to introduce more structured wellness initiatives.

One evening, after a particularly rewarding meditation session at work, Emily sat at her desk, her thoughts drifting towards the possibilities ahead. She envisioned a series of workshops that could cover various aspects of wellness, from stress management techniques to mindful communication. Her mind buzzed with ideas – maybe she could even invite wellness experts to lead these workshops, providing her colleagues with a variety of perspectives and practices.

The following day, Emily took her first step towards this vision. She approached her boss with a proposal for a more formal wellness program. "I've been thinking about how we can build on the success of the meditation breaks," she began, her voice tinged with excitement. "What if we organized monthly workshops on different wellness topics? I believe it could really enhance our work environment and the well-being of our team."

Her boss, impressed by the initiative and the positive feedback from the team, was receptive to the idea. "That sounds great, Emily. Let's discuss this further and see how we can implement it. Maybe we can allocate a budget for external experts or resources," he suggested.

With the green light from her boss, Emily began the planning process. She reached out to local wellness experts, explaining her vision and inviting them to collaborate. The responses were encouraging. Several experts in areas such as nutrition, yoga, and stress management expressed interest in leading sessions.

As word of these planned workshops spread through the office, the excitement was tangible. Emily's colleagues began to approach her with suggestions and topics they were interested in. "Could we have a session on balancing work and life?" one colleague asked. "I'd love to learn more about healthy eating habits," mentioned another.

Emily reflected on this new phase of her journey. She journaled her thoughts, musing on the potential of these workshops to create a more mindful and balanced work culture. She envisioned an office environment where well-being was as much a priority as productivity, where her colleagues felt supported in their personal and professional growth.

Manifestation of Harmony in Relationships and Actions

"Can a single drop of calmness ripple through an ocean of chaos?"

In the heart of Shiyuantech Solutions, Emily's presence had become an inspiration of serenity. Her journey of integrating mindfulness into her life had transformed her approach to work along with the very atmosphere around her.

On a particularly hectic Monday morning, the office was abuzz with the usual frenzy of looming deadlines and urgent meetings. Emily moved through the office with a composed grace, her steps measured, her expression serene, unaffected by the frenetic energy that characterized the start of the workweek.

As she settled into her workspace, her colleagues couldn't help but notice the stark contrast between her tranquil presence and the surrounding turmoil. Her desk, a reflection of her state of mind, was organized and uncluttered.

Throughout the day, Emily's calmness became her signature trait, particularly noticeable during a mid-morning crisis meeting. The project team had hit a snag, and tensions were high. Voices rose, and tempers flared as the team grappled with the unexpected challenge. Amid this storm, Emily remained a picture of composure.

As the meeting progressed, her colleagues found themselves inadvertently drawing from her tranquility. Her suggestions, offered in a clear, measured tone, cut through the discordance of stressed voices. She listened attentively to each team member, acknowledging their concerns with empathy, and responding with thoughtful solutions.

Her approach had a tangible effect on the room. Gradually, the heightened emotions began to subside, the team's collective anxiety giving way to a more focused and productive discussion. Emily's ability to remain centered in the face of adversity provided a grounding influence, steering the meeting back on course.

In the aftermath, several colleagues approached Emily, expressing admiration for her ability to stay calm under pressure. "How do you do it?" they asked, genuinely curious about the source of her unshakeable composure.

Emily smiled, sharing brief insights into her mindfulness practices. "It's about staying present and not getting swept away by the chaos," she explained. "Sometimes, just taking a moment to breathe and center yourself can make all the difference."

As the day ended, Emily's impact on the office was evident. The earlier tension had dissipated, replaced by a more harmonious and cooperative work environment. Her colleagues began to emulate her approach, taking short mindfulness breaks to regain focus and perspective.

In her own reflections, Emily recognized the significant role her practices played in her professional life. She saw her calmness as a tool that brought stability and clarity to her team. Her journey of personal growth had become intertwined with her role at work, making her an inadvertent catalyst for a more mindful workplace culture.

"Can the depth of listening echo louder than the might of speech?"

In the bustling corridors of Shiyuantech Solutions, Emily had carved out a niche as a skilled professional and compassionate listener. Her colleagues, once caught up in the usual corporate rush, noticed and appreciated a distinct quality in Emily – her ability to listen with empathy.

On a Tuesday afternoon, a typically busy day in the office, Emily's empathetic listening skills came to the forefront during a team brainstorming session. The team had gathered in a conference room, the walls adorned with whiteboards filled with colorful notes and diagrams. The air was thick with ideas and the usual stress of hitting creative targets.

As the team members pitched their ideas, Emily's way of listening stood out. She maintained eye contact, nodded thoughtfully, and offered encouraging smiles. She didn't just wait for her turn to speak; she truly listened, absorbing the essence of what each person was saying.

Her colleague, Mark, who was often hesitant to voice his thoughts, found himself speaking up. Emily's attentive gaze and open posture encouraged him to share an innovative idea he had been mulling over. As he spoke, Emily leaned in, genuinely interested, her demeanor conveying that what he had to say was important. The room, usually buzzing with interjections and quick-fire responses, fell into an attentive hush.

When Mark finished, Emily responded. "That's a really interesting approach, Mark. I like how you've thought this through," she said, her tone affirming and respectful. Her response sparked a constructive dialogue, with other team members building on Mark's idea, a rare occurrence in their usually competitive meetings.

Later that day, in a one-on-one meeting with a junior colleague, Emily's empathetic listening was again on display. The colleague, Sarah, was expressing concerns about managing her workload. As Sarah spoke, Emily's response was a thoughtful silence that allowed Sarah to express herself fully.

When Emily did speak, it was with insight and understanding. "It sounds like you're feeling overwhelmed. Let's see how we can break this down and make it more manageable," she offered. Her approach made Sarah feel supported and validated, transforming what could have been a stressful interaction into a collaborative problem-solving session.

Word of Emily's empathetic listening began to spread through the office. Colleagues started seeking her out, not only for professional advice but for conversations that required a thoughtful ear. They noticed how conversations with Emily left them feeling more understood and less stressed.

Emily herself began to see her ability to listen empathetically as tool that could foster a more supportive and collaborative work environment. She recognized the power of listening not just to respond but to understand, a subtle but profound shift in communication that could positively impact her team's dynamics.

"Can the stillness of mind illuminate the path through the maze of complexity?"

One Thursday morning, a significant issue arose with a key project Emily was overseeing. A crucial software component was malfunctioning, threatening to derail the project's timeline. The team gathered in a meeting room, the air thick with tension and concern.

As the team members presented the problem, Emily listened intently, her expression calm yet focused. Instead of jumping to immediate conclusions or placing blame, she took a moment to center herself, drawing on her mindfulness practices. This brief pause allowed her to approach the situation with clarity and composure.

"Let's break this down," Emily suggested, her voice steady. She initiated a systematic review of the project, asking questions that encouraged her team to look at the issue from different angles. Her approach was methodical but open-ended, inviting collaboration and creative thinking.

As the team dissected the problem, Emily encouraged them to consider the broader impact of each potential solution. She reminded them to think about the client's needs, the project's long-term goals, and the team's well-being. Her holistic perspective fostered a more inclusive and thoughtful problem-solving process.

During the discussion, a junior developer, hesitant until now, proposed an innovative but untested solution. In the past, such suggestions might have been quickly dismissed. However, Emily's open-minded approach allowed for a safe space to consider new ideas.

"That's an interesting approach," Emily acknowledged, her tone encouraging. She weighed the risks and potential of the idea, fostering a discussion that examined its feasibility. Her balanced consideration of the suggestion boosted the team's morale and sparked further creative solutions.

The meeting culminated in a decision that combined the junior developer's innovative idea with more traditional methods, creating a hybrid solution that addressed the issue effectively while minimizing risks. Emily's mindful approach to problem-solving had not only resolved the immediate issue but also promoted a sense of unity and innovation within her team.

"Can the shadow of doubt illuminate the path to understanding?"

In the ever-evolving dynamics of Shiyuantech Solutions, a notable change was occurring in the relationship between Emily and her project manager, Michael. Michael, who had initially viewed Emily's mindfulness and spiritual practices with a degree of skepticism, began to witness firsthand the positive effects of her approach on their work environment.

The shift became evident during a project planning session. The team was brainstorming ideas for a new client proposal, and the tension was high due to the challenging nature of the project. Emily, maintaining her usual calm demeanor, presented a series of innovative yet practical solutions. As she spoke, Michael listened intently, visibly impressed by her ability to think outside the box while staying grounded.

In the days that followed, Michael found himself increasingly seeking Emily's input on various aspects of the project. He started to appreciate her balanced approach to problem-solving – a blend of creativity, pragmatism, and mindfulness. This new level of professional respect began to thaw the frostiness that had previously characterized their interactions.

One afternoon, in a casual corridor conversation, Michael complimented Emily on her recent contributions. "I have to admit, I was a bit doubtful about your methods at first, Emily," he said with a candid tone. "But seeing how you handle these complex projects with such composure has changed my mind. Your approach is really making a positive impact on the team."

Emily appreciated Michael's acknowledgment. It was a sign that her efforts to integrate her personal growth into her professional life were not only being noticed but also valued. This recognition from Michael, who held a significant influence in the office, further solidified her position as a respected member of the team.

Their relationship gradually transformed from one of mere professional necessity to mutual respect and understanding. Conversations about work became more collaborative, with both Emily and Michael openly exchanging ideas and solutions. Emily's insights, often infused with her mindfulness principles, brought a new depth to their discussions, leading to more innovative and effective strategies.

Colleagues noticed the change in the atmosphere during meetings involving both Emily and Michael. The usual tension gave way to a more constructive and harmonious environment, setting a positive example for the entire team.

"Does the echo of a shared story build a bridge or a mirror?"
One Saturday evening, Emily hosted a small gathering at her apartment. The ambiance was relaxed, with soft music playing in the background and

the aroma of homemade food filling the air. As her friends arrived, there was an air of ease and anticipation, evidence of the comfortable and open environment Emily had created.

During the evening, conversations flowed effortlessly. Unlike previous gatherings, where discussions often skimmed the surface of casual topics, this time, they explored more personal and meaningful subjects. Emily listened intently to her friends, offering thoughtful responses, and sharing her own experiences with a vulnerability that was both new and refreshing.

One conversation stood out when Emily's friend, Clara, opened up about a recent challenge she was facing at work. Instead of offering quick advice, Emily listened deeply, acknowledging Clara's feelings and experiences. This empathetic listening provided Clara with a sense of being truly heard and understood, something she later expressed gratitude for.

As the night progressed, other friends began to share their stories and struggles. Emily's approach to these conversations was a blend of mindfulness and genuine interest. Her questions were thoughtful, and her responses, infused with insights from her own journey, often provided a new perspective or a moment of clarity.

These deepened interactions led to a stronger bond among the group. Friends who had known each other for years discovered new facets to one another's personalities and lives. The atmosphere was one of mutual respect and a shared journey of personal growth, fostered by Emily's approach.

By the end of the evening, as her friends began to leave, there were expressions of appreciation and hugs exchanged. The sentiment was clear: the evening had been more than just a social gathering; it had been a shared experience of connection and growth.

After the guests had left, Emily reflected on the evening. She felt a sense of fulfillment, knowing that her personal transformation was rippling out into her friendships, enriching these relationships in unexpected and beautiful ways.

"Can the roots of the past nourish the blossoms of the present?"

On a bright Saturday afternoon, Emily arranged a family gathering at her parents' home, a quaint house surrounded by a well-tended garden. The air was filled with the aroma of her mother's cooking, a comforting and familiar scent that brought back memories of her childhood. The gathering was casual, with her siblings, parents, and a few close relatives.

As they sat around the large dining table, laden with an array of dishes, the conversation flowed freely, touching upon various topics. Emily waited for the right moment to share her experiences. When the conversation naturally drifted towards how everyone was coping with their busy lives, Emily saw her opening.

She spoke of her meditation practices and the positive impact they had on her life. Her words were careful, ensuring they didn't come across as preaching, but rather sharing. She talked about the challenges she faced at work and how her mindfulness journey had helped her navigate them with more composure and clarity.

Her family listened, intrigued by the visible changes in Emily. Her father, initially a skeptic, asked thoughtful questions, showing a newfound interest in her practices. Her mother shared her experiences with traditional prayer and how it brought her peace, drawing parallels with Emily's meditation.

Emily's siblings, too, joined the conversation, sharing their own stressors and life challenges. Emily listened attentively, offering insights where appropriate, and learning from their experiences. It was a two-way exchange, marked by a genuine interest in each other's well-being.

As the gathering continued, the atmosphere became one of mutual respect and understanding. Emily's family began to appreciate her journey, seeing it not as a divergence from their values, but as an extension of the family's collective experiences and wisdom.

Later in the evening, as they gathered in the living room over tea and desserts, the conversation turned more philosophical. They discussed the importance of finding balance in life, of maintaining mental and emotional well-being amidst the pressures of modern living.

Emily's mother, reflecting on the conversation, expressed her pride in Emily's growth. "You've always been determined, but now there's a sense of calm in you," she said warmly. Emily's siblings nodded in agreement, some even expressing a desire to learn more about mindfulness techniques.

As the night ended and Emily prepared to leave, there was a sense of closeness that hadn't been there before. The gathering had strengthened their family bonds opening doors for deeper conversations and mutual growth.

Driving back to her apartment, Emily felt a deep sense of gratitude. Her spiritual journey, which had begun as a personal quest, was now enriching her family relationships, creating a space for shared experiences and mutual learning.

"Does the river of self-flow into the ocean of others, or does it find the sea within?"

The progression of Emily's journey, encompassing both her personal and professional realms, had evolved into a beautiful example of holistic growth. Her ability to seamlessly weave her spiritual insights into every aspect of her life brought a newfound depth and richness to her experiences with others.

On a quiet Saturday morning, Emily found herself in her favorite local bookstore, browsing through the spirituality section. Her eyes landed on a book about integrating mindfulness into daily life. Flipping through the pages, she felt a connection with the author's words, each sentence resonating with her own experiences. Emily decided to buy the book, envisioning how its insights could further enrich her journey.

Later that day, Emily visited a nearby park, a place where she often went to reflect and meditate. Sitting under a sprawling oak tree, she began to read. The gentle rustle of leaves in the breeze and the distant laughter of children playing created a serene backdrop. As she dived deeper into the book, she found herself drawing parallels between the author's advice and her own methods of incorporating mindfulness into her daily routine.

That evening, Emily hosted a small dinner at her apartment for a few close friends. As they enjoyed the meal, the conversation naturally steered towards personal growth. Emily shared insights from the book she had read earlier, discussing how its concepts aligned with her own practices. Her friends listened intently, some asking questions, others sharing their own experiences with mindfulness and personal development.

The discussion was rich and varied, touching on topics like work-life balance, managing stress, and the importance of self-care. Emily's friends appreciated her perspective, noting how her balanced approach to life had positively influenced their own views on personal growth. They discussed the possibility of attending a wellness retreat together, an idea that was met with enthusiasm.

At work the following week, Emily's holistic approach to personal and professional life continued to shine. In a team meeting, she proposed a new project approach that integrated mindful practices to enhance creativity and collaboration. Her colleagues were intrigued, and her boss gave her the go-ahead to develop the idea further.

Back at home, Emily reflected on the recent developments in her life. She realized how her journey had become, about how she could share and spread the insights she had gained. Her relationships, both personal and professional, had become more meaningful and fulfilling.

Emily journaled about these reflections, acknowledging the interconnectedness of all aspects of her life. She wrote about the importance of maintaining a balance between giving and receiving, learning, and teaching, growing individually, and contributing to the growth of others.

As she closed her journal, Emily felt a profound sense of gratitude. Her journey of holistic growth had transformed her life in ways she had never imagined. It had deepened her connections with others, enriched her professional life, and brought a sense of harmony to her daily existence.

Challenge Demonstrating Growth

"Can stillness calm the tempest, or does it simply dance amidst the chaos?"

Emily arrived at work to find her team in a state of turmoil. A critical system failure had occurred, jeopardizing a major project she was overseeing and sending shockwaves through her department.

Emily took a deep, steadying breath. Her team looked at her, their expressions a mix of panic and expectation. They were in the main conference room, a space typically filled with collaborative energy, now laden with anxiety. The large digital clock on the wall ticked away, underscoring the urgency of their situation.

"Let's break this down," Emily said, her voice a steady anchor in the storm. She moved to the whiteboard, marker in hand, her demeanor focused yet calm. She began to outline the problem, her hand steady as she sketched the broad strokes of the crisis. Her team gathered around, their initial shock giving way to a growing sense of purpose.

As Emily led the discussion, she integrated her mindful approach into the problem-solving process. She encouraged her team to take brief moments to center themselves, ensuring that their responses were measured and thoughtful, not reactive. "Let's tackle this one step at a time," she suggested, her presence reassuring.

The team broke into smaller groups, each tasked with addressing specific aspects of the crisis. Emily moved between the groups, offering guidance and support. Her approach was a blend of technical know-how and empathetic leadership, a combination that kept her team grounded even as they navigated the high-pressure situation.

Despite the crisis, Emily maintained a sense of composure. Her mindfulness practices were more critical than ever, providing her with the inner resilience to manage the stress of the situation. She took brief moments throughout the day to meditate, finding pockets of tranquility where she could.

As the day progressed, the team began to make headway. The atmosphere in the conference room shifted from one of distress to cautious optimism.

Emily's approach had helped to stabilize the situation while fostering a sense of collective resilience among her team.

By late afternoon, a solution was in sight. The team had identified a workaround to the system failure, as evidence of their collaborative effort and Emily's steady guidance. There was a tangible sense of relief and accomplishment as they finalized their plan to mitigate the crisis.

As the team wrapped up their emergency meeting, Emily offered words of gratitude and encouragement. "Your hard work and dedication today have made a real difference," she said, looking around at her team, who were visibly exhausted yet satisfied with their effort.

Emily reflected on the day's events. The crisis had tested her and her team in ways she hadn't anticipated. Yet, in facing this challenge, they had demonstrated resilience, adaptability, and a strong sense of unity. Emily felt a deep sense of pride in her team and in her ability to lead them through the crisis, as proof to her growth as a professional and as an individual.

"Is the leader who quiets the storm within more powerful than the one who calms the storm without?"

In the aftermath of the crisis at Shiyuantech Solutions, the need for strong, competent leadership became increasingly apparent. Emily, with her unique blend of professional acumen and emotional intelligence, found herself at the forefront of this demand.

As the office began its recovery from the system failure, the impact of the crisis lingered. There was a sense of uncertainty among the team members, many of whom looked to Emily for guidance. In response, Emily organized a series of debriefing sessions, aiming to address the technical aspects of the crisis along with the emotional fallout.

The first session was held in the main meeting room, now a space associated with the recent turmoil. Emily, aware of the room's tense atmosphere, took the initiative to transform it into a more welcoming environment. She rearranged the seating to facilitate open communication, placing chairs in a circular formation to promote inclusiveness.

As the team gathered, Emily began with a calm, reassuring tone. She acknowledged the stress and strain the crisis had put on everyone, expressing her appreciation for the team's hard work and resilience. Her opening remarks set a tone of empathy and understanding, paving the way for a candid discussion.

The session progressed with Emily facilitating a balanced review of the crisis. She encouraged each team member to share their experiences, challenges faced, and lessons learned. Her approach was methodical yet sensitive, allowing space for both technical insights and personal reflections.

Emily's emotional intelligence shone through as she listened to her team's feedback. She offered support and validation for their feelings of frustration and anxiety, while also steering them towards constructive analysis. Her ability to empathize, while maintaining focus on solutions, was a key factor in the session's effectiveness.

In the days that followed, Emily's role as a leader continued to evolve. She worked closely with the technical team to implement the necessary changes to prevent a recurrence of the crisis. At the same time, she remained attentive to her team's morale, recognizing that recovery from such an event was not just about systems and processes but also about people and their well-being.

Emily reflected on the experience. She journaled about the challenges of leading through a crisis, the importance of emotional intelligence in such situations, and her own growth as a leader. These reflections were introspective, exploring the interplay between her mindfulness practices and her professional responsibilities.

"Can a single seed grow a forest in the heart of a storm?"

One morning, as the next deadline loomed, the team convened in their usual meeting room, now transformed into a war room. The walls were plastered with timelines, flowcharts, and action plans. Emily stood at the head of the table, her demeanor calm yet resolute, a stark contrast to the frenetic energy of the room.

She initiated the meeting with a brief mindfulness exercise, a practice that had become a staple in their routine. The team closed their eyes, taking deep breaths, centering themselves for the task ahead. This moment of calm gave them the mental clarity needed for the day's intensive work.

As the team embarked on their tasks, Emily moved from one workstation to another, offering support and guidance. Her approach was hands-on yet non-intrusive, allowing her team the space to apply their skills while providing strategic oversight. She balanced her role as a leader with being a collaborator, working alongside her team to troubleshoot problems and refine solutions.

The team's response to the crisis was a blend of technical expertise and creative problem-solving, fueled by the collaborative spirit Emily had nurtured. They worked long hours, their efforts synchronized like a well-oiled machine, each member playing a crucial role in navigating the project through turbulent waters.

The turning point came late in the evening, as the team was huddled around a conference table, poring over the latest data. A breakthrough idea emerged, a solution that was both innovative and practical. The room erupted in a mix of relief and excitement. Emily's eyes shone with pride as she witnessed her team's hard work coming to fruition.

In the days that followed, the team worked relentlessly to implement the solution. Their efforts were not just about meeting deadlines; it was about proving their resilience and capability. Under Emily's leadership, they not only resolved the crisis but also enhanced the project, adding new features that significantly improved its quality.

The day of the project presentation arrived. The team, led by Emily, presented their work to the higher management. The presentation was not only a showcase of their work but an account of their journey through the crisis. Emily spoke eloquently, highlighting the team's collective effort and the innovative solutions they had developed.

The response from the management was overwhelmingly positive. They commended the team for their exceptional work, particularly praising their ability to turn a crisis into an opportunity. Emily's leadership was singled out for recognition, her ability to guide her team through adversity earning her accolades.

As the team celebrated their success, there was a sense of camaraderie and accomplishment that went beyond professional achievement. They had not only saved the project but had also grown stronger as a team, their trust in each other and in Emily's leadership solidified.

For Emily, the experience was a testament to her growth as a leader and the impact of her spiritual insights in a professional setting. She had fostered an environment where each member could thrive and contribute to their fullest potential.

"Can a shared journey through the storm weave an unbreakable tapestry?"

The following week, the team gathered for a debriefing session in their usual conference room. The air was filled with a sense of camaraderie and mutual respect. As they settled into their seats, there was an exchange of knowing smiles and nods, a silent acknowledgment of the journey they had been sharing.

Emily initiated the session with a heartfelt expression of gratitude. "I want to thank each of you for your incredible hard work and dedication," she said, her voice tinged with genuine appreciation. "We have been facing several formidable challenges lately, but we have been coming through them together, stronger and more cohesive than ever."

The team members took turns sharing their experiences and insights. As they spoke, it was evident that the experiences had fostered a deeper understanding and appreciation of each other's strengths and abilities. The atmosphere was open and reflective, with team members acknowledging how Emily's calm and inclusive leadership had been a guiding light through the turmoil.

One of the key themes that emerged from the discussion was the importance of communication and collaboration. Team members reflected on how Emily's approach had encouraged them to voice their ideas and opinions, leading to innovative solutions that might not have emerged in a more hierarchical setting.

The team also shared how the experiences had changed their perspective on handling stress and pressure. Many credited the mindfulness exercises introduced by Emily for helping them stay centered and focused during the crisis. These practices had not only been beneficial in the moment but had also provided them with tools they could use in future challenges.

As the meeting ended, the team decided to implement some of the practices they had adopted during the last several weeks as regular features in their work routine. They agreed to continue the mindfulness exercises before meetings and to maintain the open and collaborative approach to problem-solving.

The sense of unity and shared purpose was substantial as the team left the conference room. They had gone through a trial by fire and come out not just successful in their projects but also enriched in their professional relationships.

The strengthened bond within the team was evident in their interactions. There was a newfound ease and efficiency in their collaboration, as proof of the trust and respect they had built for each other.

"Can the calm within echo through the corridors of ambition?"

Late one afternoon, Emily sat in her office, reflecting on recent events. The sun cast a warm, golden light through her window, illuminating the small Zen Garden on her desk. She thought about the journey she had undertaken, both personally and professionally, and how it had culminated in her ability to lead her team with composure and insight during critical times.

Her thoughts were interrupted by a knock on the door. It was her boss, Mr. Anderson, who had come to personally commend her on her handling of their recent projects. "Emily, your approach during the past month has been exemplary," he said, his tone earnest. "You've shown not just technical expertise, but true leadership. Your ability to remain calm and think clearly under pressure, and to encourage the same in your team, is exactly what we need in this company."

Emily listened, a sense of gratitude and humility washing over her. She acknowledged Mr. Anderson's praise and shared her perspective. "I've learned that mindfulness and a balanced approach to problem-solving can make a significant difference in high-pressure situations," she explained. "It's not just about managing the project, but also about managing ourselves – our reactions, our emotions."

Her boss nodded in agreement. "That's a valuable insight," he said. "Your team's performance has demonstrated the effectiveness of your methods. We're considering incorporating some of these approaches companywide. Would you be willing to lead a workshop for other managers?"

Emily felt a surge of excitement at the prospect. This was an opportunity to extend the benefits of her journey to others in the organization. "I'd be honored," she replied, already considering how she might structure such a workshop.

In the weeks that followed, Emily worked on developing the workshop. She focused on practical aspects of mindfulness and emotional intelligence in leadership, drawing from her own experiences and the challenges faced during the crisis. She included case studies, interactive exercises, and opportunities for reflection, aiming to make the workshop both engaging and informative.

The day of the workshop arrived, and Emily stood before a room full of managers and team leaders. As she began to speak, she felt a sense of purpose. She shared her story, her journey of integrating mindfulness into her professional life, and how it had transformed her approach to leadership.

The response was overwhelmingly positive. The attendees were engaged, asking questions, and sharing their own experiences. Many expressed a desire to learn more and to start implementing similar practices in their teams.

As Emily concluded the workshop, she felt a profound sense of accomplishment. Her journey had come full circle, from seeking personal growth to sharing her insights for the betterment of others. She had evolved not just as a professional but as a leader, one who understood the value of personal well-being in achieving professional success.

Themes of Transcendence and Detachment
"The Ox Forgotten, Leaving the Man Alone"

"Where does the silence hum loudest in a world of constant sound?"

A profound integration began to unfold in Emily's life. Her spiritual practice, once a solitary pursuit, had elegantly woven itself into the very fabric of her everyday existence. The line between her meditation and the world around her had blurred, each aspect of her life now infused with a mindful presence.

The morning light spilled softly into Emily's apartment, casting a serene glow across the room where she sat in quiet meditation. The familiar hum of the city outside merged with her rhythmic breathing, creating a symphony of inner and outer worlds intertwining. As she emerged from her meditation, she carried the tranquility with her, the calmness echoing in her every step, in the way she brewed her tea, and in each word, she chose as she conversed with her neighbor in the elevator.

At work, this integration was equally profound. Emily's office, once a place of strict professional rigor, now had subtle touches of her spiritual journey. Her small Zen Garden sat on her desk, a symbol of her commitment to balance and mindfulness. Her interactions with colleagues were imbued with a deep sense of presence. Conversations transcended mere transactional exchanges; they were now opportunities for genuine connection, her listening attentive and full-hearted.

In meetings, Emily's approach was a seamless blend of professionalism and spiritual wisdom. She began each session with a moment of collective stillness, inviting her team to join in a brief grounding exercise. This practice had a transformative effect, meetings became more than agenda-driven discussions; they were gatherings where creativity and clarity flourished.

Her lunch breaks were sacred spaces of reconnection. Sometimes, she walked in the nearby park, each step a meditation, her awareness attuned to the chirping of birds and the rustling of leaves. Other times, she sat quietly in the cafeteria, her meal a practice of mindfulness, savoring each bite, fully present to the flavors and textures.

The impact of her integrated practice rippled through her personal life as well. Evenings with friends became deeper, more meaningful encounters. Conversations delved into philosophical realms, exploring themes of existence, purpose, and the interplay of the mundane and the spiritual. Emily listened and shared her insights, a reflection of her inner exploration.

In moments of solitude, Emily journaled her words the song of her journey. She wrote of the challenges and triumphs of weaving spirituality into the fabric of daily life, each entry a testimony to her evolving understanding of the interconnectedness of all aspects of her existence.

Emily's life had transformed. Her spiritual practice, once a distinct part of her routine, was now an indistinguishable thread in the fabric of her day. Each moment, whether at work, in solitude, or in the company of others, was a living meditation, a dance of the sacred and the worldly.

As the sun set, Emily sat by her window, reflecting on the journey so far. Her spiritual practice had become her way of being, not just an activity to be performed, but a lens through which she experienced every facet of her life.

"Does the stream seek the ocean, or does it simply flow?"

The conscious striving for enlightenment, once the cornerstone of her spiritual practice, had evolved into a more natural, effortless state. Her growth was no longer a separate endeavor but had become an organic part of her daily experiences, seamlessly integrated into the structure of her life.

On a crisp Tuesday morning, Emily woke to the gentle rays of sunlight filtering through her curtains. As she stretched and greeted the day, there was no deliberate shift to a meditative state; it was already there, a constant undercurrent in her being. Her morning routine was in a constant state of mindfulness, each movement, from brushing her teeth to brewing her coffee, an expression of her inner stillness.

At work, this effortless integration was equally visible. Emily walked through the corridors of Shiyuantech Solutions with a calm, grounded presence. In her interactions with her colleagues, there was a depth and attentiveness that went beyond the ordinary. In the project meetings, her insights were not just intellectually astute but also intuitively profound, reflecting her seamless blending of professional expertise and spiritual wisdom.

Emily's approach to problem-solving had changed. Gone was the frenetic energy of tackling issues; in its place was a fluid, graceful manner of navigating obstacles. Solutions emerged not from a place of anxious deliberation but from a wellspring of clarity and calm within her.

As the day transitioned to evening, Emily's interactions with friends and family mirrored this evolution. Conversations were deeper, instilled with a presence that was both grounding and elevating. Her listening was with the heart, creating a space of genuine understanding and connection.

In her quiet moments, Emily's reflections revealed the depth of her transformation. Journal entries that once detailed her efforts to attain spiritual growth now flowed with observations of the natural unfolding of her inner journey. Her insights were gentle realizations, arising from the ordinary moments of her life.

Even in moments of conflict or stress, Emily found that her responses were no longer reactive. There was a spaciousness in her reactions, a pause that allowed for compassionate and thoughtful responses. This shift was a natural byproduct of her integrated spiritual practice.

As night fell, Emily sat by her window, gazing at the stars, her mind serene. The journey that had begun with deliberate steps towards enlightenment had become a graceful, unforced exploration of the depths of her being. Every moment of her day, every interaction, every challenge, and every joy was a part of her spiritual growth, occurring not apart from but within the very heart of her life.

"Is the mountain moved by the wind, or does it simply witness the dance?"

As Emily journeyed deeper along her spiritual path, a profound sense of detachment began to manifest in her life. This detachment, far from being a sign of disinterest or apathy, was a conscious unbinding from excessive attachment to outcomes and material possessions. It was a state of being that granted her a new perspective, one that was rooted in mindfulness and presence.

On a typical Wednesday morning at Shiyuantech Solutions, Emily faced a critical project decision. In the past, such moments would have triggered a surge of stress, the weight of potential outcomes bearing down on her. But now, Emily approached these crossroads with a serene detachment. As she sat in her office, the morning light casting a soft glow on her desk, she contemplated the options with a clear mind. Her decisions were guided by a deep understanding of what was best for the project and her team.

One weekend, Emily found herself at a shopping mall, wandering among the glittering displays of luxury goods. In the past, these excursions were driven by a desire to fill a void through material possessions. Now, as she walked through the aisles, she felt a sense of liberation. The allure of these items had diminished, replaced by an appreciation for the simple, enduring joys of life - a conversation with a friend, a walk in nature, a moment of quiet reflection.

Emily's detachment also transformed her interactions with her colleagues and friends. In conversations, she was fully present, listening deeply without the distraction of forming responses in her mind. Her advice and insights were free from personal biases or desires, making her a trusted confidante and guide. Her relationships deepened, marked by a genuine connection that transcended superficial exchanges.

During a family dinner, Emily's brother remarked on the change. "You seem different, more at peace," he observed. Emily smiled, sharing how her spiritual practices had led her to a place of detachment, where she could engage with life more fully and authentically.

Emily's internal dialog reflected this transformation. Her journal entries were no longer filled with anxieties about the future or regrets about the past. Instead, they were contemplations on the present moment, expressions of gratitude, and reflections on the beauty of life's impermanence.

Detachment brought a new dimension to Emily's creativity and problem-solving. At work she approached challenges with a calm curiosity, exploring solutions without the pressure of personal attachment to a specific outcome. Her team noticed this change, finding inspiration in her balanced approach to work and life.

In a discussion with a close friend, Emily shared her insights on detachment. "It's not about renouncing the world or its experiences," she explained. "It's about experiencing everything fully, without being ensnared by it. It's a freedom that allows us to be in the world but not of it."

"Does the river seek the ocean, or does it simply flow?"

Emily's life began to unfurl in a new rhythm, marked by a profound contentment found in the simplicity of everyday moments. The once mundane facets of her daily routine transformed into wellsprings of joy and serenity, each moment a tribute to her deepened appreciation for the present.

One crisp Saturday morning, Emily embarked on a routine walk through the park. The path, familiar and often overlooked, now seemed to unveil itself anew. The rustle of leaves underfoot, the melody of birdsong, the gentle caress of the breeze against her skin – all these sensory experiences merged into a symphony of simple pleasures. Emily walked slowly, her every step an act of mindfulness, fully immersed in the beauty of the natural world around her.

This newfound contentment in simplicity permeated her interactions at work as well. In a team meeting at Shiyuantech Solutions, rather than rushing through the agenda, Emily took a moment to appreciate the collaborative spirit of her colleagues. She observed the animated expressions, the thoughtful contributions, and the shared ambition that filled the room. These observations, once lost in the rush of corporate life, now enriched her experience, filling her with a sense of gratitude for the community she was a part of.

Emily's approach to problem-solving had also shifted. Challenges that would have previously elicited stress were now met with a calm acceptance. In a meeting where a significant project setback was discussed, Emily listened intently, acknowledging the issue without panic. Her response was measured and focused on solutions, her composure emanating a reassuring calmness that influenced her team.

Even her workspace reflected this change. Her desk, once cluttered with documents and tech gadgets, was now organized with minimalism in mind.

A single potted plant sat by her computer, its green leaves a reminder of nature's simplicity and resilience. This uncluttered space was not just a physical change but a manifestation of her inner state – serene, ordered, and focused.

This transformation extended into her social life. Dinners with friends, once occasions for extravagant meals and elaborate plans, became simpler affairs. Emily found joy in cooking a modest meal together, in sharing stories over a cup of tea, in the laughter and warmth of close companionship. These gatherings, devoid of any pretense, were imbued with a genuine connection and contentment.

Even her understanding of success underwent a transformation. Success was no longer about achievements and accolades but about living a life aligned with her values, finding satisfaction in the simplicity of existence, and cultivating joy in everyday experiences.

"Does the moon seek its own reflection, or does it simply shine?"

Emily's journey into deeper spiritual attunement brought about a subtle yet profound transformation in her persona, particularly in her perception of the self. The once prominent voice of her ego, with its incessant demands for recognition and validation, began to quieten, giving way to a more humble and genuine presence.

On a sunny Tuesday morning, Emily arrived at Shiyuantech Solutions, her steps unhurried, her mind at ease. She entered the office, not with the air of someone seeking to impress or command attention, but with a quiet confidence that spoke of inner contentment. Her interactions with her colleagues were marked by a newfound humility. She listened more than she spoke, valuing others' opinions and celebrating their achievements with sincere enthusiasm.

This shift was most evident during a team meeting where a major success of the project was being discussed. In the past, Emily might have taken this opportunity to highlight her contributions. Now, she chose instead to shine the spotlight on her team, acknowledging each member's efforts. Her words were genuine, devoid of any hidden agenda, simply a leader appreciating her team.

Emily's approach to problem-solving also reflected this change. In a brainstorming session for a new project, she encouraged her team to take the lead, offering guidance only when necessary. She celebrated their creative ideas, and when a particularly innovative solution was proposed by a junior team member, Emily's praise was heartfelt and devoid of any overshadowing ego.

In her social interactions, Emily's conversations were less about her own experiences and more about understanding and learning from others. She approached discussions not as competitions to be won with wit or intellect, but as opportunities for genuine connection and growth.

Even her personal goals underwent a transformation. They were no longer centered around climbing the corporate ladder or gaining acclaim. Instead, they revolved around continuing her spiritual growth, contributing positively to her workplace and community, and nurturing her relationships.

Emily's journal entries bore witness to this evolution. She wrote not of ambitions and accolades but of gratitude, lessons learned, and moments of simple joy. Her aspirations were now about being a better person, colleague, friend, and leader – roles defined not by societal standards but by a sense of purpose and fulfillment.

"Who hears the song of a tree falling alone in the forest?"

The transformation within Emily, marked by the diminishing of her ego, ushered in a new era of service-oriented focus in her life. This shift was not a grand declaration but a subtle redirection of her energies and intentions towards the wellbeing and upliftment of those around her.

Emily arrived at her office with a clear intention to make her day meaningful through acts of service. She began by organizing a 'Lunch and Learn' session for her team, focusing on work-life balance and stress management - topics she knew were vital for her colleagues' wellbeing. As she prepared the conference room, setting out informational pamphlets and arranging the seats in a welcoming circle, her attention to detail was a quiet act of service.

During the session, Emily led by example, sharing her own experiences and strategies for maintaining mental health in a high-pressure environment. Her openness encouraged others to participate, turning the session into a collaborative exchange of ideas and support. The gratitude in her colleagues' eyes spoke volumes of the impact her initiative had on them.

In the afternoon, Emily dedicated time to mentor a junior colleague, Anna, who had recently joined the team. She listened attentively to Anna's concerns, offering guidance that was both practical and empowering. This one-on-one mentoring was evidence to Emily's commitment to nurturing the growth of those around her.

Beyond the confines of the office, Emily extended her service-oriented approach to her community. She volunteered at a local youth center, providing career guidance and life skills training to teenagers. Her weekends were often spent in these fulfilling sessions, where her experience and wisdom became invaluable resources for young minds eager to learn and grow.

Emily's home life also reflected this shift in focus. She started a small community garden in her neighborhood, bringing together residents to cultivate a shared green space. This project was not just about gardening; it was about fostering community spirit and connection, something Emily deeply valued.

This new orientation towards service brought a profound sense of fulfillment to Emily. She found that in helping others, she was not only contributing to their wellbeing but also enriching her own spiritual journey.

Emily journaled about this shift, reflecting on the satisfaction that came from being of service. "In giving, we receive" she wrote one evening, her words a mirror to her inner transformation. This principle became her guiding light, illuminating her path with the joy of giving and the grace of humility.

"Can the silence shared between two souls be the loudest conversation?"

In the city park Emily found herself surrounded by the lush tranquility of nature, a stark contrast to the bustling streets just beyond. It was here, under the shade of an old oak tree, where she often met with her friends for heartfelt conversations and moments of shared silence.

As the golden sun filtered through the leaves, casting dappled shadows on the ground, Emily waited for her friend Sarah. The time spent in these serene surroundings had become a cherished ritual, a space where both could share their thoughts and experiences without the trappings of everyday pretense.

Sarah arrived; her face etched with the stress of the week. Emily greeted her with a gentle smile. They sat on a weathered bench, its wooden slats warmed by the afternoon sun. As they talked, Emily's demeanor was a blend of attentiveness and tranquility, her presence a comforting balm to Sarah's frayed nerves.

The conversation meandered from mundane topics to deeper, more personal matters. Sarah spoke about a recent struggle at work, her words laden with frustration and doubt. Emily listened with her whole being. She offered no quick solutions or dismissive reassurances. Instead, she provided a space for Sarah to express herself fully, her responses thoughtful and devoid of judgment.

This was the essence of Emily's new approach to relationships. Her spiritual journey had cultivated in her a profound sense of detachment, not from the people she cared about, but from the ego-driven need to fix or control situations. Her humility allowed her to be fully present with others, offering genuine care and understanding.

As the afternoon waned, Emily shared her own experiences, speaking of her spiritual practices with a quiet passion. She talked about how these practices had brought a sense of peace and contentment to her life, a contentment that was not contingent on external achievements or recognition.

The conversation flowed naturally into a discussion about life's simple pleasures. Emily spoke of her newfound appreciation for moments like these, where the beauty of nature and the richness of human connection coalesced into something truly meaningful. She expressed how these moments, once overlooked, had now become sources of deep joy and serenity.

As they parted ways, there was a sense of renewed connection between them. Sarah left feeling lighter, her burdens eased by the shared experience. Emily watched her leave, a feeling of gratitude filling her heart. Her journey had not only transformed her own life but was also touching the lives of those around her in subtle yet profound ways.

In these moments of connection, Emily realized the true depth of her spiritual growth. How her inner transformation enabled her to engage with the world in a more authentic, compassionate way. Her relationships, once marred by superficiality and ego, were now deep wells of genuine connection and mutual growth.

As the sun dipped below the horizon, casting a warm glow over the park, Emily sat in quiet reflection. Her life, once a pursuit of individual achievement, had transformed into a journey of shared experiences and meaningful interactions.

"Does the moon reflect in a cup of still water amidst the storm?"

The gentle hum of the city seemed distant as Emily walked through the busy streets, her steps measured and unhurried. The world around her moved at a frantic pace, yet she was an embodiment of tranquility amid the madness. Her journey towards spiritual understanding had filled her with a profound sense of inner peace, a balance that was evident in every aspect of her life.

As she passed by a lively marketplace, the harsh sounds and flurry of activity failed to disturb her serene composure. Vendors called out their wares, and shoppers bustled about, but Emily moved through it all with a quiet grace. Her mind was clear, unwavering by the whirlwind of external stimuli.

Later that day, Emily found herself in a meeting at work. The room was charged with the usual stress of corporate deadlines and high stakes, but Emily's presence brought a subtle shift in the atmosphere. She listened to her colleagues' animated discussions, her expression one of calm attentiveness. When she spoke, her words were measured and thoughtful, bringing a sense of clarity and focus to the conversation.

Her colleagues, initially caught up in their own anxieties, gradually began to mirror her composure. The meeting, which could have spiraled into a stressful affair, took on a more productive and balanced tone. Emily's inner peace had a tangible, calming influence on those around her.

In the evening, Emily engaged in a routine that had become a cornerstone of her daily life – a solitary walk in the nearby park. As she strolled along the winding paths, surrounded by the soothing sounds of nature, she reflected on her day. Her mind was at ease, free from the relentless cycle of overthinking that once plagued her.

The park, with its lush greenery and tranquil ambiance, was the perfect backdrop for her introspective journey. She found joy in the simple act of observing the sunset, its hues of orange and pink painting the sky. This appreciation of the present moment, of the beauty in the everyday, was an indication of her changed perspective.

As night fell, and the city lights began to twinkle, Emily sat on a bench, closing her eyes in meditation. The sounds of the city became a distant symphony, a backdrop to her inner stillness. In this moment of solitude, she felt a deep connection to her spiritual foundation, a source of unshakable peace and balance.

Her meditation was a bridge between the events of the day and the promise of tomorrow. It was a time to recharge, to reaffirm her commitment to living a life grounded in mindfulness and serenity. This daily practice was a way to live fully, deeply engaged with the world yet not overwhelmed by it.

As she opened her eyes, the park was bathed in soft moonlight. Emily rose from the bench, her heart filled with a quiet joy. She walked back towards her home, her steps light, her spirit at ease. Her journey had led her to a place of inner peace, a state of being that infused every aspect of her life with a calm assurance.

"Can the echo of a silent heart awaken a thousand souls?"

Emily's transformation into a model of spiritual and personal growth had become a signal of inspiration within her community. Her journey, marked by profound self-awareness and an unwavering commitment to inner growth, resonated deeply with those who crossed her path. She had become more than just a person; she was a living testament to the power of spiritual evolution.

One crisp autumn morning, Emily organized a community event at a local park, a serene haven amid the bustling city. She had meticulously planned a day of mindfulness and wellness activities, aiming to share the benefits of her journey with others. The park, with its towering trees and tranquil pond, was a perfect setting for a gathering centered around spiritual well-being.

As people arrived, drawn by flyers and word-of-mouth, they were greeted by Emily's warm smile and calm demeanor. The event began with a group meditation session, led by Emily on a grassy knoll under the gentle morning sun. She guided the attendees through a series of breathing exercises, her voice soft yet clear, inviting them to connect with the present moment.

The meditation session was followed by a series of workshops on mindfulness, healthy living, and personal growth. Emily facilitated these sessions with ease, sharing insights from her own experiences. Her approach was relatable and devoid of any pretense, making the concepts accessible to everyone, regardless of their background in spirituality.

Among the attendees was a young woman named Jean, who had been grappling with the pressures of modern life. She found herself drawn to Emily's story, particularly her emphasis on finding joy in simplicity and her detachment from material pursuits. Jean approached Emily during a break, seeking advice on how to start her own journey towards inner peace.

Emily listened to Jean with genuine interest, her eyes reflecting empathy and understanding. She shared practical tips on integrating mindfulness into daily routines, emphasizing the importance of small, consistent steps. Her advice was not prescriptive but rather an invitation to explore and discover what resonated personally.

As the day progressed, Emily's impact on the attendees became increasingly evident. People engaged in thoughtful conversations, exchanged experiences, and explored new perspectives. The atmosphere was one of collective learning and growth, spurred by Emily's example and guidance.

The event culminated with a group discussion, where participants shared their takeaways and reflections. Many expressed gratitude for the opportunity to pause and connect with themselves, something they often neglected in their busy lives. Emily's role as a facilitator and guide was unanimously appreciated, her journey serving as a powerful catalyst for others to embark on their own paths of self-discovery.

In the days following the event, Emily received messages from several attendees, thanking her for the inspiration and impact she had made. Jean reached out to share how she had started practicing mindfulness and was already noticing a positive shift in her outlook.

Emily's transformation had not only enriched her own life but had also become a source of inspiration for others. Her journey, marked by a shift from ego-driven pursuits to a focus on service and simplicity, had demonstrated the profound impact one individual's evolution can have on a community.

Behaviour Without Conscious Striving for Enlightenment

"Does the moon disturb the still water, or does it merely witness its own reflection?"

The essence of sustained calmness had seamlessly woven itself into Emily's very being. This tranquility, once an aspiration nurtured through dedicated spiritual practices, had now become her natural state, a serene backdrop to the myriad scenes of her daily existence.

As the early morning sun cast a soft glow through the blinds of her apartment, Emily awoke not to the shrill call of an alarm but to the gentle rhythm of her own serene awareness. Her movements were unhurried, each gesture a quiet demonstration of the deep calm that had taken root within her. She prepared her morning tea, the steam rising in lazy swirls, mirroring the peacefulness that enveloped her.

The walk to work was no longer just a transition from one place to another but a continuation of her state of tranquil presence. The busy city streets, with their symphony of honking cars and bustling crowds, existed around her but did not penetrate the bubble of serenity that she carried with her. Passersby, caught in their own whirlwinds of thought and concern, occasionally glanced at Emily, noting the unusual grace and calm she exuded.

At Shiyuantech Solutions, Emily's presence was a subtle force of quiet stability. In meetings, her calmness was a silent anchor, steadying the ebb and flow of corporate dynamics. Her contributions were thoughtful and measured, devoid of haste or agitation. Colleagues, initially perplexed by this unflappable demeanor, gradually began to appreciate and, in some cases, emulate her approach.

In the middle of a particularly tense project discussion, Emily's tranquility became conspicuously evident. As voices rose and opinions clashed, she remained a picture of composure, her words slicing through the chaos with clarity and purpose. Her ability to remain undisturbed under pressure was a lesson in equilibrium for her team.

Her lunch breaks were solitary retreats into mindfulness, whether spent in the small park adjoining her office or at her desk, savoring her meal with a presence that turned a simple lunch into a meditative practice. These moments of solitude were integral threads in the fabric of her balanced life.

Emily's interactions with others, too, were colored with this enduring calm. Conversations were devoid of the frenetic energy that often characterizes social exchanges; instead, they were rivers of genuine communication, flowing smoothly and deeply. Friends and acquaintances found in her a patient listener, her responses always thoughtful, never rushed, or superficial.

In the evenings, Emily's apartment became a refuge of peace. The minimalistic décor, the soft lighting, and the absence of intrusive technology all reflected her inner state. Here, she indulged in activities that reinforced her tranquility – reading, writing, or simply sitting in silence, fully content in her own company.

As she retired each night, Emily's thoughts were not a tangle of worries or plans but quiet reflections on the day's experiences. Lying in bed, she felt the same peace that greeted her at dawn, a full circle of serene existence.

"Does the mind lead, or does it follow the silent whispers of the heart?"

Emily moved with a purpose that was both deliberate and serene. Her days, once meticulously planned and executed solely based on logic and data, had taken on a new dimension. Now, her decisions were increasingly guided by an inner compass, an intuition that seemed to draw from a deeper well of understanding.

One morning, as the soft glow of dawn illuminated her office, Emily sat at her desk, a complex problem laid out before her. The project she was overseeing had hit an unexpected snag, one that defied straightforward solutions. The data and analyses, spread across her desk, offered no clear path forward. In the past, this would have triggered a storm of analytical thinking, but now, Emily closed her eyes, taking a moment to turn inwards, seeking guidance from a place beyond the spreadsheets and graphs.

As she sat in stillness, the noise of the office faded into a distant hum. Her mind, usually a whirlwind of thoughts and calculations, settled into a tranquil clarity. It was in this stillness that an insight emerged, a solution that was as creative as it was unexpected. Trusting this flash of intuition, Emily began to map out a new strategy, one that diverged from conventional approaches but felt inherently right.

During the weekly team meeting, as they discussed potential solutions, Emily encouraged them to look beyond the obvious, to tap into their own intuition. "Let's not just think outside the box," she urged, "Remember there is no box." her voice infused with a quiet confidence. "Sometimes the best solutions come from a place of intuition, not just analysis."

This approach led to a dynamic change in team interactions. Ideas flowed more freely, unencumbered by the strict confines of traditional logic. The team began to trust their instincts, finding innovative solutions that combined practical knowledge with intuitive insights.

Emily's intuition also began to influence her interactions outside of work. In conversations with friends, she found herself offering advice that was less about giving direct answers and more about helping them connect with their own inner wisdom. Her words seemed to carry a depth that resonated deeply, often leading to moments of profound realization for those she spoke with.

This new reliance on intuition also brought a sense of harmony to her personal life. Decisions about her lifestyle, relationships, and personal growth were made with a newfound ease, as if she was in tune with a rhythm that guided her towards choices that were in alignment with her true self.

Her weekends, once filled with activities and social engagements planned out of habit or obligation, now unfolded more organically. She found herself drawn to activities that nurtured her soul – a walk in nature, a quiet afternoon with a book, or a spontaneous meet-up with a friend that left both parties enriched.

Emily reflected on this shift. Her journal entries, once dominated by logical analyses of her day-to-day experiences, now brimmed with observations on the interplay between intuition and rationality. She wrote of the synchronicities that seemed to occur more frequently, of decisions that felt aligned with a greater flow, of a life that felt more authentic and fulfilling.

"Can a single calm breath still the winds of a storm?"

Within the corridors of Shiyuantech Solutions, Emily's presence had become a source of stability and inspiration. The once frenetic pace that defined her work life had transformed into a rhythm of thoughtful composure, influencing those around her in subtle yet profound ways.

One Monday morning, as the office buzzed with the start-of-week energy, Emily's calm demeanor stood in stark contrast to the usual rush. Her colleagues, often caught up in the whirlwind of deadlines and meetings, found themselves gravitating towards her, seeking a moment of respite in her tranquil aura.

In a project meeting that week, tensions were high. A looming deadline and unexpected technical issues had the team on edge. Emily, leading the session, exuded a composed confidence that seemed to permeate the room. As voices rose in frustration, she listened patiently, acknowledging each concern with empathy. Then, with measured words, she guided the conversation towards collaborative solutions. Her ability to maintain composure under pressure had a ripple effect, calming frayed nerves and refocusing the team on the task at hand.

Outside of work, Emily's influence was equally notable. During a family gathering, her role as a stabilizing force was evident. Emily's interactions were islands of calm. Her genuine interest in her family members' lives, coupled with her unhurried responses, brought a sense of harmony to the gathering. Relatives who were initially caught up in the stress of their own stories found themselves opening to her, drawn to her serene presence.

Emily's influence extended to her volunteer work as well. At a local community center where she led mindfulness workshops, attendees were drawn to her balanced approach to teaching. Her sessions, a blend of practical exercises and philosophical discussions, offered a haven for those seeking peace in a hectic world. Participants left her workshops feeling grounded and rejuvenated, often expressing their appreciation for the sense of stability and clarity she brought into their lives.

Even in moments of solitude, Emily's role as a source of stability was evident in her internal reflections. Her journal entries, once a place for personal contemplation, now included thoughts on how her journey could benefit others. She pondered ways to extend the sense of peace she had found to those around her, be it through her work, her community involvement, or her personal relationships.

"Does the melody of life echo in a single laughter?"

On a typical Thursday, as Emily commuted to work, her attention was captivated not by the usual distractions of her phone or the stresses of the day ahead, but by the vibrant play of colors in the sky. The sunrise, a spectacular array of oranges and pinks, transformed the cityscape into a canvas of natural art. She watched, mesmerized, as the hues shifted and danced with the clouds. This moment, a routine part of her daily commute, had become a source of wonder and contemplation, a reminder of nature's effortless beauty.

At Shiyuantech Solutions, even in that very structured environment of her workplace, Emily found delight in the small, often unnoticed details. A shared joke with a colleague by the coffee machine, the satisfying click of keys as she typed an email, even the rhythmic sound of footsteps in the hallway – all these sounds and interactions, once background noise, now played a symphony of everyday life that she appreciated deeply.

During lunch, Emily chose to sit outside, embracing the opportunity to connect with the world around her. The park adjacent to her office was her sanctuary. She savored her meal, each bite a mindful experience, heightened by the fresh air and the gentle rustle of leaves. The simple act of eating lunch, a routine often rushed through, had become a moment of tranquility and presence.

In the afternoon, as a brief rain shower passed over the city, Emily paused to watch from her office window. The smell of rain, earthy and refreshing, wafted in, stirring memories and a sense of calm. She smiled, taking a moment to breathe in the scent, allowing it to anchor her in the present.

Her workday ended with a collaborative session with her team. During the brainstorming and discussion, Emily found joy in the collective energy and creativity of the group. The exchange of ideas, the ebb and flow of conversation, and the shared goal of problem-solving – these aspects of her job, once sources of stress, were now appreciated as opportunities for connection and growth.

On her way home, Emily stopped by a local market. The vibrant colors and textures of fresh produce, the hum of conversations between vendors and customers, the warmth of the setting sun casting long shadows – all these elements combined to create a sensory experience that Emily immersed herself in. She chose her groceries with care, each selection an acknowledgment of the nourishment and pleasure they would bring.

Evenings at home were a continuation of this mindful appreciation. Whether she was reading, practicing yoga, or simply sitting with a cup of tea, Emily found joy in these quiet moments. They were opportunities to reflect, to unwind, and to simply be.

As she prepared for bed, Emily's thoughts often turned reflective. In her journal, she expressed her gratitude for the day's simple joys – a practice that had become as essential as the experiences themselves. She wrote of laughter shared, beauty witnessed, and moments cherished, each entry a celebration of the ordinary transformed into the extraordinary.

"Can a single act of kindness echo through a forest of indifference?"

Emily's spontaneous acts of kindness, both big and small, had become a defining trait, painting her days with strokes of compassion and selflessness. These gestures, uncalculated and genuine, arose from her deep sense of connection to those around her and her commitment to making a positive impact in their lives.

Monday morning, as Emily made her way through the crowded streets to work, she noticed an elderly man struggling to carry a heavy bag of groceries. Without a second thought, she approached him, offering a helping hand. Her offer was met with a grateful smile, and together they navigated the busy sidewalk. The man's stories, shared during their brief walk, added an unexpected richness to Emily's morning, a reminder of the joy found in human connection.

At Shiyuantech Solutions, Emily's acts of kindness were subtle yet impactful. In a project meeting, when she noticed a colleague, Mark, seemed particularly stressed, she took a moment after the meeting to check in on him. Her listening ear and words of encouragement provided Mark with much-needed support, a simple gesture that lightened his burden and strengthened their professional bond.

During lunch, Emily spontaneously decided to buy coffee for the office receptionist, a gesture of appreciation for her often-unacknowledged hard work. The receptionist's surprised and delighted reaction was a reward in itself, reinforcing Emily's belief in the power of small acts of kindness.

Emily's acts of kindness extended beyond her immediate circle. One evening, on her way home, she passed by a homeless individual she often saw on her route. On impulse, she bought him a meal from a nearby restaurant, sitting with him as he ate, sharing stories and laughter. This interaction, though brief, was a profound exchange of humanity and respect.

Even in her interactions with strangers, Emily's kindness shone through. She made a habit of offering her seat to others on the bus, holding doors open for people behind her, and offering a warm smile to passersby. These small gestures, often overlooked in the rush of daily life, were Emily's way of spreading positivity and warmth in a world that often felt cold and indifferent.

In her personal life, Emily's kindness took on a more intimate form. She organized a surprise birthday celebration for her close friend, Sarah, knowing she had been feeling down lately. The effort Emily put into planning the event, from decorating Sarah's apartment to baking her favorite cake, was a demonstration to her deep care and attention to the wellbeing of her friends.

Emily's acts of kindness were not limited to grand gestures. They were woven into the fabric of her daily life, from the way she interacted with her neighbors to her conscious efforts to be environmentally friendly. Her lifestyle choices, from supporting local businesses to volunteering at community events, were reflections of her desire to contribute positively to the world around her.

In her moments of solitude, Emily reflected on these acts of kindness in her journal. She wrote not with a sense of pride or self-congratulation but with a deep understanding of the interconnectedness of all beings. For Emily, these acts were not just about helping others; they were a way of living in harmony with her values, an expression of her spiritual growth and her commitment to making the world a kinder, more compassionate place.

"Does the echo of one calm voice still the storm of many?"

One Thursday morning, the usual office stress was noticeably muted. As employees navigated their daily tasks, there was an undercurrent of tranquility, a reflection of Emily's composed demeanor. Her desk, situated in the heart of the open-plan office, had become a symbol of this new culture. Neatly organized, adorned with a small, vibrant plant, it exuded a sense of peaceful orderliness.

In the morning team meeting, the impact of Emily's influence was particularly evident. The room, once a battleground of competing ideas and stress-induced arguments, now resonated with constructive discussion and mutual respect. Emily, leading the meeting, set the tone with her approach. She started with a moment of collective silence, allowing her team to center themselves before diving into the agenda.

As the meeting progressed, Emily's way of navigating complex issues with a calm and pragmatic approach inspired her colleagues. Her ability to listen attentively, acknowledge varying viewpoints, and steer conversations towards productive outcomes had a visible effect on her team. The atmosphere was no longer tense but charged with a collaborative spirit.

This change was not confined to meetings. In the office, Emily's positive attitude and readiness to assist her colleagues with a smile or a word of encouragement were contagious. Her desk became a frequent stop for many, seeking advice or simply a moment of respite from the day's challenges.

The lunch break, a time traditionally dominated by hurried meals and office gossip, transformed into an opportunity for genuine connection. Emily often initiated group lunches in the office cafeteria, where conversations revolved around personal interests and positive experiences, rather than work-related stresses or complaints.

Other departments, observing the changes, began to adopt similar practices. It wasn't unusual to see other teams incorporating moments of mindfulness into their routines or adopting a more empathetic and supportive approach in their interactions.

This shift in workplace culture also manifested in how the office space was utilized. Areas that were once empty or used for hurried, informal meetings were now spots for quiet reflection or relaxed, informal collaboration. The office library, previously seldom used, saw an increase in activity, with employees taking short breaks to read or simply sit in silence.

Emily's impact on the work environment was also noticed by the higher management. Her department consistently showed high levels of team satisfaction and productivity, prompting the company to consider implementing some of her practices company wide.

In her personal reflections, Emily acknowledged the transformation she had witnessed. Her journal entries, once focused solely on her individual journey, now included observations on the positive changes in her workplace. She wrote about the joy of seeing her colleagues embrace a more balanced approach to work and the satisfaction of contributing to a more harmonious work environment.

"Can a single heart's warmth light a thousand candles?"

One tranquil Saturday evening, Emily hosted a small gathering at her apartment. The setting was intimate, with soft lighting and comfortable seating arranged to foster closeness and warmth. As her guests arrived, they were greeted by her sincere smile and a hug that conveyed more than words could. The atmosphere was charged with anticipation, not for a night of mere socializing but for an experience of true connection.

As they settled in, the conversation flowed naturally. Emily listened intently, not just to respond, but to understand, her eyes reflecting a deep sense of empathy. Her responses were thoughtful and insightful, often sparking deeper dialogues about life, dreams, and challenges.

Her friend, Anna, shared a recent struggle she was facing at work. Emily's response was sympathetic but also empowering. She asked probing questions, helping Anna to see her situation from different perspectives. Emily's empathy was profound, as she shared similar experiences, not to overshadow Anna's story but to let her know she was not alone.

The evening was interspersed with moments of light-heartedness and laughter. Emily's ability to be fully present made each joke more humorous, each story more engaging. Her laughter was infectious, filling the room with a sense of joy and ease.

Later in the night, as they gathered around the dinner table, the conversation turned to memories and shared experiences. Emily's family members expressed their admiration for the changes they had seen in her. Her brother commented on how her journey had inspired him to embark on his own path of self-discovery.

Emily's mother shared how proud she was of Emily's growth, not just in her career but as a person. She spoke of Emily's increased empathy and understanding, qualities that had strengthened their mother-daughter bond. Emily listened, her heart swelling with gratitude and love, her eyes glistening with unshed tears.

As the night came to a close, each goodbye was heartfelt. Her friends and family left with a sense of fulfillment, not just from the evening but from the deeper connections they had formed with Emily. She stood at the door, watching them leave, a feeling of contentment enveloping her.

That night Emily journaled about these deepened relationships. She wrote about the joy of being truly present with her loved ones, of being able to offer empathy and understanding. Her entries were filled with gratitude for the ability to connect on a more profound level, a testament to the impact of her spiritual journey on her personal life.

In her daily interactions, whether a quick phone call to check on a friend or a thoughtful message to a family member, Emily's genuine care and presence were evident. Her relationships had transformed from superficial exchanges to deep, meaningful connections, enriching her life and those around her.

"Can the stillness within stir the world without?"

On a particularly luminous Thursday, Emily's workplace became a stage where her mindful presence shone brightly. The usual discord of office life seemed to pause momentarily as she walked through the halls, her steps a silent witness to tranquility amidst the mundane. Her desk, once a typical corporate workspace, now exuded a sense of calm, with its organized simplicity and the quiet presence of her small thriving plant that reflected her love for life's subtle beauties.

The air was thick with the usual stress of deadlines and project hurdles, but her calm demeanor infused the room with a serene energy. As she led a discussion, her words were not only insightful but also reflective of a deep inner calm. She encouraged her team to approach each challenge with a sense of presence and patience, transforming the meeting from a stressful confrontation into a constructive dialogue.

In the lunchroom, Emily's interactions were a quiet lesson in mindfulness. Whether she was engaging with a colleague over a simple meal or offering a listening ear to someone's concerns, her actions were imbued with genuine care and attentiveness. These moments, seemingly insignificant, became profound experiences for those who interacted with her, a reminder of the power of presence in everyday life.

In her neighborhood, she organized regular meditation sessions at a local park, inviting residents to join her in experiencing the tranquility of being in the moment. These sessions, often attended by a diverse group of individuals, became a sanctuary of peace in the hustle of city life. Emily's guidance in these sessions was gentle yet profound, leading others to discover the transformative power of mindfulness in their own lives.

Even in her quieter moments, Emily's role as a model of mindfulness was evident. Her evening strolls in the neighborhood were a study in presence. Neighbors often observed her walking at an unhurried pace, her eyes taking in the beauty of her surroundings with a quiet appreciation that was infectious.

Emily started a blog to share her insights and experiences on living a mindful life. Her words, infused with wisdom and authenticity, reached far beyond her physical presence, inspiring a wider audience to explore the depths of mindfulness in their own lives.

In these varied facets of her life, Emily's journey was living proof of the profound impact of a life guided by spiritual principles and inner harmony. Her transformation from a seeker of personal growth to a beacon of mindfulness was not just a personal achievement but a gift to those around her. She showed that mindfulness was not an esoteric practice confined to meditation cushions but a tangible, practical approach to living that could transform the very fabric of everyday life.

Testing Detachment

"Can a single leaf, trembling in the storm, still find solace in the roots it shares with the mighty oak?"

The serene landscape of Emily's life was suddenly overshadowed by a cloud of distress when she received a call late one Tuesday evening. The voice on the other end, trembling with emotion, conveyed the news that Mrs. Kaur, Emily's mentor was seriously ill. The words pierced through Emily's calm façade, sending ripples of shock and sorrow through her being.

As the phone call ended, Emily sat motionless, the receiver still in her hand, her mind grappling with the reality of the situation. Mrs. Kaur had been more than a mentor to her; she was a confidante, a source of wisdom, and a pillar of strength. The thought of her in a state of fragility was inconceivable, yet here it was, a truth that she couldn't turn away from.

The following day at Shiyuantech Solutions, Emily's usual composed demeanor was replaced by a quiet somberness. Her colleagues, accustomed to her consistent calm and warmth, noticed the change. Inquiries of concern were met with a gentle smile and a brief explanation, revealing just enough to explain her altered state but not enough to invite further probing.

In her office, Emily found it hard to concentrate. Her gaze often drifted to the small plant on her desk, a gift from Mrs. Kaur, now a poignant reminder of their connection. Memories flooded back – the countless conversations, the shared moments of laughter and introspection, the lessons learned. Each memory was a tribute to the profound impact Mrs. Kaur had on her life.

Feeling a need to escape the confines of her office, Emily decided to take a walk in the nearby park during her lunch break. The familiar paths and the rustling leaves offered little comfort today. She found a secluded bench and sat down, her thoughts a turbulent sea of emotions.

As she sat there, Emily's mind wrestled with philosophical questions about life, suffering, and impermanence. The teachings and practices that had brought her peace seemed distant now, obscured by the storm of her emotions. The tranquility she had cultivated felt fragile in the face of this personal crisis.

Emily turned to her mentor's words, trying to recall the lessons on coping with adversity. But the comfort they usually provided seemed elusive, the words echoing hollowly in her mind.

The hours passed, and the park began to empty as evening approached. Emily remained on the bench, the sky above transitioning from the bright blue of day to the muted tones of dusk. Her internal dialog continued, a mixture of memories, grief, and attempts to regain her composure.

As she finally stood to leave, a sense of resolve began to form within her. She decided to visit Mrs. Kaur the following day, to be by her side, to offer support and love, just as her mentor had done for her countless times.

That night, in her apartment, Emily's preparations for the visit were quiet and reflective. She packed a small bag with things she thought Mrs. Kaur might need, each item chosen with care. As she did so, her thoughts turned inward, reflecting on the impermanence of life and the preciousness of the connections we forge.

"Does the river lose its essence when it embraces the banks that guide its course?"

The news of Mrs. Kaur's illness presented a profound challenge to Emily, testing the very foundations of her spiritual practice. The principle of detachment, which she had embraced and cultivated, now seemed to be at odds with the deep attachment and affection she felt for her mentor. This conflict created turbulence within her, a storm that threatened to unsettle the balance and composure she had worked so hard to achieve.

In the days following the news, Emily found herself in a state of internal conflict. At work, she mechanically went through her tasks, her usual efficiency overshadowed by a pervasive sense of disquiet. Her interactions with colleagues were polite but distant, as she struggled to keep her emotions in check. The calm demeanor she was known for was now a mask, concealing the turmoil beneath.

Emily found herself staring at a project plan on her computer screen, unable to focus. The lines and numbers blurred as her thoughts drifted to Mrs. Kaur, lying in a hospital bed, her health waning. A sense of helplessness washed over Emily, a stark contrast to the control and clarity she usually exuded.

Emily turned to her spiritual practices with an intensity born of desperation. She meditated more frequently, hoping to find some relief from the emotional storm. But the usual tranquility that meditation brought her was elusive. Her sessions were marred by a relentless stream of thoughts and worries about Mrs. Kaur, making it difficult for her to find the inner peace she so desperately sought.

Conversations with friends and family, usually a source of comfort, now only served to amplify her distress. Well-meaning inquiries about Mrs. Kaur's health and expressions of sympathy seemed to deepen her sense of attachment, making the practice of detachment feel almost unattainable.

One evening, while visiting Mrs. Kaur in the hospital, Emily grappled with these conflicting emotions. Sitting by her mentor's bedside, holding her frail hand, she was struck by the fragility of life. Mrs. Kaur, once a tower of strength and wisdom, now lay weak and vulnerable. The sight filled Emily with a profound sadness, a stark reminder of the impermanence of human existence.

During the visit, Mrs. Kaur, sensing Emily's distress, whispered words of comfort. "Remember, my dear, that attachment and love are not the same as clinging. It's okay to care deeply, to love deeply. True detachment is not about indifference; it's about loving without being bound by that love."

These words, though spoken softly, had a profound impact on Emily. They echoed in her mind as she left the hospital. The distinction between attachment and love, between caring and clinging, was a nuanced aspect of detachment that she had not fully considered.

In the following days, Emily reflected on Mrs. Kaur's words. She realized that her struggle was not just with detachment but with understanding the true nature of it. Her thoughts, once dominated by attempts to suppress her emotions, now shifted towards exploring a balance between caring deeply and maintaining her inner peace.

"Does the river question where it flows when it reaches the sea?"

Emily sat enveloped in silence, a stark contrast to the turmoil raging within her. The news of Mrs. Kaur's illness had struck a deep chord, stirring a storm of emotions that she found increasingly difficult to quell. Her struggle with acceptance was substantial, a battle between her profound emotional pain and her spiritual understanding of life's impermanence.

The usually comforting ritual of morning meditation became a battleground for her conflicting feelings. As she attempted to center her thoughts, images of Mrs. Kaur, frail and ill, intruded, shattering her calm with sharp shards of fear and sorrow. Each breath, meant to bring peace, instead seemed to draw her deeper into the abyss of her anguish.

At work, Emily's usual poise and concentration were noticeably diminished. The vibrant energy of Shiyuantech Solutions, which she had always thrived in, now felt overwhelming. Her interactions with her team were tinged with a subtle detachment, her smiles a little more forced, her responses a tad slower.

In her office, surrounded by the familiar trappings of her professional life, Emily wrestled with her emotions. The logical part of her mind, honed by years of spiritual practice, whispered truths about the nature of life and the inevitability of loss. Yet, her heart rebelled, unable to reconcile these truths with the raw, aching sense of impending loss.

This inner turmoil spilled over into her after-work activities. The yoga classes she taught, once a source of joy and fulfillment, now felt like a chore. Her movements were mechanical, her usual vibrant energy subdued. The mantras and teachings she imparted to her students sounded hollow in her own ears, a stark reminder of the gulf between knowledge and experience.

Conversations with friends became exercises in evasion. She found herself skirting around the topic of Mrs. Kaur's illness, unwilling to voice her fears and doubts. Her friends noticed her reticence and responded with gentle concern, but Emily felt trapped in a shell of her own making, unable to express the depth of her turmoil.

Her nightly journaling, once a haven for her thoughts, became a canvas for her struggle with acceptance. The pages were filled with questions that had no easy answers. How could she reconcile her belief in life's transient nature with the sharp sting of potential loss? How could she maintain her spiritual equilibrium in the face of such personal grief?

Sleep, when it came, was fitful. Haunted by dreams of hospitals and whispered goodbyes, Emily would wake up feeling drained, the new day offering no break from her inner conflict. Her struggle with acceptance was a poignant reminder of the complexities of the human heart, a heart that, despite its capacity for growth and understanding, remained vulnerable to the profound impact of love and loss.

"Can the moon's reflection be separated from the water?"

In the stillness of her early morning routine, Emily sought refuge in the familiar embrace of meditation. The dim light of dawn crept through the blinds, casting a serene glow across her sparsely furnished living room. She sat cross-legged on her cushion, her posture erect yet relaxed, a physical manifestation of her struggle to maintain equilibrium amid emotional turmoil.

The silence of the room was profound, broken only by the soft rhythm of her breathing. As she closed her eyes, her mind, usually a harbor of tranquility, was awash with tumultuous thoughts of Mrs. Kaur's illness. Each breath became an effort in mindfulness, a deliberate attempt to anchor herself in the present, to find relief amid the storm raging within.

Emily's days at work were marked by a renewed commitment to her spiritual principles. During breaks, she would find a quiet corner in the office garden, immersing herself in brief meditation sessions. These moments of solitude were bridges to inner strength, reinforcing her belief in the power of mindfulness to navigate life's most challenging trials.

The office environment, with its constant buzz of activity and deadlines, functioned as a backdrop to Emily's personal test of faith. In meetings, she practiced deep listening, focusing fully on her colleagues' words, using their voices as anchors to the present, pulling her back from the whirl of her own troubled thoughts. Her responses, though measured and thoughtful, carried an underlying current of her inner struggle.

Emily's interactions with her team took on a new depth. She found herself sharing snippets of wisdom about the impermanence of life and the importance of finding peace within. These conversations, once purely professional, now touched on philosophical themes, reflecting her own grappling with these universal truths.

In her personal life, Emily turned to mindfulness as a source of comfort. Her evening walks, once a time for quiet reflection, now became a practice in mindfulness. With each step, she focused on the sensation of the pavement beneath her feet, the gentle breeze against her skin, the myriad sounds of the city around her. These sensory experiences grounded her in the here and now, providing a brief interval from her emotional pain.

Her weekly yoga classes, which she both attended and taught, became a physical manifestation of her inner journey. The mat was her sanctuary, each pose a tribute to her resilience, her body bending and stretching in harmony with her breath, a dance of strength and vulnerability.

The pages of her journal bore witness to this period of profound testing. Her words, usually flowing with ease, now trembled with the weight of her emotions. She wrote of her struggles and her victories, of moments when her principles seemed like a distant shore and others when they were her lifeline. Her entries were a song of introspection, a chronicle of her journey back to inner peace.

Even her diet and daily habits reflected this deepening commitment to her spiritual path. She chose foods that nourished her body and soul, and routines that fostered serenity and balance. Her apartment, always a space of minimalistic calm, became even more of a haven, filled with soothing music, the scent of incense, and the soft glow of candles.

Throughout this challenging period, Emily's resolve was tested at every turn. Yet, with each passing day, her dedication to her spiritual principles grew stronger. She found solace in the teachings that had guided her thus far, leaning on them not just as practical tools for navigating the rough waters of her emotional journey.

"Does the echo of a tree falling in a forest resound in the hearts of those who have known its shade?"

In the wake of Mrs. Kaur's illness, Emily's role in her community took on a new dimension. She found herself at the intersection of her own grief and the need to provide support for those who had also been touched by Mrs. Kaur's wisdom.

One crisp autumn afternoon, Emily organized a small gathering at her apartment for those in her community who knew Mrs. Kaur. The room was filled with soft, comforting music and the subtle scent of jasmine, creating a space that was both reflective and soothing. As her guests arrived, each carrying their own bundle of emotions, Emily welcomed them with a gentle, understanding smile.

They sat in a loose circle, the atmosphere heavy with unspoken sorrow yet tinged with a sense of communal support. Emily initiated the gathering by sharing her feelings about Mrs. Kaur, her voice wavering slightly as she spoke. "Mrs. Kaur has been a guiding light for us all," she began, "and it's in times like these that we need to come together, to share and support each other."

As others began to share their experiences and memories of Mrs. Kaur, Emily listened intently, offering words of comfort, and understanding. Each story revealed the profound impact Mrs. Kaur had had on their lives, from offering sage advice to being a compassionate listener. Emily found herself both offering and receiving support, a reciprocal flow of empathy and care.

In the following days at work, Emily continued to balance her personal grief with her professional responsibilities. Her colleagues, aware of her close relationship with Mrs. Kaur, offered their support, but also looked to her for guidance on how to handle challenging situations, drawing on the wisdom she had learned from her mentor.

Back at home, Emily's quiet moments were spent in reflection and journaling. Her writings became a dialogue with her emotions, a way to process her grief while also documenting the lessons she had learned from Mrs. Kaur. These sessions were purifying, helping Emily navigate her feelings and emerge with a clearer perspective.

Her evenings were often spent on long walks, where she allowed herself to fully experience her grief. The crisp air and the rhythm of her steps provided a backdrop for her to reflect on Mrs. Kaur's teachings, finding peace in the memories and guidance she had received.

During this period, Emily also reached out to Mrs. Kaur's family, offering her support and assistance. She helped organize a small, intimate vigil, bringing together those close to Mrs. Kaur to celebrate her life and legacy.

This event was a legacy to the strength of the community she had helped nurture.

"If a tree falls and becomes the soil, does its essence nurture new growth?"

The passing of Mrs. Kaur left a substantial void in the community, and in the days that followed, Emily found herself naturally stepping into the mentorship role her beloved guide had once filled. This new responsibility, while daunting, also felt like a tribute to Mrs. Kaur's enduring influence on her life.

In the softly lit meeting room of Shiyuantech Solutions, Emily initiated a new series of weekly sessions, designed to offer guidance and support to her colleagues. The first session was an emotional affair, with Emily sharing poignant lessons she had learned from Mrs. Kaur. Her voice, laced with reverence for her mentor, resonated with her audience, many of whom were grappling with their own challenges.

Emily's approach to these sessions was a blend of practical advice and philosophical insight. She encouraged open discussions, creating a safe space for her colleagues to share their struggles and aspirations. Her words, infused with Mrs. Kaur's wisdom, provided both comfort and direction, helping her colleagues navigate both professional and personal landscapes.

Emily began to be sought after in her broader community, her reputation as a source of sage advice growing. One evening, under the warm glow of her living room lights, she hosted a small group from her neighborhood, discussing topics ranging from mindfulness to coping with life's uncertainties. The atmosphere was one of mutual respect and learning, with Emily facilitating the conversation with a gentle hand.

Emily found herself reflecting on her new role. Her journal entries, once a canvas for her personal thoughts and experiences, now included reflections on her mentoring sessions, the insights she shared, and the feedback she received. These reflections were a means to continuously improve her approach to mentorship.

One significant development was Emily's decision to start a blog. She wanted to extend the reach of her mentorship, sharing the lessons she had learned from Mrs. Kaur with a wider audience. The blog quickly gained a following, with readers drawn to her authentic voice and the practical wisdom she shared.

In a heartfelt post, Emily wrote about stepping into the role of a mentor. She expressed how this journey was her way of honoring Mrs. Kaur's legacy, of passing on the knowledge and kindness she had received. Her words, filled with emotion and gratitude, struck a chord with her readers, many of whom shared their own stories of growth and transformation in the comments.

As time passed, Emily's role as a mentor became an integral part of her identity. She found joy and purpose in guiding others, in being a guiding light as Mrs. Kaur had been for her.

"Does the river know the thirst it quenches, or does it simply flow?"

At Shiyuantech Solutions, Emily initiated a peer-support group, a space where colleagues could share their struggles and seek collective wisdom. The first session, held in a small, sunlit conference room, was a blend of vulnerability and courage. Emily led by example, sharing her own feelings of loss following the death of Mrs. Kaur's. Her openness set the tone, encouraging others to open up about their challenges. The group quickly evolved into a supportive network, providing comfort and strength not just to its members, but also to Emily herself.

This sense of service extended into her community work. Emily started volunteering at a local hospice, offering companionship and empathy to those facing their final journey. Each visit provided Emily with a profound sense of purpose. In helping others navigate their farewells, Emily found a way to process her own grief and find acceptance in the cycle of life and loss.

Her home became a hub for friends seeking guidance and support. One evening, as gentle music played in the background and candles flickered softly, Emily hosted a small gathering. The conversation naturally gravitated towards dealing with loss and change. Emily, drawing from her own experiences and the wisdom she had gleaned from Mrs. Kaur, shared insights on coping with grief. The evening, filled with shared stories and mutual support, ended with a group meditation session, leaving everyone, including Emily, feeling more grounded and connected.

In her personal relationships, Emily found that her efforts to support others were reciprocated. Her family, recognizing her emotional turmoil, rallied around her, offering love and support in quiet, unassuming ways. Her friends also shared their experiences creating a blanket of mutual care and understanding.

Emily's newfound role as a mentor and supporter had a significant impact on her emotional well-being. She found that in giving support, she was weaving a network of interconnectedness, one that not only helped others but also provided her with a sense of belonging and resilience. Her conversations, whether with a colleague in need of advice or a friend sharing a personal dilemma, became opportunities for mutual healing and growth.

Through these acts of service and support, Emily discovered a profound truth – that in the interconnected web of human experience, giving and receiving are not separate acts, but parts of a whole.

"Is the echo aware of the voice that birthed it?"

The local community center, where Emily had previously volunteered only occasionally, now saw her more frequent presence. She initiated a weekly mindfulness session, a space where people from various walks of life came together to find comfort and strength. Emily, with her gentle guidance, created an atmosphere of tranquility and shared understanding. The diversity of the group, ranging from busy professionals to retired seniors, added depth to the discussions, allowing for a rich tapestry of experiences and perspectives.

She began to participate in community decision-making forums, her voice and insights adding value to discussions on neighborhood projects and initiatives. Her balanced and compassionate approach to issues earned her respect and admiration, drawing more people to seek her counsel.

In one significant instance, a conflict arose in the community regarding the development of a local park. Emily played a crucial role in mediating the discussions, helping to find a solution that honored the concerns of all parties involved. Her ability to listen, empathize, and provide thoughtful input was instrumental in reaching a peaceful resolution.

Emily's deepened connection with her community began to influence her professional interactions as well. She started a community outreach program, encouraging her colleagues to engage in local service projects. This initiative improved the company's relationship with the community and also fostered a sense of team spirit and social responsibility among her colleagues.

Through these varied interactions and initiatives, Emily not only found healing for herself but also became a source of support and inspiration for others. Her journey through personal crisis had led her to a deeper understanding of the interdependence of individual and community well-being. She had stepped into the role once filled by Mrs. Kaur, not merely as a replacement but as a unique and compassionate presence in her own right.

Complete Enlightenment
"The Ox and Man Both Gone Out of Sight"

"Can the mind's whisper be heard in the symphony of the universe?"

In the tranquility of early dawn, as the first rays of sunlight gently kissed the horizon, Emily found herself in a state of profound contemplation. The world around her was still asleep, but within her, a vibrant awakening was taking place. This moment marked the beginning of a transcendent awakening, a pivotal point in her spiritual journey where the ordinary boundaries of perception began to blur and expand into realms beyond.

As she sat in her favorite chair by the window, Emily's gaze was fixed on the changing colors of the sky. The hues of pink and orange melted into each other, painting a canvas of delicate beauty. In this moment, something within her shifted. It was as if the external beauty of the dawn had triggered an internal illumination, a spark of enlightenment that transcended her usual sensory experiences.

Her apartment, a space that had always been a sanctuary for her, now seemed to resonate with a new energy. The walls, the furniture, even the air around her, felt alive, pulsing with an unseen rhythm. Emily's mind, which had always been a wellspring of thoughts and reflections, quieted to an almost surreal calm. It was as if her thoughts had dissolved, leaving behind a vast expanse of clear, unobstructed awareness.

In this heightened state of consciousness, Emily's perception of time and space altered. The ticking of the clock, the familiar marker of passing time, seemed inconsequential. She felt a profound connection with something eternal, a timeless essence that lay beyond the physical confines of her surroundings.

Her senses, too, were heightened in a way she had never experienced. The aroma of her morning tea, the texture of the fabric of her chair, the distant sound of a bird singing – each sensation was magnified, imbued with a depth and richness that was almost overwhelming.

As she sat in this state of expanded awareness, Emily's mind began to explore philosophical and spiritual realms that she had only read about in books. Concepts like interconnectedness, the nature of consciousness, and the illusion of the self were no longer just intellectual ideas. They became vivid, experiential realities, as tangible to her in that moment as the chair she sat in.

This transcendent awakening brought with it a cascade of revelations. Emily realized that her journey until now, though filled with growth and learning, had been just the surface of a vast ocean of consciousness waiting to be explored. She understood that her experiences, her struggles, and her triumphs were all part of a larger web of existence, interconnected and permeated with profound meaning.

As the morning progressed, the ordinary world began to stir. The sun climbed higher in the sky, casting its warm glow into her apartment. But for Emily, the world she was returning to was not the same. She had glimpsed something beyond the ordinary, a realm of higher consciousness that had forever altered her perception of reality.

"Does the leaf know it dances with the wind, or does the wind dance with the leaf?"

Emily meditated on the heightened state of enlightenment, sitting enveloped by an overwhelming sense of unity with the universe. The walls of her apartment, once defining her personal space, now seemed inconsequential, as if they were mere illusions separating her from the vast expanse of the cosmos. The morning light streaming through her window bathed the room in a golden hue, blurring the boundaries between the inside and the outside, between herself and the world.

As she breathed in deeply, each breath seemed to synchronize with the rhythm of the universe. It was as if the air she inhaled was not just filling her lungs, but also her soul, connecting her to an intricate network of life that extended far beyond her physical presence. The sounds of the city, the distant hum of traffic, the chirping of birds, all merged into a harmonious symphony, echoing the interconnectedness of all things.

Emily's mind, usually a core of thoughts and plans, was now quiet, awash in a sea of tranquility and profound understanding. The mental chatter that had once occupied her thoughts had dissipated, leaving a clear, unobstructed view of a deeper truth – the oneness of her being with the universe.

In this state of oneness, Emily felt a profound empathy for all living beings. She sensed their joys and sorrows, hopes, and fears, as if they were her own. This empathy was not overwhelming; rather, it was a natural extension of her expanded consciousness, as evidence of the interconnected nature of all existence.

As she sat there, Emily's perception of time altered. The past and the future, concepts that had once governed her life, now seemed like mere constructs of the human mind. She was fully immersed in the present, in the eternal now, where every moment was complete and perfect.

Her surroundings took on a new dimension. The objects in her apartment, the furniture, the plants, the artworks, were no longer inanimate. They pulsated with energy, each piece a part of the cosmic dance of creation and destruction. The plant on her windowsill, a gift from a friend, was a living embodiment of the cycle of life, its green leaves a symbol of growth and renewal.

Emily's philosophical and spiritual musings reached new depths. She contemplated the nature of existence, the purpose of life, and the ultimate destiny of the universe. These were not fearful inquiries but joyful explorations, a natural curiosity arising from her newfound understanding of her place in the cosmos.

As the day progressed, Emily maintained this deep connection with the universe. Whether she was engaging in her daily activities, interacting with colleagues at Shiyuantech Solutions, or walking through the bustling city streets, she carried with her this sense of oneness. Her interactions with others were more heartfelt and genuine, as she recognized the universal spirit that dwelled within each person she met.

In the evening, as she prepared for bed, Emily reflected on her transcendent experience. Her journal, usually filled with daily reflections and insights, now contained descriptions of her profound connection with the universe. She wrote about the dissolution of her individual self into the greater whole, the deep sense of peace and fulfillment that came with this realization, and her newfound perspective on life.

"Is the flutter of a leaf felt by the tree, or does the tree sway the leaf?"

In this heightened state of awareness, Emily walked through the world with a profound sense of interconnectedness. Her perception of life and existence had transformed, allowing her to see and feel the invisible threads that connected her to everything around her.

One morning, Emily arrived at Shiyuantech Solutions with a serene smile, her eyes reflecting a deep understanding. As she interacted with her colleagues, she could sense the interplay of their emotions and thoughts. Her responses to them were more thoughtful and compassionate, acknowledging not just their words but the unspoken feelings behind them.

In a team meeting, as her colleagues presented their ideas and concerns, Emily perceived the underlying connections between their thoughts and the project at hand. She gently guided the discussion, weaving their diverse perspectives into a cohesive strategy. Her colleagues, initially puzzled by her new approach, soon found themselves inspired by her ability to see the bigger picture and how each of their roles played a part in it.

During her daily walks in the park, Emily felt an intense connection with nature. She noticed the intricate patterns of the leaves, the dance of the birds, and the rhythmic flow of the wind. Each element of nature spoke to her of a grand, harmonious design, a symphony in which she was both a spectator and a participant.

Emily's interactions with her friends and family took on a new dimension. She listened to them with a deeper empathy, understanding their joys and sorrows as reflections of universal experiences. Her advice to them was filled with wisdom that spoke of the interconnectedness of all life, helping them see their challenges and triumphs as part of a larger design.

Emily journaled about this profound realization. Her words captured the essence of unity, expressing how the separation between self and other, between humanity and nature, was an illusion. She wrote about her experiences with a poetic depth, exploring the philosophical implications of this newfound understanding.

At a community event, Emily shared her insights on interconnectedness. Her speech, delivered with quiet conviction, captivated her audience. She spoke of the unity of life, how each individual's actions and thoughts contributed to the collective well-being of the community and the world. Her message resonated with many, sparking discussions and reflections on how to live more harmoniously with each other and the planet.

This perception of interconnectedness also influenced Emily's approach to challenges. She tackled problems, both at work and in her personal life, with a holistic perspective. She considered the wider implications of her decisions, always mindful of how her actions would affect the intricate web of life around her.

Emily's relationships deepened as she engaged with others from a place of profound connection. Conversations with colleagues, friends, and family became more meaningful, each interaction an opportunity to honor and celebrate the shared journey of life.

Emily felt a deep sense of unity with the universe. She experienced moments of transcendence, where the boundaries of self dissolved, and she became one with the cosmos. These experiences were both humbling and empowering, filling her with a sense of awe and responsibility towards all existence.

"Can a moment linger where time has no trace?"

In her transcendent state of consciousness, Emily began to perceive the world in a way that defied conventional understanding. The constructs of time and space, once solid and unyielding, now seemed fluid and permeable, leading her to experiences where the linear progression of time blurred and distances shrank into insignificance.

One morning, as Emily sat in her living room, bathed in the soft light of dawn, she closed her eyes for meditation. Instead of the usual sense of peace and stillness, she found herself on a journey where moments from her past, present, and imagined future intertwined seamlessly. Childhood memories, current realities, and visions of what could be, all danced together in a harmonious ballet of time. These experiences were not mere reflections but vivid, immersive moments where she could feel, see, and even touch the essence of those times.

At work, this new perception of time and space began to influence her approach to projects and interactions. In a strategic planning meeting at Shiyuantech Solutions, Emily guided her team through an exercise that transcended traditional thinking. She encouraged them to envision the project not just as a linear progression but as a dynamic entity that existed across different timelines. Her colleagues were initially baffled, but as they engaged with the exercise, they began to appreciate this unconventional approach, finding innovative solutions that spanned beyond the immediate scope of the project.

Emily's altered perception also transformed her interactions with the physical world. During her walks in the city park, distances that once took minutes to traverse now felt like mere steps. She would set out towards a distant tree, and in what felt like a blink, she would be standing beside it, the space between having contracted in a way that defied logic. This phenomenon was not frightening to Emily but filled her with awe and a deep sense of connection with the universe.

Conversations with friends and family took on a new dimension, as Emily found herself able to connect with them on a level that transcended physical presence. During phone calls or video chats, she felt as though she was right there with them, experiencing their environments and emotions as if no physical barriers existed.

This dissolution of time and space extended to her professional mentoring sessions. As she spoke with mentees, she found herself able to tap into their past experiences and potential futures, offering guidance that was deeply resonant and profoundly impactful. Her advice seemed to come from a place of understanding that transcended the immediate moment, drawing from a well of wisdom that encompassed the totality of their journeys.

Emily journaled about these experiences with a sense of wonder. She wrote about the fluidity of time, the interconnectedness of all moments, and the illusion of distance. Her entries were explorations of a reality that was expansive and boundless.

Emily also started to explore these concepts in her community work. She organized workshops where she shared her insights on the non-linear nature of time and space, encouraging participants to open their minds to the infinite possibilities of existence. These workshops became popular, drawing people curious to understand and experience this new way of perceiving the world.

As Emily continued to navigate this extraordinary state of being, her understanding of reality deepened. She saw the world not as a series of isolated incidents and locations but as a continuum of interconnected events and places, a continuous flow of existence without the constraints of time and space.

"Does the self expand, or does it fall, when it echoes the universe's call?"

In this transformative phase of her journey, Emily experienced a profound shift in her sense of self. The solid boundaries that once defined her individual identity began to dissolve, merging her consciousness with the greater matrix of life. This change was not just philosophical but a tangible alteration in how she experienced her existence.

Her daily commute through the city streets became a journey of deep connection. Each person she passed, each bird that flew overhead, every gust of wind felt like a part of her own being. The artificial divide between herself and the world around her was fading, revealing a profound unity with all forms of life.

Conversations became more than exchanges of words; they were energetic dialogues where she felt deeply intertwined with the experiences and emotions of the other person. Her ability to empathize reached new heights, as she began to experience their joys, sorrows, and fears as if they were her own.

During her mindfulness sessions at the local community center, Emily guided participants through explorations of their interconnectedness with the universe. The sessions became powerful experiences of collective awakening, with participants reporting a heightened sense of oneness with the world around them.

Emily's internal dialog took on a new dimension. Her thoughts and reflections were no longer centered on her personal experiences but expanded to include the experiences of others. Her journal entries reflected this shift, with passages that explored the interconnectedness of all beings and the illusion of separateness.

Even her artistic expressions, such as her paintings and poetry, began to capture this sense of universal connection. Her art became a medium to convey the intricate web of life, where every line, color, and word was a part of a larger, more encompassing reality.

As Emily navigated this new phase of her life, her sense of purpose and understanding deepened. She no longer saw herself as a solitary traveler on a personal journey but as a vital part of a grand, interconnected dance of existence. This altered sense of identity was not a loss of self but an expansion into a greater self, a self that was boundless and intimately connected to the fabric of life.

"Is reality woven from threads of the dream, or do dreams unfold from the reel's unseen seam?"

In this extraordinary phase of her journey, Emily found herself traversing a landscape that was both surreal and deeply illuminating. Her experiences transcended the mundane, weaving together the threads of dream and reality into a rich tapestry of symbolic imagery and insight.

One night, under the canopy of a star-filled sky, Emily embarked on a solitary walk through the city park. The world around her seemed to shift, the familiar paths transforming into delicate trails, illuminated by a luminescent glow that seemed to emanate from the earth itself. The trees whispered ancient secrets in a language beyond words, their leaves shimmering with an otherworldly light. Emily felt as if she were walking in a living dream, where every element of nature communicated with her in a symphony of profound insights.

In these surreal sequences, Emily encountered symbolic figures that spoke to her innermost thoughts and feelings. One evening, while meditating in her apartment, she visualized a majestic phoenix rising from ashes, its wings ablaze with vibrant colors. This vision filled her with a deep understanding of transformation and renewal, a reflection of her own journey through adversity.

Interactions with friends and family were imbued with this dreamlike quality. Conversations flowed like rivers, meandering through landscapes of emotion, and thought, revealing hidden depths and connections. Emily found herself able to perceive the unspoken feelings and desires of those she spoke with, offering empathy and understanding that transcended ordinary communication.

In one particularly vivid experience, Emily found herself in a vast field, surrounded by a sea of wildflowers under a twilight sky. Here, time seemed to stand still, and she felt an overwhelming sense of unity with the cosmos. The flowers whispered messages of love and interconnectedness, their fragrance a reminder of the beauty and fragility of life.

Her dreams became vivid journeys into fantastical realms, each dream a chapter in a larger story of self-discovery. In one dream, she flew over a city of crystal, its structures reflecting the myriad possibilities of existence. The sensation of flight filled her with exhilaration and freedom, a metaphor for her own liberation from limiting beliefs.

Preparing a meal became a ritual of gratitude, each ingredient a gift from the earth, each flavor a note in a symphony of sensory delight. Her daily routines were no longer chores but opportunities to engage with the world in a state of heightened awareness and appreciation.

Emily began to see the world not just as a physical space but as a setting for the expression of deeper truths. Her experiences, though defying logical explanation, were instilled with profound insights into the nature of existence and her place within it.

"Is each vivid sensation a brushstroke of truth, or are we painters lost in the hues of youth?"

Emily experienced the world through a lens of heightened sensory perception that brought a vivid intensity to her everyday experiences. The mundane became magical, as her senses were amplified, revealing the intricate tapestry of life in astonishing detail.

At Shiyuantech Solutions, these enhanced perceptions transformed her workspace into a kaleidoscope of experiences. The hum of the computers and the murmur of her colleagues' conversations blended into a symphony of sounds, each note distinct and resonant. The clicking of keyboards was no longer just a background noise but a rhythmic beat that seemed to sync with the pulse of the office.

Emily found herself acutely aware of the subtleties in her colleagues' voices – the slight inflections, the pauses, the breaths taken between words. This heightened auditory sensitivity allowed her to perceive the emotions and intentions behind the words, giving her a deeper understanding of her team's dynamics and concerns.

The tactile world also took on a new dimension for Emily. The feel of her smartphone's surface, the texture of her office chair, the smoothness of the papers she handled – every touch was a rich sensory experience, filled with nuance and depth. Even the air she breathed felt different, as if each breath was a communion with the life force that surrounded her.

Lunchtime became an adventure in taste and aroma. Foods she had eaten many times before now exploded with flavors, each ingredient telling its own story. The aroma of coffee from the office machine was intoxicating, carrying hints of distant lands and the hands that had harvested and prepared the beans. Eating was no longer just a routine part of her day but a journey into the essence of nourishment and pleasure.

In her evening meditations, these enhanced perceptions took her deep into the realm of her inner world. She could feel the flow of energy in her body, each breath a wave of sensation, each heartbeat a drum in the symphony of her existence. Her meditation sessions became journeys into the core of her being, revealing layers of consciousness she had never accessed before.

This period of enhanced sensory perception was a deepening of her connection to the world around her. It was as if a veil had been lifted, revealing the intricate beauty and complexity of the universe in every moment. Her experiences became a source of wonder and exploration, an invitation to probe deeper into the mystery of existence.

"Does the leaf that falls in timeless grace know its journey, or does it simply embrace the space?"

Emily began to experience moments of timelessness that transcended the conventional understanding of time. These instances, occurring sporadically yet with profound impact, altered her perception and brought insights that seemed to originate from a plane of higher consciousness.

Sunday morning, Emily was in the community garden, engaged in her routine of tending to her plants. As she delicately pruned the leaves and watered the soil, time seemed to dilate around her. The routine task, typically a matter of minutes, stretched into what felt like hours. Each drop of water shimmering on the leaves, each rustle of the branches in the gentle morning breeze, was a universe unto itself, rich with detail and significance. In this expanded state of awareness, Emily felt a deep connection to the cycle of life, understanding the intricate interplay of growth, decay, and renewal.

During a deep conversation with a friend over lunch, time seemed to warp. What was a simple chat transformed into a profound exchange, where every word and silence was laden with meaning. In these suspended moments, Emily found herself offering advice that seemed to stem from a deeper well of wisdom, providing comfort and guidance that resonated deeply with her friend.

In her quiet moments of reflection at home, Emily would ponder these experiences, writing about them in her journal. She described the sensation of being both a part of the world and, apart from it, of seeing the dance of time from a vantage point of stillness. Her writings became explorations of these experiences, attempts to understand, and integrate the profound lessons they offered.

These moments of timeless awareness were more than just anomalies in Emily's perception; they were gateways to deeper understanding and cognition. They brought her a sense of peace and clarity, a reminder of the fluid nature of time and the limitless potential of the human mind.

"Can the song of the unseen be heard in the silence of the known?"

Emily found herself increasingly immersed in mystical experiences, each encounter deepening her understanding and acceptance of life's enigmatic nature. These experiences, ethereal and profound, became a source of joy and wonder.

One evening, under the canopy of stars, Emily participated in a guided meditation session held in a tranquil park. As the facilitator's voice wove through the gentle rustling of leaves, Emily felt herself slipping into a deep state of relaxation. Gradually, her awareness expanded, transcending the physical boundaries of her body. She felt as if she were floating, her spirit mingling with the night sky. In this state, she experienced a profound sense of unity with the cosmos, a feeling that lingered long after the meditation concluded.

During a weekend retreat, Emily led a discussion on the mysteries of existence, sharing her experiences and insights. The conversation unfolded into a deep philosophical dialogue, with each participant sharing their perspectives and experiences. Emily's ability to articulate her mystical experiences and the lessons learned from them provided a fresh perspective, sparking curiosity and wonder among her friends.

Emily's encounters with the mystical found expression in her art. She began to create abstract paintings, each canvas a vivid portrayal of her spiritual experiences. These paintings were vibrant and dynamic, filled with colors and forms that seemed to capture the essence of her mystical encounters. Displaying them in her living room, they became conversation pieces, piquing the interest of visitors and serving as gateways to discussions about spirituality and the unseen aspects of life.

In her personal study, surrounded by books and her own artworks, Emily searched deeper into mystical literature. She explored texts from various spiritual traditions, finding parallels and insights that resonated with her experiences. Her journal entries from this period were filled with reflections on these readings, weaving together her personal experiences with the wisdom of sages and mystics from different eras.

This exploration led Emily to organize a series of workshops on mystical experiences and spiritual growth. Held at a local community center, these workshops attracted a diverse group of participants, eager to explore the mystical dimensions of life. Emily's sessions were a blend of guided meditations, discussions, and creative expression activities, designed to help participants tap into their own spiritual experiences.

Emily found herself anchored in a profound inner peace, a tranquility that transcended the ordinary realms of understanding. This peace was a deep, resonant connection with the universe, a serene acceptance of its vast and inexplicable beauty.

Changed Perception of Reality

"Is compassion a gift given, or a mirror held?"

Emily's approach to life was filled with a profound compassion that touched everyone she interacted with. This compassion extended into her daily interactions.

Her volunteer work at a local homeless shelter was another avenue where her compassion shone brightly. Emily not only served meals but also took the time to engage in conversations with the shelter's visitors. She treated everyone with dignity and respect, recognizing their humanity beyond their current circumstances. Her interactions were heartfelt, leaving a lasting impact on those she connected with.

At home, Emily's compassion was reflected in her care for her elderly neighbor. She often checked in on him, assisting with small chores or simply sharing a cup of tea. These moments were precious, filled with laughter and stories, forging a bond that transcended generational divides.

Emily's compassion extended to herself as well. She practiced self-care, recognizing that nurturing her own well-being was essential to continue offering kindness to others. Her evenings were spent in peaceful solitude or engaged in activities that replenished her spirit, such as meditation, reading, or yoga.

On a weekend retreat, Emily facilitated a workshop on compassion and mindfulness. The attendees, diverse in backgrounds and experiences, were drawn into a journey of introspection and empathy. Through guided meditations and group activities, Emily helped them explore the depths of compassion, not just as a concept but as a practical, daily practice.

"Is the voice within a guide or an echo of the heart's desires?"

Emily's intuition became her compass, guiding her actions with a clarity that stemmed from deep within. This new alignment with her higher self was evident in the choices she made, whether it was work related or personal.

This intuitive guidance permeated her daily interactions. While walking through a lively market, Emily's attention was drawn to a young artist selling handmade jewelry. Something about the artist's work resonated with her deeply. Trusting her intuition, Emily struck up a conversation, which led to a collaboration where the artist designed unique pieces for an event at Shiyuantech Solutions. The collaboration was not only a success but also a significant boost for the young artist's career.

Intuition played a key role in deepening her relationships. During a weekend visit with her sister, Emily sensed an unspoken tension. Rather than confronting it directly, she intuitively chose to spend the day engaging in shared activities they both loved. This gentle approach allowed her sister to share her concerns in her own time, leading to a heartfelt conversation that strengthened their bond.

Her intuitive guidance also manifested in her community work. Emily felt a strong inner push to start a mindfulness program for teenagers at the local community center. Despite initial doubts about its reception, she followed her intuition. The program turned out to be a resounding success, providing a much-needed space for young people to explore mindfulness practices.

One evening, while evaluating a philosophical text, she felt an inner nudge to write a reflective piece on her blog. This post, seemingly written on a whim, resonated with her readers, sparking a series of meaningful online discussions about spirituality and personal growth.

Emily's growing trust in her intuition was a deeper alignment with her true self. It was the movement of synchronicity, where the right people, opportunities, and experiences seemed to appear at the perfect time. Her life became a series of serendipitous events, each guided by the subtle, yet powerful, voice of her intuition.

"Is the path discovered by walking, or does walking create the path?"
Emily's life took on a quality of spontaneity that was both liberating and profound. Gone were the days of meticulous planning and strict adherence to schedules. Instead, Emily embraced the natural flow of life, finding joy in the unexpected and beauty in the unplanned.

One Tuesday morning, at Shiyuantech Solutions, Emily's newfound spontaneity became evident. Instead of her usual structured agenda for the team meeting, she introduced an open forum. Colleagues were invited to share any ideas or concerns spontaneously. This approach led to a burst of creativity and problem-solving that had previously been stifled by rigid meeting structures. Emily's ability to adapt and respond in the moment brought a dynamic energy to the team, fostering a culture of innovation and open communication.

Emily's spontaneity brought a freshness and authenticity to their relationships. Impromptu gatherings, surprise visits, and unexpected outings became the norm, creating memories filled with laughter and genuine connection. Her willingness to embrace the moment led to deeper, more meaningful exchanges, where conversations flowed naturally and unguardedly.

Even in her community work, Emily began to incorporate more spontaneous elements. During a mindfulness workshop, she abandoned her planned script, choosing instead to tailor the session based on the energy and needs of the participants. This approach resonated with the attendees, who found the experience more engaging and personal.

Emily set aside rigid meditation schedules, opting instead to meditate whenever she felt the need or inspiration. This spontaneity in her practice deepened her connection to her inner self, allowing her to be more in tune with her spiritual needs.

This spontaneous approach to life did not mean Emily shunned all forms of structure. Instead, she found a balance, knowing when to plan and when to let go. This balance was evident in her project management at work, where she skillfully combined strategic planning with the flexibility to adapt to changing circumstances.

In her philosophical explorations, Emily began to delve into texts and teachings about the Taoist concept of Wu Wei, or effortless action. This philosophy resonated with her new approach to life, reinforcing her belief in the power of going with the flow and trusting in the natural course of things.

Through her spontaneous approach, Emily discovered a profound truth about life: that often, the most meaningful experiences come not from meticulous planning, but from the willingness to embrace the unknown and trust in the journey. Her life became a witness to the beauty of living in the moment rich with unexpected twists and turns, each one a step in her ever-evolving journey of self-discovery and growth.

"Is the dance led by the music, or does the dancer inspire the melody?"

Emily's embrace of spontaneity ushered in a harmonious existence, aligning her rhythm with the universe's. This harmony radiated outward, touching every aspect of her life.

Emily approached her projects with a fluidity that amazed her colleagues. She seemed to intuitively sense the right moment to push forward or when to allow ideas to simmer. In one instance, during a critical project phase, instead of enforcing the original strict deadline, Emily sensed the team's need for more creative space. This decision paid off as the team delivered an innovative solution that surpassed expectations.

Emily rearranged her home to create an environment that flowed seamlessly with her daily activities. Her mornings were no longer rushed; she began her day with a gentle yoga routine, moving in sync with her breath, each pose a physical expression of her inner balance.

Conversations with loved ones became more meaningful. During a weekend family gathering, Emily, sensing a simmering tension, gracefully steered the conversation towards shared memories and laughter, diffusing the situation effortlessly. Her ability to read the room and act intuitively nurtured a more profound sense of understanding and closeness within her family.

In her philosophical studies, Emily explored texts on synchronicity and the law of attraction, deepening her understanding of how her inner state influenced her external world. Her journal entries from this period reflected a blend of personal insights and philosophical musings, weaving together her experiences with universal concepts.

One Saturday, on a whim, Emily visited a local jazz club. The improvisational nature of jazz, with its fluid and unpredictable melodies, resonated deeply with her. She felt as though the music mirrored her life's new rhythm. Emily's harmonious existence was a dance with life, a graceful interplay of action and intuition.

Her life had become a demonstration to the beauty of living in alignment with the universe's rhythms, a life where each moment was embraced with openness and trust, and where the journey itself became a destination of peace and fulfillment.

"Does the calm sea reflect the sky, or does the sky find stillness in the sea?"

Emily's life embodied a balanced emotional state, a serene contentment that gracefully navigated the ebb and flow of life's varied experiences. Although she still started her day with a period of meditation, she now welcomed thoughts and emotions like passing clouds, observing them without attachment. This practice set the tone for her day, grounding her in a state of mindful presence.

This emotional balance also played out in her painting. Emily explored themes of harmony and contrast, her brush strokes capturing the fluid dance between light and shadow, movement, and stillness. The canvases were reflections of her inner state – vibrant yet tranquil, dynamic yet composed.

Emily's balanced emotional state was apparent. Her evening walks were times of reflection, where she acknowledged her feelings – joy, sadness, or contemplation – with a gentle acceptance, understanding their impermanent nature.

Her journal entries from this period illustrated her journey towards emotional balance. The pages were filled with introspective musings, where she explored the nuances of her emotional landscape, acknowledging the beauty in both the highs and lows, and the wisdom in their transience.

Emily's approach to life's challenges showcased her emotional maturity. When faced with an unexpected setback at work, she navigated the situation with a steady hand, her calm approach mitigating stress and inspiring confidence in her team. Her ability to maintain composure under pressure was a tribute to her inner stability.

Emily's balanced emotional state became the ideal of stability and wisdom. It was evidence of her spiritual growth, illustrating how a deep understanding of life's transient nature could foster a peaceful contentment, making her not just a participant in life's journey but a serene navigator of its many tides.

"Is the melody of the moment found in the note or in the silence between?"

Emily's life became a living embodiment of mindfulness, with each moment cherished as a unique and precious gift. Even her lunch breaks were times of quiet reflection. Instead of eating at her desk, she made it a point to step outside, where she would find a peaceful spot to enjoy her meal. Here, in the noise of the city, she still found tranquility, observing the world around her with a curious and non-judgmental eye. The chirping of birds, the rustle of leaves, and the distant hum of city life became part of her mindful experience, enriching her connection with the present moment.

Conversations were no longer mere exchanges of words but opportunities for genuine connection. Emily's ability to be fully present allowed her to understand and empathize with others on a deeper level, creating bonds of trust and openness.

Her evening walks were not just physical exercises but sensory journeys. She noticed the changing colors of the sky, the patterns of shadows on the pavement, and the varied textures of the cityscape. Each step was an acknowledgment of the present moment, a celebration of life's ever-changing beauty.

Emily created a space that was both calming and invigorating, filled with items that had personal significance. Her choice of décor, from the art on the walls to the books on her shelves, reflected her journey and her commitment to living fully in each moment.

In her journal, she recorded her thoughts and feelings about them, capturing the essence of her daily experiences. This practice helped her to process and appreciate the richness of her life, turning ordinary moments into profound insights.

Even in moments of challenge or stress, Emily maintained her mindful approach. When faced with difficulties, she took time to pause, breathe, and center herself, allowing her to respond with clarity and calmness. This ability to remain anchored in the present, even under pressure, was confirmation to the strength of her practice.

She shared her insights and experiences with others, encouraging them to explore the beauty of the present moment. Whether through casual conversations or structured workshops, she became a guide for those seeking to embrace a more mindful way of life.

"Can the silence of one seed awaken the forest?"

Emily's transformed state began to subtly influence those in her orbit, creating ripples of positive change and inspiration. Her colleagues at Shiyuantech Solutions, friends, and even casual acquaintances were drawn to the profound calmness, clarity, and compassion that she radiated.

Emily, with her gentle guidance and insights, became a catalyst for personal growth. Her friends started exploring their own paths to enlightenment, some taking up meditation, others reaching into philosophical studies, all influenced by Emily's transformation.

No matter where she was Emily's presence was impactful. At a local environmental initiative, she spoke about sustainability and about the interconnectedness of all life. Her words resonated with the audience, moving many to reconsider their lifestyles and their relationship with the environment. Emily's approach, which combined practical advice with a deeper spiritual perspective, inspired others to see the world in a new light.

In her apartment building, Emily's neighbors were drawn to her tranquil presence. Simple interactions in the elevator or the hallway left them feeling calmer and more centered. Some neighbors started joining her in the small meditation sessions she held in the rooftop garden, finding peace and inspiration in the practice.

Everyone she met felt the influence of her transformation. Conversations became more meaningful and supportive. Friends, family, and coworkers began to open up about their own struggles and aspirations, seeking Emily's advice and perspective. Her balanced and compassionate approach helped them all to navigate their challenges.

Emily embodied the possibility of profound personal transformation, inspiring others to embark on their own journeys of self-discovery and growth. Her life was a message of mindfulness, compassion, and wisdom, for anyone seeking a deeper understanding of themselves and the world around them.

"Is the dance of a leaf separate from the wind?"

Emily's sense of unity with the universe permeated every aspect of her existence. She walked through life with a deep awareness that everything was interconnected, that she was a part of a larger cosmic play.

At Shiyuantech Solutions, this profound connection influenced her approach to leadership and collaboration. She guided her team with wisdom that transcended conventional management practices. In meetings, Emily fostered a sense of unity, emphasizing that each member's contribution was vital to the collective success of their projects. Her approach inspired her colleagues to work harmoniously, viewing their individual tasks as integral parts of a cohesive whole.

Her interactions with friends and family were imparted with a deep empathy. She listened with an open heart, understanding that their joys' and challenges were reflections of universal human experiences. Her advice, always thoughtful and infused with kindness, helped her loved ones navigate their own paths with greater clarity and purpose.

Her morning prayers were experiences of cosmic communion. In the quiet of dawn, she felt a deep resonance with the rhythm of the universe, gaining insights and inspirations that she carried throughout her day.

Her paintings depicting the interconnectedness of all life. These works of art resonated with those who experienced them, often serving as catalysts for their own reflections on life and existence.

Emily faced life's ups and downs with equanimity, understanding them as part of the natural flow of existence. This perspective allowed her to navigate tough situations with grace and resilience, often finding innovative solutions that benefited not just her but the greater good.

Resolution of Conflicts and Relationships

"Can a single drop of purpose quench the thirst of a parched world, or does it evaporate before touching the ground?"

On a bright Monday morning, with the sun casting golden beams through her office window, Emily reviewed a project proposal that had landed on her desk. It was a bold initiative aimed at using technology to improve access to clean water in underdeveloped regions. As she examined the document, her mind raced with ideas. She visualized the faces of people whose lives could be transformed by this project, a stark contrast to the profit-driven ventures that once consumed her attention.

Later that day, Emily called a meeting with her team. The conference room buzzed with anticipation as her colleagues filed in, each curious about the new direction their leader was taking. Emily began, her voice steady yet filled with a passion that was contagious. She spoke of the water project, outlining both its financial viability and its humanitarian impact. Her words painted a vivid picture of the project's potential, inspiring her team with a sense of purpose that went beyond the walls of Shiyuantech.

During the discussion, a junior analyst named Sam voiced concern. "Emily, this project is ambitious, but what about the risks? The investment is significant, and the returns are not guaranteed." The room fell silent, the question hanging in the air like a challenge.

Emily nodded, acknowledging the concern. "Sam, you're right. The risks are real, but let's consider the impact. This isn't just about returns. It's about making a difference, about leveraging our skills for a greater cause." Her response was not a dismissal but an invitation to view their work through a different lens.

The meeting ended with the team feeling a mix of apprehension and excitement. They were stepping into uncharted territory, but under Emily's guidance, they felt a renewed sense of purpose.

As the days passed, Emily found herself in deep philosophical discussions with her colleagues. Lunch breaks turned into impromptu debates about corporate responsibility and the role of technology in society. Emily listened, shared, and gently guided these conversations, sowing seeds of awareness and compassion.

One evening, as she walked through the now-quiet office, Emily paused by a window overlooking the city. The sprawling urban landscape, with its twinkling lights, seemed to mirror the complexity of her own journey. She reflected on the path that had brought her here, the choices she had made, and the impact she hoped to create. A sense of serenity enveloped her, confirmation that her professional life was now aligned with her inner values.

As weeks turned into months, the water project began to take shape. Challenges arose, as they inevitably do, but each obstacle was met with a collective determination to succeed. Emily's leadership, once defined by efficiency and competitiveness, was now marked by empathy and collaboration. She had become not just a manager but a mentor, guiding her team through both professional and personal growth.

In this environment of shared purpose and deep reflection, the boundaries between professional and personal life began to blur. Emily's colleagues started to bring their whole selves to work, sharing their aspirations, fears, and joys. The office became a community, a place where personal transformation and professional ambition coexisted.

As Emily looked ahead, she knew that this was just the beginning. There were more projects to undertake, more lives to touch, more lessons to learn. But in this moment, she felt a profound sense of fulfillment, knowing that her professional life was now a true reflection of her deepest values. The journey ahead was uncertain, but Emily embraced it with an open heart.

"Is the voice of discord a clamor to be silenced, or a melody seeking harmony?"

As the sun cast its early rays over the city, Emily arrived at Shiyuantech Solutions, her mind already turning over the day's agenda. Among the tasks awaiting her was a meeting with Michael, a senior project manager known for his sharp mind but equally sharp temper. Their recent disagreements over project priorities had created an undercurrent of tension, one that Emily was determined to address today.

Walking through the quiet office, Emily took deep, deliberate breaths, centering herself in preparation for the conversation. She believed in the power of empathy and understanding, tools she had sharpened in her journey of self-discovery.

Michael was already in the meeting room, his brow furrowed as he reviewed some documents. As Emily entered, he looked up, his expression a mix of defensiveness and curiosity.

"Good morning, Michael," Emily greeted warmly, taking a seat across from him. "Thank you for meeting with me. I know we've had our differences regarding the Henderson project, and I'd like us to find a way forward together."

Michael's posture stiffened. "Emily, I respect your perspective, but I firmly believe that my approach is what's best for the project."

Emily nodded, acknowledging his viewpoint. "I understand, Michael. Let's explore our approaches together. I want to understand your perspective more deeply."

As they dove into the discussion, Emily listened intently, to Michael's words, as well as the emotions and concerns underlying them. She realized that his insistence stemmed not from stubbornness but from a deep commitment to the project's success.

"Michael, I see your dedication, and it's invaluable," Emily said sincerely. "What if we combine elements of both our plans? We could leverage your detailed risk analysis with my focus on sustainable practices. It could make the project more robust and innovative."

Michael paused, considering her words. The defensive edge in his voice softened. "That... could work. I hadn't considered integrating sustainability as a core component. It might actually open up new avenues."

The conversation shifted, becoming more collaborative. They began to weave their ideas together, creating a plan that was stronger and more comprehensive than either could have developed alone.

As the meeting concluded, Michael extended his hand, a gesture of respect. "Thank you, Emily. This was a productive discussion. I'm looking forward to seeing where this new direction takes us."

After Michael left, Emily sat back, reflecting on the encounter. She had not only navigated a conflict but had turned it into an opportunity for growth and innovation. Her approach had transformed a potential confrontation into a collaborative exchange.

This resolution rippled through the office. News of their successful meeting spread, and soon other team members began to approach conflicts with a similar mindset. The atmosphere in the office shifted; where there had once been pockets of tension, there was now a growing sense of unity and openness.

Emily's non-confrontational, empathetic approach was becoming a cornerstone of the company culture. It encouraged open dialogue, mutual respect, and a willingness to see beyond one's own perspective.

In the weeks that followed, this cultural shift led to several innovative solutions to long-standing problems. The team worked more cohesively, and their projects reflected this harmony, both in their process and outcomes.

Emily's leadership had catalyzed a positive change throughout Shiyuantech Solutions. She had demonstrated that empathy and collaboration were not just idealistic values but powerful tools for creating a thriving, innovative workplace.

As Emily looked out of her office window at the end of the day, she felt a deep sense of satisfaction. She had navigated the challenges of the day with grace and had fostered an environment where empathy and understanding were the foundations of success. This was more than just a professional achievement; it reflected her personal growth and her commitment to creating a world where people worked together for the greater good.

"Can the light of a single candle illuminate the path for two, or does each journey require its own flame?"

In the soft glow of the evening, Emily sat in the cozy living room of her best friend, Sarah. The room was filled with the comforting scent of jasmine tea and the quiet hum of a distant city. Around them, the walls were adorned with photos capturing their shared memories, each an indication of a friendship that had weathered many seasons.

Sarah, looking more wearied than usual, cradled her tea, her eyes reflecting a quiet turmoil. Emily, with her newly found depth of empathy, sensed her friend's unspoken distress. She reached across the small coffee table, placing her hand over Sarah's.

"Sarah, you've always been there for me," Emily began, her voice soft but steady. "I can tell something's weighing on you. I'm here, just like you've always been for me."

Sarah's eyes welled up, and she took a deep breath, finding courage in Emily's sincere gaze. "It's my mom, Em. Her health isn't going well, and I'm struggling to juggle work, caring for her, and just... keeping myself together."

Emily listened, her heart aching for her friend. She remembered her own struggles and how Sarah had been a pillar of support. It was now her turn to be that pillar.

"Sarah, let's figure this out together. Maybe I can help with some of your workload, or we can find a care service for your mom. You're not alone in this."

As they looked into possible solutions, Emily's mind was fully present, her suggestions thoughtful and practical. But beyond the practicalities, it was her presence, her unwavering support, that provided Sarah with a sense of comfort and strength.

The conversation gradually shifted, not just dwelling on the challenges but also reminiscing about the joyful moments they had shared. Laughter began to weave its way into their dialogue, lightening the heaviness in the room.

"Remember our road trip to the coast?" Emily said with a smile, stirring a shared nostalgia.

Sarah's laughter rang out, genuine and free. "How could I forget? You trying to set up that tent was a comedy show on its own!"

In these moments of shared laughter and tears, their bond deepened, rooted in a genuine understanding and love. Emily's journey of personal growth had transformed her along with enriching the lives of those around her.

As the night wore on, they continued to talk, sometimes in earnest, sometimes in jest, always with a profound sense of connection. Emily felt a deep contentment, knowing that her presence was a source of strength and joy for Sarah.

When it was time to leave, Emily hugged Sarah tightly. "Call me, anytime, for anything," she said earnestly.

Walking back to her home under the starlit sky, Emily reflected on the evening. Her relationships, she realized, were the threads that wove the tapestry of her life. Each connection, each moment of shared vulnerability and joy, added richness and depth to her existence.

This newfound depth in her personal relationships was not just a change in her behavior but a reflection of her inner transformation. Emily's journey had taught her the value of presence, of truly being there for others, not just in body but in spirit.

As she lay in bed that night, Emily felt a profound gratitude for the journey she had embarked upon. It had led her to a place where she could be a source of strength and love for others, where her relationships were defined by a deep, authentic connection.

Tomorrow would bring its own challenges and triumphs, but for now, Emily rested in the peace of knowing that she was living a life of genuine love and presence, touching the lives of those she cared for in the most meaningful ways.

"Does the fading echo of a bell still resonate within the silence, or does its sound vanish into the void?"

Emily sat quietly in her apartment, Mrs. Kaur's passing still echoing in her mind. The room was dimly lit, shadows playing on the walls, reflecting the somber mood that enveloped her. Outside, the city carried on, oblivious to the loss of a soul that had touched Emily deeply.

Mrs. Kaur, her elderly neighbor, had been more than just a friendly face in her life. She had been a source of wisdom, sharing stories of her life that were woven with threads of resilience and grace. Emily remembered their long conversations, often over cups of steaming chai, where Mrs. Kaur would impart bits of her life's philosophy.

Now, as she sat enveloped in the quiet of her apartment, Emily felt the weight of loss but also a profound sense of acceptance. She gazed out of the window, watching the sun setting in the distance, painting the sky in hues of orange and pink. In that moment, the beauty of the sunset seemed to echo the beauty of life's impermanence.

She reflected on the conversations she had with Mrs. Kaur, especially on their discussions about the nature of life and death. Mrs. Kaur often spoke of life as a fleeting journey, a transient passage that one must traverse with grace and gratitude. "Life," Mrs. Kaur would say, "is like the seasons. It changes, it evolves, and eventually, it transitions into something else."

Emily closed her eyes, taking a deep breath, allowing these thoughts to sink in. She realized that accepting Mrs. Kaur's passing was also accepting the natural cycle of life. It was about embracing the impermanence of existence, the constant ebb and flow that defined the human experience.

In her mind's eye, Emily revisited the many moments she shared with Mrs. Kaur. Each memory was a precious keepsake, a reminder of the lessons learned, and the warmth shared. She smiled gently, acknowledging that while Mrs. Kaur was no longer physically present, her spirit and teachings would continue to live on within her.

The room grew darker as the night crept in, as a sense of peace settled over Emily. She understood that grief was a part of loving someone, but so was the celebration of their life and the acceptance of their departure.

With a renewed sense of clarity, Emily lit a candle in honor of Mrs. Kaur. The flame flickered gently, casting a soft, warm glow in the room. She sat there for a while, watching the flame, feeling a connection to Mrs. Kaur's spirit.

As the night wore on, Emily penned down her thoughts in her journal. She wrote about the transient nature of life, about love, loss, and the lessons imbued within each experience. This act of writing was therapeutic, a way to process her emotions and pay tribute to a cherished soul.

Eventually, Emily prepared for bed, her heart still heavy but also filled with gratitude. She realized that Mrs. Kaur's passing was not just an end but also a part of a larger, ongoing cycle of life. In her dreams that night, she saw Mrs. Kaur, smiling and serene, surrounded by a garden of blooming flowers.

When Emily awoke the next morning, she felt a sense of calm acceptance. She knew that the journey ahead would have its share of challenges and joys, but she was ready to embrace them all, carrying with her the wisdom and love imparted by Mrs. Kaur. In this way, she honored the memory of her beloved mentor, not just in grief, but in living a life full of purpose and compassion.

"Can a single seed, once planted in the heart, grow forests in the souls of others?"

As the first rays of dawn cast a gentle glow through her window, Emily rose from her bed, the events of the previous night still vivid in her mind. The loss of Mrs. Kaur had left an indelible mark on her, a profound sorrow tempered by an equally profound sense of purpose. She stood there for a moment, watching the play of light on the walls of her room, contemplating the day ahead.

She made her way to the small desk by the window, where she kept her journal. Flipping through the pages filled with thoughts and reflections, Emily paused at a section where she had transcribed some of Mrs. Kaur's most impactful teachings. These words, once mere ink on paper, now seemed to pulse with life and urgency.

"Compassion is not just an emotion; it's an action," Mrs. Kaur had said during one of their long conversations. Emily pondered this, realizing that to truly honor Mrs. Kaur's memory, she needed to embody this principle in her daily life.

As the morning progressed, Emily set out on a walk through the neighborhood. The streets, lined with trees gently swaying in the breeze, seemed to resonate with her newfound resolve. She greeted her neighbors with a warmth and presence that she had learned from Mrs. Kaur, listening intently to their stories, and offering words of encouragement and support. In these interactions, she felt Mrs. Kaur's spirit guiding her, urging her to spread kindness and understanding.

Later that day, Emily visited the community center, a place where Mrs. Kaur had spent much of her time volunteering. The staff, who knew Emily as Mrs. Kaur's protégé, welcomed her with open arms. Emily offered to take over some of the classes Mrs. Kaur used to conduct, sharing not just practical skills but also the life lessons that she had been fortunate enough to learn from her.

As she engaged with the people at the center, Emily found herself involved in discussions that mirrored the philosophical dialogues she once had with Mrs. Kaur. She spoke of empathy, resilience, and the beauty of life's impermanence, channeling the wisdom of her late mentor. The attendees, captivated by her words, felt a connection to Mrs. Kaur's teachings, creating a ripple effect of her legacy.

In the evening, Emily returned home, her heart full. She sat by her window, pen in hand, ready to journal about the day. But this time, it wasn't just a personal reflection; it was a testament to the impact Mrs. Kaur had on her life and the lives of others.

As she wrote, Emily realized that honoring Mrs. Kaur's legacy was not a singular act but a lifelong journey. It was about living with intention, being a source of light in the world, just as Mrs. Kaur had been. She vowed to continue this journey, carrying the torch of compassion and wisdom forward.

The moon rose high in the sky as Emily closed her journal, a sense of peace enveloping her. In the quiet of the night, she whispered a thank you to Mrs. Kaur, promising to keep her spirit alive in memory, and in action. With this promise, Emily drifted off to sleep, the legacy of her mentor forever etched in her heart, guiding her steps into the future.

"Can the stillness of one heart quell the storms in another?"

Emily's presence emanated a sense of calm and steadiness that belied the chaos around her. She had become a ideal of support and inspiration to those in her life, as evidence of her profound personal evolution. Each step she took, each word she spoke, carried with it the weight of her journey and the depth of her empathy.

On a crisp Wednesday afternoon, Emily found herself in a quaint café, the aroma of freshly brewed coffee mingling with the murmur of conversations around her. Across the table sat her friend, Anna, whose eyes were rimmed with the telltale signs of sleepless nights and worry. As Anna poured her heart out about the struggles she faced in her relationship, Emily listened intently, her gaze unwavering, her mind fully present.

The conversation meandered through the labyrinths of heartache and healing, with Emily interjecting occasionally, not to advise, but to reflect back Anna's own strength and wisdom. Her words were carefully chosen, permeated with the insight gleaned from her own experiences, guiding Anna to see her situation in a new light.

In a corner of the lively Shiyuantech Solutions office, a junior colleague was visibly frustrated, the lines of code on his screen a jumble of confusion. Emily approached him with a gentle smile, offering not just technical guidance but also a listening ear to his concerns about meeting project deadlines. Her approach was not of superiority, but of collaboration, her calm demeanor helping to alleviate his anxiety and refocus his efforts.

One evening, as she shared a meal with her younger brother, James, Emily noticed a certain restlessness in him. Through subtle questions and patient listening, she unraveled his apprehensions about his upcoming college decisions. Her responses were not prescriptive but exploratory, encouraging James to trust in his abilities and to follow his passions.

At a local book club meeting, when a heated debate arose over the interpretation of a novel's theme, Emily steered the discussion away from conflict and towards a deeper understanding of the diverse perspectives. Her ability to acknowledge and validate each member's viewpoint fostered a sense of respect and unity among the group.

Each of these moments reflected Emily's inner transformation. Gone were the days of uncertainty and self-doubt. In their place stood a woman who, through her journey of self-discovery, had cultivated a deep well of empathy and balance. Her words, her actions, her very being, became a source of comfort and inspiration to those around her.

Friends began to seek her out not just in times of distress but also to share their joys and triumphs, knowing that she would revel in their happiness just as she empathized with their pain. Colleagues at work respected her for her knowledge and admired her for her compassion, often turning to her for guidance in both professional and personal matters.

As Emily lay in bed that night, the moon casting a soft glow through her window, she reflected on the impact she had on the lives of those around her. Her journey, marked by trials and triumphs, had led her to this place of balance and empathy.

"Can a single flower's fragrance be where the garden begins?"

Emily's newfound approach to life continued to cast ripples of positive change within her social and professional circles, subtly yet significantly altering the dynamics and inspiring others to embrace their own journeys of growth and self-improvement.

At the local community center, where Emily volunteered, her influence was increasingly evident. The once mundane and routine meetings of the volunteer group had transformed into vibrant brainstorming sessions. Her ideas, brimming with creativity and empathy, sparked enthusiasm among her fellow volunteers. They began to approach community issues with a renewed vigor, often seeking Emily's insights. The center, which had once struggled to engage the local youth, was now buzzing with activity, drawing in teenagers and young adults inspired by Emily's dedication and innovative approach.

Even in her interactions with acquaintances and strangers, Emily's impact was tangible. Her open demeanor and willingness to listen attracted people from various walks of life, sharing their stories and seeking her perspective. Emily's approach to life's challenges, grounded in empathy and introspection, became an example for those grappling with their own struggles.

As Emily navigated her day-to-day life, her mind often reflected on the profound nature of her influence. She pondered the interconnectedness of human experiences and the power of individual transformation to inspire collective change. Her thoughts reached into philosophical realms, contemplating the ripple effect of one's actions and the shared journey of growth and self-improvement.

Her personal transformation had evolved into a story of communal growth. Each interaction, each piece of advice she shared, became a catalyst for change in others. Emily realized that her commitment to personal growth had inadvertently turned her into a lighthouse, guiding others through the turbulent waters of their own lives.

As she lay in bed each night, reflecting on the day's events, Emily felt a profound sense of fulfillment. The knowledge that her journey was not only reshaping her life but also touching the lives of others filled her with a deep sense of purpose. She understood that the positive changes she had fostered in herself were now creating a chain of transformations, a series of positive ripples that extended far beyond her immediate surroundings.

"Does the light that shines through the window illuminate the room, or does it reveal the family within?"

On a crisp Saturday morning, the sun filtering through the curtains of her childhood home, Emily sat at the kitchen table with her parents. The aroma of freshly brewed coffee mingled with the scent of her mother's homemade cinnamon rolls, a nostalgic reminder of simpler times. The scene was familiar, yet there was an undeniable change in the air. The conversations that once skirted the surface of polite inquiries now reached into deeper, more meaningful territories.

Her father, a man of few words, talked about his recent retirement, sharing his fears and uncertainties about this new phase of life. Emily listened intently, her eyes reflecting a genuine understanding. She shared insights from her own journey, about embracing change and finding purpose in every stage of life. Her words, infused with empathy and wisdom,

seemed to comfort her father, his usual stoic demeanor softening as he considered her perspective.

Her mother, always the more expressive of the two, spoke about her aspirations to start a small business, something she had put on hold for years. Emily's encouragement was palpable, her enthusiasm infectious. She offered to help her mother draft a business plan, her professional skills blending seamlessly with her personal desire to support her family. The conversation flowed naturally, with laughter and shared dreams filling the room.

As the day progressed, Emily's younger brother arrived, his usual aloofness replaced with a curious openness. He had always admired Emily but had never quite understood her journey. Now, as they sat together, Emily spoke candidly about her challenges and triumphs, her words bridging the gap that had long existed between them. Her brother, inspired by her authenticity, shared his own struggles with finding direction in life. Emily listened, her responses thoughtful and encouraging, fostering a newfound connection between them.

Emily pondered the intricate web of family dynamics, the delicate balance between giving support and receiving it. Her thoughts often wandered to the concept of emotional inheritance - how families pass down not just genetic traits but emotional patterns and coping mechanisms. She recognized how her own growth was helping to break certain cycles, paving the way for healthier family relationships.

As the day turned to evening, the family gathered in the living room, a place where, in the past, silence had often reigned. Now, the space was filled with warm chatter, an exchange of stories and plans for the future. Emily's parents shared anecdotes from their past, revealing layers of their personalities that Emily had never known. This newfound openness was authentication to the trust and comfort that had grown between them.

In these moments, Emily realized the profound impact her journey had on her family. Her growth had not only transformed her but had also acted as a catalyst for her family's evolution. Each conversation, each shared experience, was strengthening the bonds that held them together. The familial ties, once tenuous, were now deepening, built on a foundation of mutual understanding and unconditional support.

As the night drew to a close, and Emily bid her family goodbye, there was a sense of fulfillment in her heart. The family she had once struggled to connect with was now a source of strength and inspiration. The journey she had embarked on had come full circle, not only changing her but also enriching the lives of those she held dear.

Reintegration into Society with New Understanding

"Returning to the Origin, Back to the Source"

"In the forest where paths diverge, can a whisper among the trees inspire the journey, without a word being spoken?

The morning sun streamed through the windows of Emily's apartment, cast a warm, golden light that seemed to dance upon the walls. It was a new day, and for Emily, it marked the beginning of a new chapter in her life, one filled with a profound sense of clarity and purpose.

As she sat at her breakfast table, Emily's mind was alive with thoughts and reflections. She sipped her tea slowly, savoring its warmth and flavor. Her usual rush to start the day had transformed into a tranquil appreciation of each moment.

Her phone buzzed with a reminder of a meeting at Shiyuantech Solutions. In the past, such notifications would have stirred a sense of urgency in her, but today, they brought a sense of anticipation. She was eager to bring her new perspective to her professional life.

Arriving at the office, Emily greeted her colleagues with genuine warmth. Her interactions were no longer superficial; they were imbued with a sincere interest in their well-being. In her office, she paused to organize her thoughts before the meeting.

The meeting was about a new project, one that Emily had proposed, focusing on sustainable technology solutions. As she presented her ideas, her passion was evident. She spoke about the potential impact on communities and the environment. Her words resonated with the team, and their responses were enthusiastic, a clear shift from the usual skepticism that greeted new initiatives.

The dialogue that followed was rich and engaging. Emily listened attentively to her colleagues' inputs, integrating their ideas with her vision.

The discussion was a collective brainstorming that tapped into the team's creativity and expertise.

Post-meeting, Emily's colleague, Tom, approached her. "Emily, your idea about integrating local artisans in our tech solutions is brilliant. It gives a whole new dimension to our work," he said, admiration evident in his voice. Emily smiled, grateful for the acknowledgment but more so for the shared enthusiasm.

Back in her office, Emily took a moment to reflect. She opened her journal, a leather-bound book that had become her companion on this journey of self-discovery. She penned down her thoughts about the meeting, the ideas discussed, and her feelings about this new chapter in her career. Writing was no longer just a way to record events; it was a process of introspection and understanding.

Later, Emily decided to take a walk in the nearby park. As she strolled among the trees, her mind wandered to the philosophical aspects of her journey. She pondered the interconnectedness of all actions, how her personal transformation was influencing her professional life, and vice versa. The walk was a meditation, a communion with nature that recharged her spirit.

In the evening, Emily met with her friend, Lisa, for dinner. The conversation naturally drifted to Emily's recent changes. "I see a new light in you, Em. It's inspiring," Lisa remarked. Emily shared her experiences, the lessons learned, and her aspirations for the future. The discussion delved into topics of personal growth, purpose, and the pursuit of meaningful work.

As Emily returned to her apartment, she felt a deep sense of fulfillment. Her life, once a quest for external achievements, had become a journey of meaningful pursuits. She realized that her renewed clarity and sense of purpose were not just guiding her actions but were also inspiring those around her.

Lying in bed, Emily looked out at the city skyline. She closed her eyes, content in the knowledge that she was on a path that was true to her heart and spirit.

"In a world where code weaves reality and dreams, how can the architect of change build bridges without crossing the river herself?"

The morning light filtered through the blinds of Emily's office at Shiyuantech Solutions, casting a lattice of shadows across her desk. Today was not just another day at work; it was a continuation of her transformative journey. Emily, once content with meeting targets and deadlines, now viewed her role through a new lens — as a vehicle for positive societal change.

As she logged onto her computer, her mind was abuzz with ideas. She had been working on a new software project, one that could potentially revolutionize access to education in remote areas. The idea had come to her in a moment of inspiration, a blend of her technical skills and her desire to make a real difference in the world.

Her first task of the day was a meeting with her project team. As she walked to the conference room, her steps were purposeful, her demeanor calm yet charged with a quiet energy. She greeted each member of her team as they arrived, her warmth and sincerity setting a tone of collaboration and respect.

"Good morning, everyone," Emily began, her eyes reflecting the passion she felt for the project. "Today, we're not just software developers; we're architects of change. Our project has the potential to touch lives, to bridge educational gaps, and to open doors of opportunity for those who need it most."

The team listened, captivated. Emily's enthusiasm was infectious, her vision clear and compelling. She outlined the project's objectives, emphasizing its social impact. The discussion that followed was dynamic, with team members contributing innovative ideas and solutions. The atmosphere was electric, a fusion of creativity and a shared sense of purpose.

Later, Emily had a meeting with the company's CEO, Mr. Anderson, to discuss the project's funding and implementation. She entered his office with a sense of resolve, ready to present her case. Mr. Anderson listened intently as Emily spoke.

"Mr. Anderson, this project is more than just a technological advancement; it's an opportunity for us to lead in corporate social responsibility. We have the chance to make a real difference, to set an example in the industry," Emily explained, her voice steady and convincing.

Mr. Anderson nodded thoughtfully. "Emily, I'm impressed with your vision. Let's explore this further. If we can align it with our business goals, I see no reason why we can't pursue this path."

Buoyed by Mr. Anderson's positive response, Emily left the meeting feeling hopeful. She knew there were challenges ahead, but she also knew she had the conviction and the support to overcome them.

Back in her office, Emily took a moment to reflect. She gazed out of her window at the cityscape below, her thoughts deep and introspective. She realized that her work had become a reflection of her inner transformation — a blend of her skills, her values, and her aspirations to contribute to a better world.

Emily's approach to her work had transformed, and with it, her sense of self. She was no longer just a professional in the tech industry; she was a catalyst for change, a beacon of hope and innovation. Her journey at Shiyuantech Solutions had become an integral part of her larger journey of personal and societal transformation.

"In a forest where trees whisper secrets of the earth, can the gardener plant seeds of change without touching the soil?"

The early morning light bathed Emily's office at Shiyuantech Solutions in a serene glow, symbolizing a new dawn in her professional journey. Today, she was to lead the first meeting for a project close to her heart — one focused on developing eco-friendly technologies that could reduce the company's carbon footprint. This project was a manifestation of her commitment to making a positive impact through her work.

As she reviewed her notes, Emily's mind was a whirlwind of ideas and strategies. She envisioned a range of sustainable tech solutions, from energy-efficient software to waste reduction algorithms. These innovations had the potential to set new industry standards, and Emily was determined to see them come to fruition.

The meeting room gradually filled with team members, each carrying their own expertise and viewpoints. Emily greeted them with a warm smile, her demeanor exuding confidence and passion. She began the meeting with a question that set the tone for the discussion.

"How can we, as a tech company, become leaders in sustainability and social responsibility?" Emily asked, her eyes scanning the room, inviting her team to ponder this fundamental question.

The response was a mix of curiosity and enthusiasm. The team members began to share their thoughts, sparking a lively debate. Emily facilitated the discussion, ensuring every voice was heard, every idea considered. Her approach was collaborative, seeking to harness the collective intelligence of the group.

As the meeting progressed, Emily outlined her vision for the project. She spoke about integrating sustainable practices into every stage of development, from design to deployment. She discussed partnerships with environmental organizations and the potential for community outreach programs. Her presentation was not just about the 'what' and the 'how' but also about the 'why' — emphasizing the moral imperative of their endeavor.

The team's response was overwhelmingly positive. They were inspired by Emily's vision and motivated by the challenge. Ideas flowed freely, from using renewable energy sources in their data centers to implementing a company-wide recycling program. The atmosphere was electric, charged with the potential for real, tangible change.

As the meeting ended, Emily assigned roles and set deadlines, but not before expressing her gratitude for the team's enthusiasm and commitment. She knew the road ahead would be challenging, but with a team united by a common purpose, she was confident they could achieve their goals.

The rest of the day was spent in a flurry of activity, planning the project's next steps, and coordinating with other departments. Emily's interactions were marked by a sense of purpose and clarity. She was not just a project manager; she was a catalyst for change, guiding her team towards a future where technology and sustainability went hand in hand.

That evening, as she walked home, Emily's thoughts were filled with plans and possibilities. She was excited about the impact their project could have — not just on the company but on the community and the environment. She felt a profound connection to her work, a sense that she was contributing to something much larger than herself.

"In the stillness of dawn and the rush of day, where does the dancer rest her feet?"

The quiet hours of the early morning had become her cherished time for reflection and introspection. Today, she was engrossed in a book about the balance between action and contemplation, a theme that deeply resonated with her current life philosophy.

As the clock neared eight, Emily closed her book and transitioned into her daily yoga routine. Each movement was deliberate, a physical manifestation of her commitment to maintaining balance in her life. Her mind was clear, focused on the present moment, the stretches providing not just physical but mental flexibility.

Later, at Shiyuantech Solutions, Emily's day was a whirlwind of activity. Her role as a project manager had her juggling multiple tasks, from team meetings to client consultations. Despite the hectic pace, Emily's demeanor remained calm and composed. She had learned to find a rhythm in the chaos, her morning reflections providing the anchor she needed to navigate the busy workday.

Emily chose to spend her break in her favorite nearby park. She found a quiet bench under a sprawling oak tree, where she could enjoy her meal and the beauty of nature around her. This time away from the office was not just a break from work; it was an integral part of her balanced approach to life. The sounds of the city mingled with the rustling leaves, reminding her of the interconnectedness of all things.

After work, Emily attended a community book club meeting. The group was discussing a novel that explored the themes of ambition and contentment, topics that spurred a lively debate. Emily shared her perspectives, drawing parallels between the characters' struggles and her own experiences. The discussion was a way for Emily to engage with her community and enrich her understanding of different viewpoints.

Returning home, Emily spent the evening working on a painting, her brush strokes reflecting the emotions and thoughts of the day. Art was her way of processing her experiences, a creative outlet that complemented her analytical work life. The canvas came alive with colors and forms, each representing a facet of her day's journey.

Before bed, Emily wrote in her journal. This nightly ritual was her time to reflect on the day's events, to acknowledge her feelings, and to plan for the days ahead. Her entries were a mix of personal insights, philosophical thoughts, and practical considerations, a mirror of her balanced approach to life.

As she turned off the bedside lamp, Emily felt a sense of contentment. Her life was a harmonious blend of action and reflection, engagement, and introspection. Each day was an opportunity to live fully, to learn, to grow, and to contribute to the world around her. Her journey had taught her the value of balance, and she embraced this philosophy in every aspect of her life, ensuring a rich, fulfilling, and well-rounded existence.

"In the chorus of dawn, does the robin sing for the sky or for the silent listener?"

The morning sun streamed through the kitchen window, casting a warm glow on the small, yet cozy space where Emily stood preparing her breakfast. The aroma of freshly ground coffee filled the air, mingling with the scent of toast. Emily moved with a sense of contentment, relishing these simple, everyday rituals that had become sources of immense joy.

As she sat at her dining table, savoring the rich flavor of her coffee, Emily gazed out the window, observing the world awakening. She watched as a robin perched on the fence, its cheerful song adding to the serene ambiance of the morning. These moments of quiet observation, once overlooked in her busy life, now held a special place in her heart.

Later, as Emily walked to work, she took a new route through the park. The vibrant green of the grass, the rustling of leaves in the gentle breeze, and the laughter of children playing in the distance filled her with a sense of peace. She found joy in these simple sights and sounds, a stark contrast to the days when her mind was too preoccupied to notice the beauty around her.

Emily visited a local bookstore after work, a place she found inspiration. She wandered through the aisles, running her fingers over the spines of books, each a gateway to another world. The musty smell of old books and the quiet ambiance of the store, and the joy of discovering a new book filled her with a sense of wonder and contentment.

Returning home that evening, Emily prepared a simple meal, taking pleasure in the process of cooking. The act of chopping vegetables, the sizzle of food in the pan, and the blend of flavors and aromas transformed cooking from a routine task into a delightful experience. She ate her dinner at her dining table, savoring each bite, grateful for the nourishment and the pleasure it brought.

As she lay in bed, Emily felt a deep sense of gratitude for the day. The simple pleasures and moments, once unnoticed, now brought her immense joy. She realized that happiness was not in grand gestures or extraordinary events, but in the beauty and simplicity of everyday life. Her journey had taught her to cherish these moments, to find wonder in the ordinary, creating a life full of simple, yet profound, joys.

Her life had become a harmonious blend of action and reflection, of engaging with the world while maintaining an inner serenity. Emily's life was no longer about overcoming personal challenges; it had evolved into a story of uplifting others, of being a serene beacon in the tumultuous sea of life. She understood that her journey had given her not just the gift of inner peace but the ability to share that peace with the world around her.

"In a garden of silence, where thoughts bloom like flowers, can the mind's stillness be both the seed and the gardener?"

At her local community center, Emily stood surrounded by a group of eager attendees, her expression a blend of calm and excitement. The room was set up simply yet invitingly, with mats spread out on the floor and soft, ambient music playing in the background. This was one of many mindfulness workshops Emily had organized, a project close to her heart aimed at promoting mental and emotional well-being in her community.

As people began to settle in, Emily took a deep breath and began to speak, her voice resonating with a warmth that immediately put the room at ease. "Welcome, everyone," she started, "Today, we embark on a journey together—a journey towards greater mindfulness and understanding of our mental and emotional landscapes."

The workshop was a mix of guided meditation, group discussions, and interactive activities. Emily led the meditation with a natural grace, her words guiding the attendees through a process of mindful breathing and awareness. The room fell into a deep silence, punctuated only by the gentle sound of breathing and the soft melody in the background.

After the meditation, Emily encouraged open discussions. She shared her own experiences with mindfulness, speaking candidly about the challenges she faced and how these practices had helped her find balance and clarity. Her honesty and vulnerability resonated with the group, sparking a sense of connection and openness among the participants.

One of the attendees, a young man named Jeff, shared his struggle with anxiety. Emily listened intently, her responses showing a deep understanding and empathy. She suggested practical mindfulness techniques that Jeff could incorporate into his daily routine, emphasizing the importance of self-compassion and patience in the process.

As the workshop progressed, Emily introduced an interactive activity focused on emotional awareness. She distributed cards with various emotions written on them and asked the participants to choose one that resonated with them at that moment. This exercise led to profound conversations about emotional health, coping mechanisms, and the importance of acknowledging and expressing one's feelings.

In between the sessions, Emily engaged in one-on-one conversations with the attendees, her demeanor both reassuring and inspiring. Her ability to connect with people from all walks of life, to listen without judgment and offer thoughtful advice, made her a beloved figure in the community.

The workshop concluded with a group reflection, where attendees shared their experiences and takeaways. Many expressed gratitude for the safe space Emily had created a place where they could explore their inner worlds without fear or hesitation.

After the event, Emily sat in the now-empty room, reflecting on the day. She pondered the ripple effect of such gatherings, how promoting mindfulness and well-being could transform not only individual lives but entire communities.

In the weeks that followed, Emily continued to advocate for mental and emotional health in various ways. She organized regular meetups for meditation and discussion, participated in panel discussions on well-being, and collaborated with local organizations to raise awareness about mental health.

"Can a single seed planted in silence blossom in a forest of noise?"

Emily sat at her kitchen table, the gentle light of dawn streaming through the window, casting a soft glow on the pages of her journal. Today, like every day, she began with a moment of introspection, reflecting on her path towards enlightenment and the profound impact it had on every aspect of her life.

As she penned down her thoughts, Emily's mind wandered to the day ahead. First on her agenda was a visit to the local school, where she had volunteered to lead a mindfulness session for teenagers. This was a project close to her heart, driven by her desire to contribute to the well-being of others, especially the younger generation. She believed in the power of early intervention, in equipping young minds with the tools to navigate life's complexities with grace and awareness.

Throughout her day, Emily's interactions with people, whether they were school children, colleagues, or strangers at the coffee shop, were filled with a sense of purpose and empathy. She listened more than she spoke, offering words of encouragement and wisdom when needed. Her presence was calming, her demeanor a balance of strength and gentleness.

As night fell, Emily would return home where she would often spend time in quiet reflection, sometimes meditating or simply sitting in silence, absorbing the tranquility of her surroundings. These moments of solitude were crucial for her, a time to recharge and connect with her inner self.

Before bed, Emily always took a moment to express gratitude for the day's experiences. She understood that every encounter, every challenge, and every triumph was a part of her ongoing journey towards a life of meaning. Her path was not about her own enlightenment alone, but also about inspiring and uplifting those around her.

In her room, with the soft light of the moon shining through the window, Emily would finally close her eyes, her mind and heart filled with a sense of fulfillment. She had come to realize that living a life of meaning wasn't about grand gestures or monumental achievements; it was about the small, everyday choices to live consciously, to grow continuously, and to contribute positively to the world.

As she drifted off to sleep, Emily's last thoughts were of the future, of the endless possibilities that awaited her on this path of enlightenment—a path that she walked for herself, and for the greater good of all who crossed her journey.

Impact on Community and Wider World

"In a hall where many sit in silence, can the echo of one heart awaken a thousand others?"

Within a tranquil community center, the meditation and discussion groups initiated by Emily flourished, transforming from intimate gatherings into a thriving community pulsating with the energy of collective spiritual and personal growth.

Each Thursday evening individuals from diverse walks of life congregated in the spacious hall Emily had arranged for the meetings. The room, once echoing with the silence of a few, now hummed with the anticipatory chatter of many. Cushions were laid out in a large circle, and in the center, a small table held a flickering candle, its flame a symbol of hope in a vigorous city.

Emily, wearing a serene smile, welcomed each member. Her eyes, reflecting a deep sense of purpose, met each gaze with warmth and recognition. Among the attendees were familiar faces, regulars who had been with Emily since the inception of the group, and new seekers, drawn by the growing reputation of the gatherings as a haven for introspection and connection.

As the session commenced, Emily's voice, gentle yet resonant, guided the group through a meditation. Her words, carefully chosen, wove through the air, inviting the participants to journey inwards. The collective breaths of the group synced with her rhythm, creating a symphony of peacefulness that enveloped the room.

Post meditation, the floor opened for discussion. Tonight's topic, suggested by a long-time member, Samuel, was 'The Power of Now'. Emily, leading the dialogue, shared her insights, drawing on her own experiences and the teachings that had guided her. Her perspective was not prescriptive but exploratory, encouraging a diversity of viewpoints and revelations.

The conversation ebbed and flowed, from personal anecdotes to philosophical musings. Laura, a new member, tentatively voiced her struggles with living in the moment, her words resonating with many. Emily listened, then responded with empathy, her advice a blend of practicality and wisdom.

It was moments like these that underscored the value of the group — a place where vulnerability was met with understanding and support.

As the evening ended, the group engaged in a closing ritual, a circle of gratitude, where each person shared something, they were thankful for. The ritual, introduced by Emily as a way to foster a sense of community and positivity, had become a cherished part of the gatherings.

After the session, the members lingered, not eager to leave the sanctuary they had found. Conversations continued in smaller clusters, connections deepening, the seeds of friendships taking root. Emily moved among them, her presence a comforting and unifying force.

In the weeks that followed, the group's impact rippled beyond the confines of the community center. Members started to implement the practices and insights gained from the sessions into their daily lives, leading to transformations both subtle and profound. The group's reputation spread, attracting more individuals seeking guidance and community.

Emily, witnessing the growth and evolution of the group, felt a deep sense of fulfillment. Her vision of creating a space for collective growth had materialized into a reality far beyond her initial expectations. The group was no longer just a gathering; it had become a movement, a community dedicated to the shared journey of personal and spiritual evolution.

As she walked home after each session Emily's heart swelled with gratitude. She realized that her journey, which had started as a solitary quest, had grown into something much larger — an inspiration for others seeking their path.

"In a forest where trees speak in silence, does the wind know the stories they tell?"

Emily's dedication to making mindfulness and meditation accessible to diverse groups led her to a busy Saturday morning at the community center, where she was scheduled to meet representatives from various local organizations. Her aim was to collaborate and create tailored programs that addressed the unique needs and backgrounds of their respective communities.

As she set up for the meeting in a spacious, sunlit room, Emily arranged chairs in a circle, creating an atmosphere of equality and openness. The walls of the room were adorned with serene artwork, setting a peaceful tone. She placed informational brochures and her own carefully prepared notes on each chair.

The representatives began to arrive, each bringing a unique perspective to the table. There was David from the local senior center, Alisha from the women's shelter, and Greg from the youth mentoring program, among others. Emily greeted each of them warmly, her genuine enthusiasm evident.

Once everyone was settled, Emily initiated the meeting with a brief mindfulness exercise. She guided the group through a few minutes of deep breathing and centering, demonstrating a practice they could potentially share with their communities. This icebreaker gave the attendees a firsthand experience of the benefits of mindfulness.

After the exercise, Emily began the discussion. "Mindfulness has the power to transform lives," she started, her tone both passionate and sincere. "But it's crucial that we make these practices accessible and relevant to all. I'd love to hear about the specific needs and challenges of your communities."

David shared his concerns about seniors feeling isolated and struggling with mobility issues. Alisha spoke about the need for trauma-informed mindfulness practices at the women's shelter. Greg discussed the challenges of engaging at-risk youth and the importance of making meditation relatable to them.

Emily listened attentively, jotting down notes. She then proposed ideas for customized programs: chair yoga and guided meditation for seniors, mindfulness sessions for trauma survivors with a focus on safety and empowerment, and engaging, activity-based mindfulness practices for the youth.

The representatives were receptive and enthusiastic. They discussed logistics, potential challenges, and ways to integrate these practices into their existing programs. Emily offered to conduct initial sessions herself and train volunteers. The energy in the room was collaborative and hopeful, with a shared vision of bringing positive change to diverse groups.

The plans they had laid out represented a real opportunity to impact lives positively. She stayed back to chat with the representatives individually, offering further insights and strengthening her commitment to this inclusive approach.

The following weeks were a flurry of activity for Emily. She conducted training sessions at the senior center, where she adapted yoga and meditation to be accessible for older adults. At the women's shelter, she led gentle mindfulness sessions, creating a safe space for healing and self-compassion. With the youth, she used interactive methods, incorporating mindfulness into art and music activities, making the sessions engaging and relevant.

Through her work, Emily saw firsthand the transformative power of these practices. Seniors reported feeling more connected and less anxious, women at the shelter found a sense of peace and empowerment, and the youth began to show improvements in focus and emotional regulation.

Back at her apartment, Emily updated her blog, sharing stories and insights from these experiences. Her posts were invitations to a wider audience to explore and embrace mindfulness, regardless of their background or circumstances.

In her journal that night, Emily reflected on the day's achievements and the journey ahead. She felt a deep connection to her purpose, a drive to continue breaking barriers and making mindfulness a universal tool for wellbeing. Her efforts were creating a ripple effect, reaching far beyond the walls of the community center, touching lives, and fostering a culture of inclusivity and compassion.

"In a world where every screen mirrors a soul, can the silence of a forest still be heard?"

Emily's blog, aptly named "Journey to Mindfulness," had quickly gained a following. Each post was a blend of personal anecdotes, practical advice, and philosophical musings, resonating with a wide audience seeking guidance and inspiration. Today, Emily decided to write about finding grace in chaos, a theme that mirrored her own experiences and the current state of the world.

As she typed, her words flowed effortlessly, painting a vivid picture of her journey from a life of relentless pace to one of mindful serenity. She shared stories of her struggles and triumphs, her moments of doubt, and her breakthroughs. Her narrative, deeply relatable, struck a chord with readers from all walks of life.

Alongside her blog, Emily had also ventured into social media. Her Instagram account, filled with inspiring quotes, snapshots of her daily life, and short videos of her meditation and yoga practices, had garnered a significant following. She used the platform to extend her reach, connecting with people across the globe, sharing snippets of wisdom and glimpses of her journey towards a more mindful existence.

One post, a video of Emily practicing yoga in a serene park setting, received an overwhelming response. Viewers were captivated not only by the physical aspect of her practice but also by the sense of peace that emanated from her. In the accompanying caption, Emily wrote about the importance of connecting with nature and finding moments of stillness within daily life. The comments section was filled with gratitude and stories of how her post had inspired others to find their own moments of tranquility.

In the following weeks, Emily dedicated time to engage with her online community. She responded to comments, shared resources, and even hosted live Q&A sessions. Her digital presence became a source of inspiration for many, a digital sanctuary where people could find support and guidance.

A local online magazine, intrigued by her growing influence, reached out for an interview. The article, titled "The Mindful Innovator," detailed Emily's journey and her mission to spread mindfulness. The feature amplified her reach, attracting more followers and sparking conversations about mental health and personal growth.

One evening, as Emily scrolled through the messages and comments from her readers, she realized the profound impact of her digital presence. People from different countries and backgrounds were connecting with her story, finding motivation in her words, and implementing her advice in their own lives. Her insights creating a ripple effect that extended far beyond her immediate physical community.

As she sat by her window, journal in hand, Emily reflected on this new chapter of her journey. Her digital platforms had become more than spaces to share content; they were extensions of her mission to foster a more mindful, compassionate world. She penned down her thoughts and feelings, acknowledging the responsibility and joy that came with her widening impact.

In her moments of introspection, Emily pondered the future of her digital journey. She envisioned expanding her content, perhaps introducing a podcast or a series of mindfulness workshops. Her goal was clear — to continue using these platforms to inspire, educate, and connect with a global community seeking a path to mindfulness and well-being.

Lying in bed that night, Emily felt a profound sense of gratitude. Her digital foray, initially just an extension of her personal journey, had become a powerful tool for change, touching lives and nurturing a community of like-minded individuals. She drifted off to sleep with a heart full of hope, eager to continue this journey of digital connection and impact.

"In a room filled with voices, can silence be the loudest sound?"

The soft hum of anticipation filled the auditorium as Emily stepped onto the stage, her presence immediately capturing the attention of the audience. This was her first major public speaking engagement, an opportunity to share her journey and insights at a prominent wellness seminar. The room, bathed in warm, inviting light, was filled with people from various walks of life, all gathered to hear Emily speak.

As Emily began her presentation, her voice was clear and resonant, carrying a sense of calm confidence. She opened with a personal anecdote, a story about her initial struggles with finding balance in life, and how this quest led her to embrace mindfulness and personal growth. The audience listened intently, drawn in by the authenticity and relatability of her story.

The theme of her talk was "The Art of Mindful Living," and as she plunged deeper into the topic, Emily skillfully wove together her personal experiences with practical advice. She spoke about the importance of self-awareness, the power of presence, and the transformative impact of adopting a mindful approach to everyday life. Her words were informative and deeply inspiring, encouraging listeners to reflect on their own lives and choices.

During the interactive segment of her talk, Emily engaged directly with the audience, fielding questions with thoughtfulness and empathy. One attendee asked about managing stress in a high-pressure work environment. Emily responded with insights from her own professional life, sharing strategies for maintaining calm and focus within the disorder. Her response resonated with many in the room, evident from the nods and murmurs of agreement.

The seminar concluded with a guided meditation led by Emily. As she instructed the audience to close their eyes and focus on their breathing, a collective sense of peace descended upon the room. It was a powerful moment, one that exemplified the essence of Emily's message — finding tranquility and clarity within oneself.

Following the seminar, Emily found herself surrounded by attendees, each eager to share their stories or seek further guidance. She listened and responded with genuine interest, her ability to connect with individuals on a personal level reinforcing her role as a guide and mentor.

Word of Emily's impactful presentation spread, leading to more invitations to speak at various workshops and conferences. She participated in a panel discussion at a mindfulness conference, where she discussed the intersection of technology and well-being. Her perspective, informed by her background in tech and her personal journey, offered a unique and valuable viewpoint that intrigued and enlightened the audience.

Her involvement in these public speaking engagements not only broadened her impact but also deepened her own understanding and practice. Each event was an opportunity for her to learn from others, to refine her message, and to further her mission of promoting mindfulness and personal growth.

"In a forest of unique trees, does the wind whisper the same song to each leaf?"

At the beginning of a subsequent workshop, the facilitator, a close friend of Emily's named Sarah, introduced herself. Sarah had been deeply influenced by Emily's path and had embarked on her own journey of self-discovery. She started the session with a brief recount of Emily's story, highlighting the pivotal moments that had led to her profound transformation.

"Emily's journey is a testament to the power of self-reflection and courage in the face of change," Sarah shared, her eyes shining with admiration and respect. The attendees listened, captivated by the account, seeing echoes of their own aspirations in Emily's story.

The workshop unfolded with discussions, activities, and exercises designed to encourage introspection and personal growth. Sarah guided the participants through a series of reflective questions, urging them to explore their values, their fears, and their dreams. The room was filled with a sense of openness and vulnerability, as people shared their stories and insights.

In a different part of the city, at a small coffee shop, a group of young professionals gathered around a table, animatedly discussing a blog post they had all read. The post, written by Emily, detailed her journey and the lessons she had learned along the way. It had resonated deeply with them, sparking conversations about their own life choices and goals.

One of the group members, a young woman named Ava, spoke about how Emily's story had inspired her to pursue a long-neglected passion for art. "Her journey made me realize that it's never too late to follow your dreams," Ava said, her voice filled with newfound determination.

Meanwhile, at a local university, a professor of psychology referenced Emily's journey in a lecture about personal development and mental well-being. The students listened intently, intrigued by the real-life example of the concepts they were studying. Emily's story served as a powerful illustration of the theories they were discussing, making the abstract ideas concrete and relatable.

As word of Emily's journey spread, more and more people found inspiration in her story. Book clubs discussed her blog posts, social media groups were formed to share insights inspired by her journey, and local communities organized events to promote self-awareness and growth.

One evening, as Emily walked home, she passed by the community center where the workshop inspired by her journey was taking place. She paused for a moment, observing the light and energy emanating from the building. A smile touched her lips as she realized the impact her story was having, far beyond her immediate circle.

Back in her apartment, Emily felt a sense of awe and humility at the thought of her personal journey inspiring others. Her story had become a catalyst, sparking a collective movement towards self-discovery and personal growth.

Emily's influence had transcended her immediate presence, touching the lives of people she had never met. Her journey had ignited a spark in others, encouraging them to embark on their own paths of self-exploration and transformation. As she journaled about these reflections, Emily felt a deep sense of connection and purpose, knowing that her journey was contributing to a larger narrative of growth and self-realization.

"In a room filled with mirrors, can one's reflection guide another's journey?"

In a small, sunlit office at Shiyuantech Solutions, Emily sat across from a young intern named Mia. The office was quiet, a stark contrast to the usual hum of activity. Today was special – it was the first official meeting in Emily's new role as a mentor in the company's personal development program.

Mia, a recent graduate with bright eyes and a nervous smile, fidgeted with her pen. "I'm just not sure which direction to take, Emily. I feel lost," she confessed, her voice tinged with uncertainty.

Emily's response was measured and kind, her experience as a mentor shining through. "Let's explore that together, Mia. Sometimes, understanding where we are lost can help us find our way," she said, her tone both comforting and encouraging.

They reached into a deep conversation, with Emily asking thoughtful questions that prompted Mia to reflect on her goals, fears, and passions. Emily shared anecdotes from her journey, offering insights without imposing her own views. Her guidance was like providing a flashlight, illuminating paths but allowing Mia the freedom to choose her own way.

Across town, in the community center adorned with vibrant art and cozy furniture, Emily led a group session for individuals seeking personal growth. She stood before the group, her presence commanding yet gentle. "Today, we'll explore the power of self-awareness," she announced, her voice resonating in the warm, inviting space.

The session unfolded with a series of interactive exercises designed to foster introspection and self-discovery. Emily moved among the participants, offering support and insights. Her ability to connect with each person, to hear their stories and offer tailored guidance, was remarkable.

Among the participants was an older gentleman, Richard, who had recently retired and found himself grappling with a loss of purpose. Emily sat beside him, listening intently as he shared his story. Her response was infused with empathy and wisdom, helping Richard explore new possibilities for this phase of his life.

Emily's mentorship extended beyond these structured sessions. She often received messages and emails from people who had been touched by her blog or public speaking engagements. Each message was met with a thoughtful response, her words a blend of encouragement and practical advice.

One such message came from a young woman, Elise, who had been inspired by Emily's story to embark on her own journey of self-discovery. They arranged to meet at a local café, a quiet spot where the clink of coffee cups and soft murmur of conversations created a backdrop for meaningful dialogue.

As they sat together, Emily's demeanor was attentive and nurturing. "It's about taking that first step, Elise. Trust in your journey," she advised, her own experiences providing a foundation for her guidance.

In these moments of mentorship, Emily's thoughts often reflected on the responsibility and privilege of guiding others. She pondered the delicate balance between offering support and empowering others to find their own strength.

As days turned into weeks, Emily's role as a mentor grew, touching the lives of many. Her office, the community center, the local café – these became spaces where conversations unfolded, where paths were explored, and where growth was nurtured.

"In a forest where different trees grow, can their roots entwine without losing their individual nature?"

In the tranquil early hours of a crisp autumn morning, Emily sat at her desk, bathed in the soft light filtering through her window. Her home office, a sanctuary of serenity and focus, was the perfect setting for the day's important task. She was preparing for a groundbreaking collaboration with other thought leaders in the wellness and personal development sphere.

Her computer screen displayed a list of names, each a renowned figure in their respective fields – from mindfulness coaches to motivational speakers. Emily felt a wave of excitement as she pondered the potential of this collaboration. Today, they were to have their first virtual meeting, setting the stage for a joint initiative that could revolutionize the way people approach personal growth and well-being.

As the clock struck the hour, Emily initiated the video call. One by one, the participants' faces appeared on her screen, each greeting the others with smiles and warm nods. The group included Julian, a yoga instructor known for his innovative approaches to mental health; Dr. Lena, a psychologist with a focus on holistic therapy; and Marcus, a life coach with a flair for motivational strategies.

"Thank you all for joining me today," Emily began, her voice calm yet filled with enthusiasm. "Our combined expertise has the potential to create something truly impactful. I believe together, we can bring new perspectives to those seeking growth and well-being."

The meeting unfolded with a vibrant exchange of ideas. Julian shared his vision of integrating yoga with mental health practices, while Dr. Lena discussed the importance of psychological frameworks in personal development. Marcus talked about the power of storytelling in motivating change. Emily listened intently, her mind alight with possibilities, interweaving her experiences with their ideas.

The collaboration took shape as they discussed creating a series of workshops and online content, blending their unique approaches into a holistic program. Emily proposed a series of webinars that would cover various aspects of well-being, from mindfulness and mental health to motivation and goal setting. The idea was met with unanimous enthusiasm.

As the meeting ended, the group had laid the groundwork for what promised to be a transformative collaboration. They agreed on a series of follow-up sessions to refine their approach and develop a cohesive strategy.

In the days that followed, Emily found herself immersed in this new venture. She spent hours brainstorming, planning, and coordinating with her collaborators. Her office became a hub of creativity and innovation, with notes and mind maps adorning the walls.

One afternoon, Emily met with Julian at a local park to discuss integrating mindfulness into physical wellness practices. They walked along the winding paths, surrounded by the vibrant colors of autumn, their conversation a lively blend of professional insights and personal experiences.

Later that week, Emily and Dr. Lena convened at a cozy tearoom to outline a framework for incorporating psychological well-being into their program. Over cups of steaming chai, they delved into discussions on emotional intelligence, resilience, and the importance of self-care.

The collaboration also led Emily to host a series of interviews on her blog, featuring each of her collaborators. These interviews offered her audience a glimpse into the diverse approaches to well-being and personal growth, further expanding her reach and impact.

As the collaborative project took shape, Emily's role as a connector and facilitator became increasingly evident. Her ability to bring together different perspectives and weave them into a cohesive narrative was a demonstration to her skills as a leader in the realm of personal development.

Each interaction, each planning session, was a step towards creating a platform that could change lives. Emily's vision of a collaborative approach to well-being was becoming a reality, a confluence of minds and talents dedicated to fostering growth, healing, and transformation.

"In a city of endless lights, does the single candle on the rooftop still make a difference?"

The sun was setting, casting a warm, golden hue over the city as Emily stood on the rooftop of her apartment building, gazing out at the sprawling urban landscape. This moment, like so many others in her life now, was reflective and filled with gratitude. Emily's journey of self-discovery and personal growth had touched the lives of countless others, creating a legacy of positive change.

In the quiet of the evening, Emily thought about the early days of her transformation, the challenges she had faced, and the milestones she had achieved. Each step on her path had been like a pebble dropped in a pond, the ripples extending far beyond her immediate reach.

Her mindfulness and meditation groups, once small gatherings in her living room, had grown into a thriving community. What started as a few interested individuals had blossomed into a network of people, each on their own journey towards self-improvement and inner peace. Emily had witnessed remarkable transformations within this group – from individuals overcoming personal challenges to forming deep, supportive relationships that transcended the sessions.

Emily's involvement in local initiatives had also flourished. She had become a recognized figure in promoting mindfulness and mental health in her community. Her collaborations with schools, healthcare centers, and local businesses had brought about a greater awareness of mental well-being and the importance of self-care. She had successfully bridged the gap between various demographics, making mindfulness practices accessible and relevant to all.

Her digital presence had expanded significantly. Emily's blog and social media platforms had become sources of inspiration and guidance for a global audience. Her posts, infused with personal anecdotes and practical advice, resonated with people from different walks of life. She received messages from followers around the world, sharing their stories of how her words had inspired them to embark on their paths of personal growth.

Emily's public speaking engagements had further amplified her impact. She had spoken at seminars, workshops, and conferences, sharing her experiences and insights. Her talks were not just speeches; they were conversations with her audience, engaging them in a dialogue about personal growth, resilience, and the power of positive change.

The most profound aspect of Emily's legacy was the inspiration she had instilled in others. People beyond her immediate circle had begun to take steps towards their self-discovery and personal growth, influenced by her journey. Emily had become a symbol of hope and transformation, demonstrating how one person's journey could spark a collective movement towards betterment.

In her role as a mentor, Emily had guided numerous individuals on their paths. Her empathetic and approachable nature made her an ideal figure for those seeking direction and support. She had become a beacon of wisdom and encouragement, helping others navigate their challenges and celebrate their triumphs.

Emily's collaborations with other thought leaders and wellness practitioners had created a synergy of ideas and practices. Together, they had developed programs and strategies that catered to a diverse range of needs, fostering well-being and personal growth on a larger scale.

As she stood there, Emily realized the magnitude of her journey. It was no longer about her transformation; it was about the collective growth and well-being she had helped cultivate. She had ignited a flame of positive change, a legacy that would continue to inspire and impact lives long into the future.

With a heart full of gratitude and a mind at peace, Emily turned to go back inside. Her journey was far from over; it was an ongoing process of learning, growing, and contributing. But at this moment, she knew she had made a difference, not just in her life but in the world around her.

Wisdom Gained Through Experience

"In the city's symphony, where each voice sings a different tune, how does silence teach the same lesson?"

Early one morning, Emily sat on the balcony of her apartment, a notebook in her hand and a contemplative look in her eyes. The city was slowly awakening, its myriad sounds and movements a beautiful backdrop of everyday life. For Emily, each sound, each movement, was a lesson, a reminder that wisdom was found in the very act of living.

Her balcony, overlooking the busy streets below, was her perch for reflection. Here, Emily often pondered the day ahead, thinking about the interactions and experiences that awaited her, each an opportunity for learning and growth. The chirping of birds, the rustling of leaves in the gentle breeze, and the distant hum of traffic all contributed to her thoughts, enriching her understanding of the world.

Later that day, Emily found herself in a lively market, the air filled with the aroma of fresh produce and the sounds of vendors and shoppers. She moved through the stalls, her senses alert to the vibrant colors and textures around her. Each interaction with the vendors, each exchange of smiles and pleasantries, was a lesson in human connection and the simple joys of everyday interactions.

In the afternoon, Emily visited a local nursing home, where she volunteered her time. As she sat with the elderly residents, listening to their stories, and sharing in their laughter and sometimes their tears, she found herself learning about resilience, about the passage of time, and the invaluable wisdom that comes with age. Their stories, rich with experiences and insights, were a testimony to the depth and diversity of life's lessons.

The evening saw Emily at a community meeting, where local residents gathered to discuss neighborhood issues. As she listened to the various concerns and opinions, Emily observed the dynamics of communication and negotiation. The meeting was both a forum for problem-solving and a live lesson in empathy, leadership, and the importance of community engagement.

Back in her apartment, Emily took time to reflect on the day's events. She wrote in her journal recording the day's occurrences and delving into the lessons each experience had imparted. Her writing was introspective, exploring the nuances of human behavior, the complexities of emotions, and the interconnectedness of all things.

She remembered an unexpected encounter with a young artist in the park that afternoon. The artist, with her bold colors and abstract designs, spoke to Emily about the courage to express oneself and the beauty of seeing the world through a different lens. This conversation led Emily to ponder the role of creativity and imagination in understanding the world.

Emily continued to embrace life's experiences as her greatest teachers. She engaged in conversations with strangers, observed the natural world, and even took up new hobbies, each providing unique insights and perspectives.

Her approach to life had become a rich mosaic of experiences, a blend of observation, participation, and reflection. Emily understood that wisdom was not a destination but a journey, one enriched by the diversity of life's experiences. Her path was one of continuous learning, a journey marked not by the accumulation of knowledge but by the depth of understanding gained through the act of living itself.

"In the stillness of dawn, where thoughts echo loudest, how does silence speak wisdom?"

The early morning hours found Emily in her favorite corner of her apartment, a space dedicated to reflection and introspection. Outside, the city was still asleep, wrapped in the quiet of dawn. Inside, Emily sat cross-legged on a comfortable cushion, a steaming cup of herbal tea by her side and her worn journal in her lap.

Today, she was looking into a reflective exercise, a regular practice that had become a cornerstone of her personal growth. The journal, filled with entries spanning years, was a chronicle of her journey - each page witness to her evolution. This morning, she decided to revisit some of her earlier entries, to understand and appreciate the depth of her transformation.

As she leafed through the pages, Emily's eyes fell upon an entry dated several years back, marked by a sense of struggle and uncertainty. Reading her own words, she recalled the challenges she faced during that period - the self-doubt, the fear of the unknown, and the overwhelming sense of being lost. Yet, within those lines of struggle, there was also a hint of determination, a budding recognition of her own resilience.

Turning the pages further, Emily observed the gradual shift in her tone and perspective. The entries began to reflect a growing sense of self-awareness, a newfound ability to embrace her vulnerabilities and transform them into strengths. It was fascinating for her to see how her past challenges, once overwhelming, had become valuable lessons, each contributing to her current state of wisdom and balance.

Midway through her journal, Emily found an entry that marked a significant turning point - the day she began her mindfulness practice. She remembered the initial difficulty of quieting her mind, the frustration of confronting her restless thoughts. But as she persisted, the practice had slowly woven itself into the fabric of her being, becoming a source of calm and clarity.

As the sun began to rise, casting a soft glow through her window, Emily reflected on the impact of these practices on her life. Her journey a continuous process of learning and unlearning, of adapting and evolving. It was a journey marked by moments of joy and pain, success, and failure, each equally important in shaping her path.

In this moment of reflection, Emily also pondered the future. She contemplated the possibilities that lay ahead, the lessons yet to be learned, and the experiences yet to be lived. Her journey a story still being written with each passing day.

Emily often shared her insights with others, whether it was through her blog, during her meditation sessions, or in casual conversations with friends. She believed in the power of sharing experiences, in the collective wisdom that emerged from open and honest dialogues.

As Emily closed her journal and sipped the last of her tea, she felt a deep sense of gratitude. The journey, with all its twists and turns, had brought her to a place of understanding and peace. It had taught her the importance of embracing every experience, the good and the bad, as integral parts of her growth.

With the city now awakening, Emily prepared for the day ahead, carrying with her the lessons of the past and the hope for the future. Her path of reflective understanding illuminating her way forward, and in turn, offering illumination to those who shared in her journey.

"Where many voices weave a single tapestry, how does one voice find its true echo?"

Amidst the clinking of coffee cups and the low hum of conversation, Emily sat across from a young woman named Clara. Clara, a recent college graduate, had reached out to Emily after reading her blog, seeking guidance on navigating the uncertainties of post-graduation life.

Emily listened attentively to Clara's concerns about the future, her fears of making the wrong choices, and her struggle to find a sense of direction. Emily's response was thoughtful and empathetic, mirroring her own experiences with similar challenges. She spoke of the times when she too had stood at life's crossroads, uncertain of which path to choose.

"Trust in the journey, even when the destination isn't clear," Emily advised, her voice a mix of assurance and understanding. "Each choice, each experience, whether it seems right or wrong at the time, is a step towards discovering who you are and what you truly want."

Their conversation dug into deeper topics, such as finding purpose and cultivating resilience. Emily shared anecdotes from her life, illustrating how embracing change and learning from failures had been crucial in shaping her path. Her words, reflections of a life lived with intention and awareness.

In all her interactions throughout the day Emily's approach was consistent - she shared her insights with a balance of empathy and realism, always drawing from her own journey. Her advice was not prescriptive but rather a sharing of wisdom gleaned from a life dedicated to personal growth and mindfulness.

"In the library's hush, where words are often silent, how does one voice echo through unseen struggles?"

In the softly lit ambiance of a local library's community room, Emily stood before a small, attentive audience. It was an intimate setting, perfect for the kind of honest, heart-to-heart conversation she was about to have. Today's talk was titled "The Unseen Struggles of Growth," a topic Emily had chosen to shed light on the often overlooked challenges of personal development.

As the attendees settled into their seats, Emily began her talk. Her voice was steady, imbued with the kind of authenticity that comes from lived experience. "Often, we see the results of growth, but not the struggles that forge it," she started, her gaze sweeping across the room, connecting with her audience.

She spoke about her past, recounting the early days of her journey when doubt and fear were constant companions. Emily described the sleepless nights filled with anxiety about the future, the overwhelming sense of being lost, and the painful process of letting go of long-held beliefs that no longer served her. Her honesty struck a chord with the audience, many of whom nodded in understanding, their own struggles mirrored in her words.

"In every challenge, there was a lesson," Emily continued, her tone shifting to one of reflection. She spoke of the critical turning points in her life, how confronting her fears and embracing uncertainty had been pivotal in her transformation. She emphasized that growth wasn't a linear journey but a series of ups and downs, each with its own set of lessons.

The floor was then opened for a Q&A session, and a young man raised his hand. "How do you find the strength to keep going when everything seems against you?" he asked, his voice tinged with the frustration of someone who was in the middle of his struggle.

Emily's response was thoughtful and empathetic. "It's about finding your 'why,'" she explained. "Your reason for moving forward, even when the path is obscured. For me, it was the belief that there was more to my life than my fears and doubts."

As the event ended, many attendees lingered, eager to speak with Emily personally. One woman, her eyes brimming with tears, shared how Emily's openness about her struggles had given her hope during a particularly challenging time in her life. Emily listened intently, offering words of encouragement, her presence a comfort.

The following week, Emily visited a high school to speak to a group of students about resilience and perseverance. Standing in the auditorium, she shared her story, focusing on the challenges she faced during her own school years — the pressure to succeed, the fear of failure, and the journey to self-acceptance.

Her message was clear: it's okay to struggle, it's okay to fail, and it's through these experiences that we grow. Her words resonated with the students, many of whom were grappling with their own pressures and expectations.

Lying in bed that night, Emily thought about the power of vulnerability. By sharing her struggles, she had not only connected with others but had also reaffirmed her own growth. She realized that acknowledging and embracing adversity was an integral part of her journey.

"In the park's whisper, where each step and chirp blends, how does one's path sing its own song?"

In the gentle glow of early evening, Emily walked along the winding path of a lush, serene park, her footsteps in harmony with the rhythmic chirping of the birds. She was on her way to a special event she had organized, titled "Embracing Your Journey." The event was designed to inspire and guide others in accepting and appreciating their life's path, just as she had learned to embrace hers.

As she arrived at the open-air pavilion, she was greeted by the sight of a diverse group of individuals, some familiar faces, others new, all united by a common quest for understanding and growth. The pavilion was set up with comfortable seating, arranged in a way that encouraged openness and connection among the attendees.

Emily began the session by sharing her own story, not just the highlights, but the struggles and uncertainties that had shaped her journey. She spoke of the times she felt lost, the moments of doubt, and the breakthroughs that came from facing her challenges head-on. Her honesty created a profound sense of trust and relatability in the air.

Emily emphasized the importance of embracing every aspect of one's journey. "Each experience, pleasant or difficult, shapes us," she explained. "It's about finding meaning in the highs and the lows, and understanding that every step, every detour, is part of a more colorful picture."

The conversation then shifted to a group discussion, where attendees were encouraged to share their experiences. One by one, people told of their fears, failures, and triumphs. A young artist spoke about the uncertainty of pursuing a creative career, a middle-aged man shared his experience with starting over after a career change, and a college student talked about the pressures of expectations.

Emily listened to each story, responding with empathy and insight. She offered perspective and gentle guidance, helping each person see the value in their unique journey. Her responses were reflections that encouraged deeper self-exploration.

The event concluded with a collaborative activity where attendees created a large mural, each contributing a symbol or word that represented a significant part of their journey. The activity was both a creative expression and a physical manifestation of the collective journeys and the shared human experience of growth and change.

Afterwards attendees lingered, not wanting to leave the supportive environment they had found. Connections were made, numbers exchanged, and plans to meet again were set in motion. Emily's event had sparked a sense of community and mutual support among those who had been strangers just a few hours before.

The next morning, Emily wrote a blog post about the event, sharing the insights and stories (with permission) that had emerged. Her post resonated with her readers, many of whom reached out to share their gratitude for her openness and the encouragement to embrace their own journeys.

As Emily read through the comments and messages, she realized the impact of her work. Her story illuminated the beauty and richness of life's journey, in all its forms. Her quest had taught her that embracing one's path, with all its ups and downs, was not just a part of gaining a deeper understanding of life; it was the essence of living fully.

Using Enlightenment to Help Others
"Entering the Marketplace with Helping Hands"

"In the quiet embrace of dawn, where does the light first touch the heart of the city?"

Emily, with the soft morning light streaming through her apartment windows, sat at her oak desk, her fingers poised over a notebook filled with ideas and plans. Her commitment to community service, now a vital part of her life, stirred a newfound purpose within her. Today, she was outlining a series of workshops aimed at introducing mindfulness practices to local schools. Her passion for these initiatives shone through every word she penned.

Later that day, Emily walked the familiar streets of her neighborhood, her steps light, her heart full. She had scheduled a meeting with the principal of a nearby school to discuss her workshop proposal. The school, an old brick building with a welcoming feel, stood as a symbol of potential growth and learning.

In the principal's office, surrounded by shelves of books and student artwork, Emily shared her vision. She spoke with clarity and conviction, her words infused with the wisdom of her journey. "Mindfulness can transform the way we approach challenges," she explained, her eyes reflecting her belief in every word. "It's not just a practice but a way of living, one that can greatly benefit our students."

The principal, a middle-aged man with a kind demeanor, listened intently, nodding occasionally. "It's an intriguing idea, Emily. Our students face so much stress these days. This could be a valuable tool for them."

Encouraged by his response, Emily detailed her plan, discussing potential schedules, resources needed, and her desire to make the workshops interactive and engaging. The principal agreed to pilot the program, promising to provide feedback and support.

As she left the school, a feeling of accomplishment washed over Emily. This was just the beginning, a small step in her broader mission to bring positive change to her community. She felt a deep connection to her surroundings, each step on the pavement resonating with her intent to serve.

Over the next few weeks, Emily immersed herself in organizing the mindfulness workshops. She collaborated with teachers, designed engaging activities, and even volunteered to lead the first few sessions herself. The workshops were well-received, with students eagerly participating and teachers noticing a positive shift in the classroom atmosphere.

During one of the sessions, a young girl named Raya approached Emily. "Miss Emily," she said shyly, "I feel calmer when I do the breathing exercises you taught us. It helps when I'm feeling sad about my grandma. She's been sick."

Emily knelt down, meeting Raya's eyes. "I'm so glad to hear that, Raya. Remember, you can do these exercises anytime you feel upset. They're a way to find a quiet space inside you, even when things are tough."

As Raya smiled and ran off to join her friends, Emily felt a surge of fulfillment. Her own journey, once solitary and introspective, was now creating ripples in the lives of others.

That evening, back in her apartment, Emily reflected on the day's events. The joy in Raya's eyes, the enthusiasm of the students, the support of the teachers – all these moments were threads in the fabric of her journey. She realized that her path was about sharing the light of her own journey with others, helping them find their way through the complexities of life.

As she gazed out at the city skyline, Emily knew that her journey was evolving, taking on new dimensions and meanings. With each person she helped, each life she touched, she was living her enlightenment but more importantly spreading it, like a beacon of hope in a world that so desperately needed it.

"In a world connected by invisible threads, what illuminates the path from one heart to another?"

Emily stood before a large, interactive digital board in the well-lit community center, a hum of engaged conversation filling the room. Around her were people from all walks of life, gathered to explore the new platform she had developed - an online portal dedicated to mental health, mindfulness, and personal growth. This evening was its launch, a culmination of her efforts to create a resource that was both accessible and transformative.

The portal, named "The Mindful Path," was a vibrant mosaic of resources - interactive forums, guided meditation sessions, articles on mental wellness, and personal growth stories. Emily had poured her expertise as a software developer into this project, ensuring it was user-friendly, engaging, and, most importantly, beneficial.

As attendees navigated through "The Mindful Path" on tablets set up around the room, Emily watched their reactions. A middle-aged man, his face usually etched with worry, lit up as he explored a section on stress management. A group of college students gathered around a module on mindfulness techniques, their youthful energy palpable. An elderly woman, her fingers trembling slightly, paused at a video on meditation for seniors.

Emily approached the woman. "How do you find it?" she asked gently.

"It's wonderful," the woman replied, her eyes moist. "I've always wanted to learn meditation, but I didn't know where to start. This... this gives me a chance."

Their conversation delved into the woman's life, her challenges, and how she hoped to find some peace through the portal. Emily listened, her heart swelling with empathy and purpose. Each story she heard that evening reaffirmed her belief in what she was doing.

Later, as the crowd thinned, Emily gathered with a small team of volunteers who had helped bring her vision to life. They shared feedback from the attendees, brainstorming ways to enhance the portal's reach and impact. Ideas flowed freely - from organizing live webinars to collaborating with local schools for mental health workshops.

The evening wound down with a sense of accomplishment and a shared vision for the future. As Emily locked up the community center, her mind was abuzz with ideas and plans. The portal was just the beginning. She envisioned a series of workshops, perhaps even a podcast, to further spread awareness and tools for mental and emotional well-being.

As she walked home, Emily pondered the profound interconnectedness of all beings. Her own journey of self-discovery had led her here, to a place where she could facilitate growth and healing in others. It was a responsibility she embraced wholeheartedly.

Back in her apartment, Emily closed her eyes, letting the events of the day wash over her. In her mind's eye, she saw the faces of those she had interacted with, each carrying their own story, their own struggles. And in that moment, she realized the true scope of her mission. It wasn't about creating digital platforms or organizing workshops; it was about touching lives, one soul at a time.

"How does the whisper of one heart find its echo in another amid life's symphony?"

Emily sat across from a young woman named Zoe at her neighborhood café. Zoe, in her early twenties, exuded a mix of eagerness and apprehension. She had reached out to Emily after attending one of her mindfulness workshops, seeking guidance on her emerging journey of self-discovery.

Emily chose it for its relaxed atmosphere, which encouraged open and heartfelt conversations. Today, the café buzzed with the energy of the morning rush, yet in their quiet corner, it felt like a private refuge.

Zoe fidgeted with her coffee cup, her eyes reflecting the turmoil within. "I just feel so lost," she began, her voice barely above a whisper. "I thought I knew what I wanted in life, but now, everything seems so uncertain."

Emily listened intently, her expression one of understanding and compassion. "It's okay to feel lost, Zoe. Sometimes, it's in those moments of uncertainty that we find our true path."

Emily shared snippets of her own journey. She spoke of her initial struggles, the moments of doubt, and how she gradually found her footing. Her words were reflective, offering Zoe a mirror to her own experiences.

"You don't have to have all the answers right now," Emily advised. "Give yourself permission to explore, to question, and to learn. Your path will unfold in its own time."

Zoe's expression softened, a hint of relief in her eyes. She asked questions about meditation, about dealing with societal pressures, and finding inner peace. Emily responded with gentle wisdom, interspersing her guidance with philosophical insights.

At one point, Emily shared a poignant memory of her mentor, Mrs. Kaur. "She once told me," Emily recalled, "that every experience, no matter how trivial it seems, holds a lesson. It's up to us to find the wisdom in it."

The conversation shifted to practical tips for integrating mindfulness into daily life. Emily suggested simple exercises, like mindful breathing and journaling, to help Zoe stay grounded.

As their meeting ended, Zoe expressed her gratitude, her initial apprehension replaced by a sense of hope. "Thank you, Emily. This has been really helpful."

Emily smiled, a sense of fulfillment washing over her. "I'm here for you, Zoe. Remember, this journey is yours, and it's as unique as you are."

Emily felt a deep connection to the world around her. The clink of coffee cups, the hum of conversation, the soft patter of rain against the café windows - it all resonated with a profound sense of being. Her journey had brought her here, to this moment, where she could serve as an example for others.

As she stood up to leave, Emily's mind was already on her next meeting, another soul seeking guidance. With each step, she carried with her the wisdom of her experiences, ready to share it with whoever crossed her path. Within the responsibility of mentorship and learning, Emily found her purpose, a purpose that extended far beyond her own enlightenment, reaching into the hearts and minds of others, helping them navigate the winding pathway of their lives.

"In a forest where each tree grows in different soils, how do their roots know the same earth?"

Later in the week, Emily visited a local university. She had been invited to collaborate with the education department to integrate mindfulness practices into their curriculum. The university, with its sprawling campus and vibrant student life.

In the lecture hall, seated with a group of educators, Emily discussed ways to incorporate mindfulness into the classroom. She proposed techniques like mindful listening, meditation breaks, and stress management workshops. The educators, enthusiastic and open-minded, shared their experiences with student anxiety and burnout, affirming the need for such practices.

One professor, a bespectacled man with a thoughtful demeanor, shared, "We've been so focused on academic achievements that we sometimes overlook the emotional well-being of our students. Your ideas could be the change we need."

As the meeting wrapped up, they agreed to start a pilot program. Emily's excitement was evident. To see her vision taking root in educational institutions was verification to the universality of her message.

That evening, as Emily walked through the university's campus, she reflected on the day's achievements. The conversations she had, the plans laid out, all were steps towards a larger goal – a world where mindfulness and compassion were integral to every aspect of life.

Her mind buzzed with ideas for future collaborations. Hospitals, non-profits, even government agencies – the possibilities were endless. With each partnership, she was weaving a fabric of change, impacting lives in ways both big and small.

In this journey of transforming societies one institution at a time, Emily found her true calling. It was about creating environments where people could thrive, find peace, and connect deeply with themselves and others. And as the sun set over the university, casting a golden glow on the buildings, Emily felt a deep sense of purpose and gratitude. She was not just walking a path of enlightenment; she was paving it for others to follow.

"In a garden where seeds of mindfulness are sown, how do the trees of understanding grow in silence?"

Emily Nguyen was embarking on a new chapter of her mission. Today, she was meeting with a team of public school educators, each dedicated to nurturing the young minds under their care. The school, a blend of tradition and innovation, was an ideal setting for Emily's latest endeavor: integrating mindfulness and compassion into the educational curriculum.

The meeting took place in a classroom, temporarily transformed into a collaborative space. Desks were arranged in a circle, fostering a sense of equality and openness among the participants. The room was filled with an air of earnest anticipation, as teachers and administrators alike recognized the potential impact of this initiative on their students' well-being.

Emily began the session with a heartfelt introduction, her tone gentle and persuasive. "Our children are growing up in a world that's more complex and demanding than ever before," she said, her gaze sweeping across the room. "By integrating mindfulness and emotional intelligence into our teaching, we can equip them with tools to navigate this world with resilience and empathy."

The educators listened, their expressions a mix of curiosity and contemplation. Emily proceeded to outline her vision: a curriculum that included daily mindfulness exercises, lessons on emotional regulation, and activities that encouraged compassion and self-awareness.

One teacher, a seasoned educator with years of experience, raised a hand. "How can we ensure these practices are effective and not just another task for the students?"

Emily acknowledged the concern with a nod. "It's about integration, not addition," she explained. "For instance, a few minutes of mindful breathing before a test can help students focus and reduce anxiety. Discussions about emotions can be woven into literature classes. It's about making these practices a natural part of their learning experience."

The discussion that followed was lively and productive. Teachers shared insights from their classrooms, discussing the challenges and needs of their students. Emily listened and responded, her suggestions a blend of practicality and compassion.

As the meeting ended, the group agreed to pilot a mindfulness program. Emily offered to conduct training sessions for the teachers, equipping them with the skills and confidence to bring these practices into their classrooms.

In the weeks that followed, Emily's vision began to take shape. She spent days at the school, leading workshops for teachers, sitting in on classes to observe and advise, and engaging with students. Her presence in the hallways, always calm and attentive, became a familiar and welcome sight.

The impact of the program was soon evident. In classrooms where mindfulness exercises were practiced, teachers reported a noticeable improvement in students' focus and participation. Students themselves shared feelings of calmness and clarity, and instances of conflict and tension in the schoolyard began to decrease.

Emily organized parent workshops, educating them on mindfulness and emotional intelligence, and how these practices could be reinforced at home. The response was overwhelmingly positive, with many parents expressing gratitude for the new insights and tools to support their children's development.

One afternoon, as Emily walked through the school garden, a group of students approached her. They were eager to share their experiences with the mindfulness exercises. "I don't get so angry anymore," one boy said, his eyes bright with the revelation. "I remember to breathe and think first."

These moments, these small yet profound revelations, were the true markers of success for Emily. As she listened to the students, her heart swelled with hope and fulfillment. She realized that she was helping shape a generation more aware, more compassionate, and better equipped to face the challenges of life.

At the playground, Emily stood for a moment, taking it all in. This was more than a project or an initiative; it was a movement, one that had the power to transform lives from the very foundation. And she was at the heart of it, her own journey of mindfulness and compassion now interwoven with the journeys of these young, vibrant souls.

"In a world where mind and heart converge, what whispers are heard in the silence of two clasped hands?"

Emily Nguyen sat in a favorite restaurant, the gentle clinking of cups and the low murmur of conversations creating a soothing backdrop. Across from her sat Dr. Anika Patel, a renowned psychologist, and advocate for mental health. They were there to discuss a partnership, one that would merge Emily's mindfulness expertise with Dr. Patel's deep understanding of mental health.

The restaurant, with its rustic charm and ambient lighting, was a place where ideas and collaborations came to life. Emily chose it for its serene atmosphere, conducive to meaningful discussions. Today, the restaurant was alive with the energy of midday patrons, but in their quiet corner, the world seemed to slow down, allowing space for their conversation.

Dr. Patel, a woman in her late forties with a warm, approachable demeanor, listened intently as Emily outlined her vision. "I believe that by combining our skills and knowledge, we can create a more holistic approach to wellness," Emily explained, her eyes alight with passion. "Your expertise in mental health and my experience in mindfulness can offer a comprehensive resource for individuals seeking balance and well-being."

Dr. Patel nodded, her expression reflecting a mix of interest and contemplation. "I've always believed in a multidisciplinary approach to mental health," she responded. "Your work in mindfulness is impressive. I think there's a lot we can do together."

They probed into the specifics of their partnership. The plan was to develop a series of workshops and online resources that addressed both mental health and mindfulness. They discussed the integration of therapeutic techniques with mindfulness exercises, aiming to offer a more rounded approach to mental health.

As the meeting progressed, Emily and Dr. Patel brainstormed ideas, each suggestion sparking new possibilities. They talked about hosting joint seminars, creating digital content, and even co-authoring a series of articles.

The conversation then shifted to the logistics of their collaboration - scheduling, resource allocation, and outreach strategies. They decided to start with a pilot workshop, combining mindfulness practices with cognitive-behavioral techniques, a blend of their respective fields.

As the restaurant's patrons ebbed and flowed, their meeting ended with a sense of accomplishment and anticipation. They parted with a firm handshake, each excited about the potential impact of their joint venture.

Over the following weeks, Emily and Dr. Patel worked tirelessly. They met regularly, either in the restaurant or Dr. Patel's office, fleshing out their ideas into tangible plans. Their collaboration was a harmony of different perspectives, each bringing their unique strengths to the table.

The day of the pilot workshop arrived. Held in a local community center, the room was set up to foster a relaxed and open environment. The attendees were a diverse group, some grappling with stress and anxiety, others simply seeking ways to enhance their well-being.

Emily led the session with a mindfulness exercise, her voice soothing and steady. Dr. Patel followed, seamlessly integrating psychological insights that complemented the mindfulness practice. The synergy between them was palpable, their respective approaches intertwining to offer a richer, more comprehensive understanding of mental wellness.

The feedback from the participants was overwhelmingly positive. Many expressed how the combination of mindfulness and psychological insights had provided them with new tools to manage their mental health.

Buoyed by the success of their first workshop, Emily and Dr. Patel planned more events and began working on their online content. Their partnership had sparked a new wave of wellness initiatives, each drawing from a well of diverse knowledge and experience.

Emily reflecting on the journey that had led her to this collaboration. Each step, each partnership, was evidence to the power of combining different perspectives for a common goal. Her path had evolved from a personal quest to a collective mission, bringing together minds and hearts in the pursuit of holistic wellness.

"Where does the river of calm flow in a world of relentless currents?"

In the spacious community hall, Emily Nguyen, with her serene demeanor and a warm, welcoming smile, was preparing to host her latest workshop. This event, titled "Journey to Empowerment: Managing Stress Through Mindfulness," was part of her ongoing commitment to bring meaningful change to her community.

As participants began to arrive, the hall transformed into a mosaic of diverse lives, each person bringing their unique story and struggles. There were young professionals, their faces etched with the pressures of corporate life; parents seeking a moment of peace away from the chaos of family life; retirees looking to find new purpose in their golden years; and even a few college students, their youthful eyes reflecting the anxiety of future uncertainties.

Emily greeted each participant at the door, making a point to exchange a few words with everyone. Her ability to connect, to make each person feel seen and acknowledged, set the tone for the workshop.

The seminar began with a brief introduction from Emily, who stood at the front of the hall, her presence both commanding and comforting. She spoke of the challenges everyone faces in managing stress and the power of mindfulness in transforming how we experience life's pressures.

"Stress isn't just about what happens to us," she explained, her voice clear and steady, "but also about how we respond to it. Mindfulness offers us a way to change that response, to bring a sense of calm and clarity to our lives."

The first half of the workshop focused on theoretical understanding. Emily discussed the science behind stress and the principles of mindfulness, using a blend of storytelling and factual information to make the concepts accessible and engaging. Her words were interspersed with quotes from renowned mindfulness practitioners, adding depth and context to her message.

As the workshop progressed, Emily shifted to more interactive exercises. She guided the group through a series of mindfulness practices, including deep breathing techniques and a short meditation session. The room, filled with the sound of synchronized breathing, took on a meditative quality, a collective experience of tranquility.

After the meditation, Emily facilitated a group discussion, encouraging participants to share their experiences and insights. The conversation flowed freely, with many expressing how the session had brought them a sense of peace they hadn't felt in a long time.

One participant, a middle-aged man with a weary look, shared, "I always thought meditation wasn't for me. But this... this was different. I felt like I could just let go of everything for a moment."

Emily listened, her responses thoughtful and empathetic, validating each person's experience. She then moved on to practical applications of mindfulness in daily life, offering tips on integrating these practices into everyday routines.

As the workshop neared its end, Emily opened the floor for a Q&A session. The questions were varied – from how to deal with stress at work to maintaining mindfulness in challenging family dynamics. Emily addressed each query with her characteristic blend of wisdom and practicality.

The event concluded with a sense of collective achievement. Participants lingered, some approaching Emily for personal advice, others simply wanting to express their gratitude. The impact of the workshop was evident in their expressions – a mix of relief, inspiration, and newfound hope.

As the hall emptied, Emily took a moment to reflect on the day. Each workshop, each seminar was a step towards fulfilling her vision – a vision of a world where mindfulness and compassion were not just concepts, but a lived reality. Her journey had led her to this point, where she was not just sharing her knowledge but also facilitating real, tangible change in people's lives.

"In the city's heart, where steel and ambition entwine, can a single seed of mindfulness transform the concrete jungle?"

In the heart of a metropolitan city, within the walls of a prominent corporate office, Emily Nguyen was making strides in influencing a significant shift in institutional culture. Her efforts, focused on integrating mindfulness and emotional well-being into the workplace, had started to yield tangible results.

The office, a symbol of traditional corporate success with its sleek design and imposing stature, had begun to embrace a new ethos. Emily had been working closely with the HR department to implement a series of wellness programs, and today marked the launch of their most ambitious project yet – a comprehensive wellness initiative that included mindfulness training, stress management workshops, and regular 'well-being hours.'

As employees gathered in the spacious atrium, transformed for the occasion with soothing colors and comfortable seating, there was an air of curiosity. The usual buzz of corporate activity had given way to a more reflective atmosphere. Emily, standing near a makeshift stage, could feel the shift in energy.

The event kicked off with a keynote speech from the CEO, a figure more known for his stern business acumen than his advocacy for mental health. Yet, his address today was a departure from the norm. "The well-being of our employees is not just a matter of productivity; it's about creating a workplace that values and nurtures each individual," he said, his words echoing Emily's influence.

Emily then took the stage, her presence commanding yet serene. She spoke about the importance of mental and emotional health, not just as a personal responsibility but as a collective one. "When we take care of our minds, we are better equipped to face challenges, both professionally and personally," she explained.

Following her speech, Emily led the group through a guided meditation session. The atrium, usually resonating with the sound of ringing phones and clicking keyboards, was now filled with the collective breath of dozens of employees. The meditation concluded to a round of soft applause, many faces reflecting a sense of peace and surprise at the experience.

The rest of the event was filled with workshops and interactive sessions. Employees engaged in discussions about stress management, participated in mindfulness exercises, and shared their personal experiences with mental health.

One particularly impactful session was a panel discussion featuring employees who had been practicing mindfulness for some time. They shared their stories of transformation, how these practices had improved their work-life balance, relationships, and overall well-being. Their testimonials, genuine and heartfelt, resonated deeply with their colleagues.

In the following weeks, the impact of the wellness initiative became increasingly evident. Meetings began with brief mindfulness exercises, 'well-being hours' were actively utilized, and conversations about mental health became more open and frequent.

Emily's work in the corporate office had started a ripple effect, reaching beyond the confines of the company. Other businesses in the area, hearing of the success of the program, reached out to Emily for guidance on implementing similar initiatives.

Meanwhile, in educational institutions where Emily had introduced mindfulness programs, similar changes were taking place. Schools reported improved student engagement, a decrease in disciplinary issues, and a more compassionate school culture. Teachers incorporated mindfulness into their lessons, and students practiced techniques to manage stress and anxiety.

Through her persistent efforts, Emily was influencing institutional change on a broader scale. Her work was contributing to a shift in societal norms, where mental and emotional well-being were becoming integral components of institutional practices.

Emily reflected on these achievements. Sitting in her apartment, gazing out at the city lights, she felt a profound sense of fulfillment. Her journey, which had started as a personal quest for meaning, had evolved into a movement, impacting lives and reshaping institutions. She realized that the true measure of her success was not just in the programs she had implemented, but in the seeds of change she had sown, seeds that were now beginning to bear fruit in ways she had never imagined.

"Where growth blooms from your touch, can a garden of mindfulness outshine the concrete sprawl?"

Emily walked down the vibrant streets that had become her canvas for change. The community, once just a backdrop to her solitary journey, was now intricately woven into the fabric of her life's work. Her dedication to promoting health, mindfulness, and personal growth had not only transformed the lives of many but had also elevated her to a position of respect and admiration in the community.

As she passed by the familiar storefronts and cafés, people greeted her with warm smiles and friendly nods. To them, Emily wasn't just a neighbor; she was a symbol of positive transformation, a beacon of hope and inspiration. The local café owner, Mrs. Marquez, waved from her doorway. "Emily, thank you for your last seminar. My customers still talk about it. You've brought something special to our community."

Emily's work had extended beyond workshops and seminars. She had initiated a community garden project, turning a neglected plot of land into a thriving green space where people could connect with nature and each other. The garden, lush with vegetables and flowers, was a tribute to the community's collective effort and Emily's vision of a healthier, more connected neighborhood.

The local school had also benefited from Emily's influence. Following the mindfulness programs she had introduced; the school had seen a noticeable improvement in student well-being and behavior. Teachers frequently invited her to speak at events, and she had become a role model for students, embodying the principles of mindfulness and compassion she taught.

One evening, at a community meeting held in the school auditorium, Emily was invited to speak about her upcoming initiatives. The auditorium was filled with residents from all walks of life, each drawn by a shared interest in Emily's message and the positive changes it had brought.

Standing on the stage, Emily looked out at the sea of faces, feeling a deep connection to each person in the room. "Our community is a tapestry of stories, each thread as important as the next," she began, her voice resonant and clear. "Together, we've started weaving a new story, one of health, mindfulness, and growth."

She unveiled her plans for more community-based programs, including a series of wellness retreats and a mentorship program for young adults. The audience listened intently, their engagement evident in their nodding heads and thoughtful expressions.

A young woman in the audience, a high school student who had attended several of Emily's workshops, raised her hand during the Q&A session. "Emily, your work has changed my life. How can we, as young people, get more involved and help spread this message?"

Emily's response was heartfelt. "Your generation has a powerful voice. Use it to share your experiences, to inspire others. Get involved in projects like the community garden or start your own. Every small action creates ripples."

The meeting ended with a standing ovation for Emily, a recognition of her impact and leadership. As people approached her with words of thanks and stories of how her work had touched their lives, Emily felt a profound sense of fulfillment.

Walking home that night, Emily reflected on her journey. What had begun as a personal search for meaning had evolved into a communal crusade for a better, healthier way of living. She had become a catalyst for change, inspiring others to take up the mantle and join in the collective effort to transform their lives and community.

Resolution

"In the quiet of dawn, where thoughts and steps synchronize, can a runner's path lead both inward and onward?"

In the early hours of a crisp morning, Alex Chen, a close friend, and colleague of Emily, laced up his running shoes, his breath visible in the cool air. The city was just waking up, its streets quiet and serene. Alex had embarked on his own journey of personal wellness, a path inspired by Emily but tailored to his own needs and interests.

As he jogged through the tree-lined streets, Alex felt a sense of clarity and purpose. Running had become a form of meditation for him, a way to clear his mind and center himself. He had always been an advocate for physical fitness, but now his approach was different. It was no longer just about staying in shape; it was a pursuit of overall well-being, a balance of body and mind.

After his run, Alex headed to a local coffee shop, a cool little spot he frequented for its quiet atmosphere and healthy menu. Over a breakfast of oatmeal and fresh fruit, he pulled out a book on psychological self-help, one of many he had been exploring. These books, covering topics from emotional intelligence to stress management, had opened a new world of understanding for him.

As he read, he thought about how these insights were changing his perspective on life. He was learning to manage his emotions better, to understand his thought patterns, and to respond to life's challenges with a more balanced approach. This psychological aspect of his wellness journey was as crucial as the physical one. It was a holistic approach, combining the strength of the body with the resilience of the mind.

Later in the day, Alex attended a mindfulness workshop led by Emily. The workshop, held in a peaceful community center decorated with calming colors and soft lights, was a gathering of diverse individuals, each on their own journey of personal growth.

Emily led the group through a series of mindfulness exercises, her voice soothing and steady. Alex, along with the others, followed her guidance, practicing deep breathing and mindful awareness. These sessions had become a regular part of his routine, a practice that complemented his physical and psychological explorations.

As the session ended, Alex stayed back to chat with Emily. They sat on a couple of comfortable chairs in the corner of the room, a space that felt detached from the rest of the world. "Your workshops have been a revelation, Emily," Alex shared, his tone sincere. "They've brought a sense of peace to my life that I didn't know I was missing."

Emily smiled, her eyes reflecting the joy of seeing a friend find his path. "I'm glad, Alex. It's about finding what works for you, what resonates with your soul."

Their conversation flowed effortlessly, touching on various aspects of wellness and personal growth. Alex spoke of his running, his reading, and his newfound appreciation for mindfulness. Emily listened, offering insights and encouragement.

As the sun began to set, casting a warm glow through the windows of the community center, Alex felt a deep sense of gratitude. His journey, inspired by Emily but shaped by his own desires and curiosities, was a tribute to the power of personal exploration.

Walking back home, Alex felt a harmonious blend of physical tiredness and mental tranquility. His journey had taught him the importance of nurturing all aspects of his being – the physical, the mental, and the spiritual. It was a journey of discovery, of pushing boundaries, and of finding balance.

In his small but cozy apartment, Alex penned down his thoughts in a journal, a practice he had adopted to reflect on his daily experiences. He wrote about his run, his readings, and the insights from Emily's workshop. Each entry was a step in his journey, a journey that was as unique as it was transformative.

Alex's path to wellness, influenced by Emily but carved by his own choices, was a journey of integration – of the body, the mind, and the spirit. It was a journey that was continuously evolving, just like him.

"In the dance of friendship, where paths intertwine and grow, can two seekers sharing the same bench see different horizons?"

In a local park, where the gentle rustling of leaves harmonized with the distant chatter of children playing, Emily Nguyen and Alex Chen sat on a worn wooden bench, their conversation a blend of reflection and camaraderie. The park, a familiar retreat for both, had witnessed many such meetings between the two friends, each encounter strengthening the bond of their friendship and shared journey.

The afternoon sun cast dappled shadows on the path, and a mild breeze carried the faint aroma of blossoming flowers. Emily and Alex were engrossed in a discussion about their recent experiences, each eager to share and learn from the other.

"I've started incorporating yoga into my routine," Alex said, his tone infused with enthusiasm. "It's amazing how it aligns so well with the mindfulness practices you've taught me."

Emily smiled, her eyes reflecting genuine interest. "Yoga is a beautiful way to connect the mind and body. I'm glad you've found it helpful," she replied. Her encouragement was always a source of motivation for Alex.

As they talked, their conversation wandered through various topics – from the challenges they faced in implementing their wellness strategies, to the small victories that kept them going. Emily shared her experiences with the latest series of workshops she had conducted, emphasizing the transformative stories of some of her participants.

"It's incredible to see the impact these workshops have," Emily remarked, a hint of pride in her voice. "There's this one participant who said the stress management techniques have changed her life. It's moments like these that remind me why I started this journey."

Alex listened intently, nodding in agreement. "And it's your guidance that inspired my own journey, Emily. Your workshops, our talks – they've been a cornerstone of my growth."

Their conversation took a deeper turn as they examined the philosophical aspects of their practices. They discussed the concept of interconnectedness, how their individual growth was not just a personal achievement, but part of a larger, communal evolution.

"As we grow individually, we contribute to the collective consciousness of our community," Emily mused, her gaze drifting to the families and individuals enjoying the park. "Our personal journeys have ripple effects, far beyond what we see."

Alex reflected on this, his mind connecting the dots between his personal changes and the broader impact on his relationships and work environment. "It's like we're all threads in a single tapestry," he added. "Our individual colors and textures add to the beauty of the whole."

The conversation shifted to future plans, with both sharing their aspirations and upcoming projects. Emily spoke about expanding her wellness initiatives to reach more diverse groups, while Alex expressed his desire to explore new dimensions of psychological self-help.

As the sun began its descent, casting a golden hue over the park, Emily and Alex stood up to leave. Their meetings always ended with a sense of renewed purpose and deepened understanding.

Walking out of the park, their steps in sync, they knew that their journeys were not parallel paths but intertwined ones, each influencing and enriching the other. Their friendship had evolved into a deep connection, a demonstration of the values of mutual support and growth.

In the quiet of the evening, as they parted ways, Emily and Alex carried with them the insights from their conversation, along with the warmth of a friendship that was a constant source of strength and inspiration. In each other, they had found a fellow traveler on the journey of life.

"In the embrace of familial roots, where understanding blossoms in the heart's soil, can a tree grow tall yet still feel the warmth of its seed's cradle?"

In the warmth of her family home, nestled in the suburbs, where the chatter of neighborhood life blended with the rustling of trees, Emily experienced a profound moment of connection and understanding. The house, with its familiar furnishings and the comforting scent of her mother's cooking, had always been a place of love, though not always of complete understanding. But today, as Emily sat around the dining table with her family, there was a tangible sense of change in the air.

The evening had begun with a casual family dinner, a routine gathering that had now taken on new significance. Emily's parents and her younger brother, Michael, gathered around the table, laden with dishes that were a reminder of their cultural heritage and familial love. The conversations, once dominated by small talk and surface-level updates, had gradually evolved to more meaningful exchanges, mirroring the deepening relationships among them.

As they enjoyed the meal, the topic naturally drifted to Emily's work and her growing role in the community. Her father, a man of few words but deep thoughts, expressed his admiration for her dedication. "Emily, we've been reading about your workshops in the local paper. Your mother and I are proud of how you're helping people find peace in their lives."

Emily, touched by her father's words, shared some of the recent experiences from her initiatives, explaining how her journey was not just about personal growth but also about fostering a collective consciousness. Her mother listened, her eyes reflecting a mix of pride and newfound understanding.

"It's wonderful to see you so passionate about your work, dear," her mother said, a soft smile gracing her lips. "I remember when you first started exploring mindfulness, we didn't quite understand it. But now, seeing the impact you're making, it's truly inspiring."

Michael, always the more skeptical one, chimed in, his tone playful yet curious. "I have to admit, sis, I didn't get all this mindfulness stuff at first. But I tried some of those breathing exercises you talked about, and they actually helped with my exam stress."

The conversation flowed, weaving through past misunderstandings, and leading to a deeper appreciation of each other's perspectives. Emily shared stories from her workshops, while her family listened, engaging with genuine interest, and asking thoughtful questions.

At one point, the discussion turned to a past tension – a period when Emily's spiritual path had seemed at odds with the family's traditional values. Her father, clearing his throat, addressed it with a sincerity that moved Emily.

"Emily, we may not have always understood your choices, but we've always wanted what's best for you. Seeing you now, so fulfilled and making a difference, it's clear you've found your path. We respect and support that."

The air in the room grew thick with emotion as Emily responded, her voice laced with gratitude. "Thank you, Dad, Mom, Michael. Your support means everything to me. My journey has taught me so much about our family's strength and love."

As dinner concluded, the family lingered at the table, reluctant to break the warmth of the moment. They laughed, reminisced, and planned future gatherings, each feeling a renewed sense of closeness.

That evening, as Emily helped her mother clear the table, a feeling of contentment enveloped her. The journey with her family, once marked by subtle tensions and misunderstandings, had blossomed into a relationship of mutual respect and admiration. Her spiritual path had not only transformed her but had also woven a deeper understanding and connection into the fabric of her family life.

In the quiet of her old bedroom, now a comforting sanctuary of memories and dreams, Emily reflected on the evening. She realized that her family's acceptance and support were integral to her journey, just as her journey had become a bridge, reconnecting her to her family in a more profound and meaningful way. This deepening of family relationships was as much a part of her spiritual growth as her workshops and meditations – a reminder that the journey to self-discovery and community impact was also about cherishing and nurturing the bonds that had supported her from the very beginning.

"In a room where ideas clash like waves against a cliff, does the tide of change erode old beliefs, or does understanding carve a new path in the stone?"

In the modern, glass-paneled conference room of Shiyuantech Solutions, where the hum of technology and the rhythm of corporate life melded seamlessly, a significant meeting was underway. Emily and Michael, the project manager with whom she had a longstanding professional conflict, were seated across from each other, a table laden with project reports and plans between them. The tension that once characterized their interactions had given way to an atmosphere charged with the possibility of resolution and understanding.

The meeting had been initiated by Michael, a shift, considering their past interactions. He had witnessed the positive changes brought about by Emily's wellness initiatives in the workplace and had begun to see the value in her approach. The room, often a witness to debates and disagreements, was now the setting for a dialogue of reconciliation and progress.

"Emily, I've been seeing the impact of your mindfulness programs on the team," Michael began, his tone more conciliatory than it had ever been. "Productivity is up, and the team seems more cohesive. I must admit, I was skeptical at first, but the results speak for themselves."

Emily, maintaining her characteristic composure, acknowledged his acknowledgment. "Thank you, Michael. I've always believed that well-being and productivity go hand in hand. I'm glad to see the positive effects on our team."

The conversation that unfolded was a balanced exchange of perspectives. Michael shared his concerns about maintaining high performance and meeting deadlines, while Emily presented how mindfulness practices could enhance focus and decision-making, ultimately benefiting the team's output.

There had been a noticeable shift in the team's dynamics. Michael began incorporating brief mindfulness exercises at the start of meetings, and team members reported feeling more relaxed and focused. Michael's interactions with the team, and particularly with Emily, became more respectful and collaborative.

Michael extended his appreciation for Emily's contributions, acknowledging how her insights had positively impacted the team's efficiency and overall morale.

"Emily, your methods have brought a new dimension to our work environment," Michael admitted, a hint of admiration in his voice. "I see now how important it is to balance productivity with well-being. Let's keep working together to continue this positive trend."

Emily, gracious in her response, expressed her willingness to collaborate further. "I'm glad to see our perspectives have aligned, Michael. I believe that we have proven how to create a work environment that not only drives success but also fosters well-being."

Emily and Michael hugged, a gesture symbolic of their understanding and respect. The resolution of their old conflicts were not just a personal victory for Emily but a verification to the power of open communication, empathy, and the willingness to embrace new approaches.

Both Emily and Michael felt a sense of accomplishment and optimism. Their journey from conflict to collaboration mirrored her broader journey of transforming workplace environments. It reinforced her belief that even in the most unlikely scenarios, change was possible, and common ground could be found.

"In a world where efficiency and profit reign, can a whisper of mindfulness transform the rhythm of corporate life?"

In the sprawling office of Shiyuantech Solutions, a quiet revolution was unfolding. It was a typical Thursday, but there was an undercurrent of change that was profound throughout the corridors and workspaces. This change, a shift towards a more mindful and compassionate work environment, was a ripple effect of Emily's influence, reaching far beyond her immediate team.

The once strictly business-focused atmosphere of the office was now interspersed with moments of mindfulness and genuine connections. Significant changes were evident – from the mindfulness tip of the day on the company intranet to the quiet zones designated for meditation and reflection. These changes marked a departure from the high-stress, high-pressure environment that had once defined Shiyuantech.

In the common area, a space usually buzzing with the clatter of coffee cups and hurried conversations, employees now gathered for a midday mindfulness session. The sessions, initially introduced by Emily, had become a regular feature, eagerly anticipated by many. Employees from various departments, some who had never spoken to each other before, now sat side by side, united in a shared experience of relaxation and rejuvenation.

The mindfulness sessions were led by different team members, a practice that encouraged participation and ownership. Today, it was led by Julia, a software developer from the research team. Her voice, calm and soothing, guided her colleagues through a breathing exercise, followed by a short meditation. The room, filled with a diverse group of individuals, fell into a serene silence, a collective pause in the day's hustle.

In the corner of the room, Emily observed quietly, her heart swelling with pride and hope. The seeds she had planted were now blossoming, nurtured by the collective desire for a healthier work environment.

The influence of mindfulness and compassion was embedded in the company's culture. Team leaders started meetings with a minute of silence, allowing everyone to settle in and focus. Decision-making processes began to reflect a consideration for employee well-being, not just the bottom line.

The HR department, inspired by the positive feedback from employees, introduced a series of workshops on emotional intelligence and stress management. These workshops, often co-facilitated by Emily, were well-attended, sparking discussions on work-life balance, mental health, and the importance of self-care.

One significant indicator of this cultural shift was the change in how the company dealt with conflicts and challenges. In a meeting addressing a project setback, instead of the usual finger-pointing and high-stress atmosphere, there was a constructive discussion on lessons learned and strategies for moving forward. The team, led by a manager who had embraced Emily's approach, focused on collaboration and support, turning a potential crisis into an opportunity for growth and learning.

This transformation was also evident in casual interactions. Conversations now included topics like meditation techniques, book recommendations on personal growth, and sharing of personal wellness goals. Employees began forming informal support groups, meeting over lunch to discuss challenges and share advice.

Emily's influence reached the upper echelons of the company as well. The executive team, noting the positive changes in employee morale and productivity, began consulting Emily on strategic initiatives related to employee wellness. Her insights were valued, and her suggestions often implemented, reflecting a company-wide commitment to fostering a mindful and compassionate work culture.

As the workday ended, a sense of calm contentment settled over Shiyuantech Solutions. The company had embarked on a journey of transformation, one that was enhancing not just the work experience but also the personal lives of its employees. The environment of mutual respect, empathy, and mindfulness had become the new norm, a testament to the enduring impact of Emily's vision and dedication.

Emily sat reflecting on the day. She realized that her influence had extended far beyond what she had initially imagined. Her commitment to bringing mindfulness and compassion into the workplace had ignited a cultural shift, transforming Shiyuantech Solutions into an example of a positive and supportive work environment. This change, she knew, was just the beginning of a broader movement, one that had the potential to reshape not just companies, but the very fabric of corporate culture.

"In a world of relentless motion, can the stillness within one's breath unlock the dance of equilibrium?"

In the softly lit tranquility of a local yoga studio, where the gentle hum of soothing music melded with the rhythmic breathing of its occupants, Alex Chen experienced a profound sense of balance and fulfillment. The studio, a haven of peace amidst the city's commotion, had become a regular part of Alex's routine, symbolizing the harmony he had achieved in his wellness journey.

The class had just ended, and as Alex rolled up his yoga mat, he reflected on the journey that had brought him to this point of equilibrium. It was a path marked by exploration, learning, and transformation, much of it inspired by his friend and mentor, Emily.

As he stepped out of the studio into the cool evening air, Alex felt a deep connection to the world around him, a feeling that extended beyond the physical benefits of his yoga practice. It was a sense of inner peace, a balance between his mind, body, and spirit that he had been seeking ever since he embarked on his wellness journey.

Walking down the busy streets, Alex headed towards a nearby restaurant where he was meeting Emily. He was eager to share his progress with her, to express his gratitude for the role she had played in his transformation.

The restaurant was a familiar spot for their meet-ups. Emily was already there, seated at their usual table by the window, a warm smile on her face as she greeted Alex.

The conversation naturally flowed to Alex's recent achievements in his journey. "Emily, I can't thank you enough for introducing me to mindfulness and meditation," Alex began, his eyes reflecting sincerity. "It's changed the way I approach life. I feel more balanced, more in tune with myself."

Emily listened intently; her heart filled with joy at seeing her friend's progress. "I'm so happy for you, Alex. It's amazing to see how far you've come. Remember, the journey is ongoing, and every day is a chance to grow and learn."

Alex nodded in agreement, sharing how he had started integrating the principles of mindfulness into his daily routine. "I've been practicing mindful eating, taking time to appreciate the flavors and textures of my food. It's made my meals more enjoyable and satisfying," he shared, a hint of enthusiasm in his voice.

He also spoke about his efforts to maintain a work-life balance, ensuring that he dedicated time for relaxation and self-care. "I've realized that taking care of myself isn't just about physical fitness. It's about nurturing my mind and respecting my emotional needs," he explained.

They started discussing how the principles of mindfulness could be applied in various aspects of life, from relationships to career choices. Emily shared her insights, offering advice and encouragement.

Before parting ways, Alex reiterated his gratitude to Emily. "Your guidance has been invaluable, Emily. I'll continue to apply what I've learned and hopefully inspire others as you've inspired me."

Emily smiled, her eyes shining with pride. "You're already on your way, Alex. Keep embracing the journey."

Walking back home, Alex felt a renewed sense of purpose and contentment. He had found a balance that resonated deeply with him, a harmony that permeated every aspect of his life. His journey of wellness, inspired by Emily but shaped by his own experiences, was proof of the transformative power of mindfulness and self-exploration.

In the quiet of his apartment, as he prepared for bed, Alex felt a profound sense of gratitude for the journey he had embarked upon. It was a journey that had brought him closer to himself and had also deepened his connection with Emily, a friend who had become a mentor along his path to wellness.

Reflections

"In the dance of shadows and light, where does the journey end and the path begin?"

In the city park, where the sunlight shining through the leaves painted shifting patterns on the ground, Emily Nguyen found herself in her favorite spot. It was here, on this very bench, where the journey of her transformation had begun years ago. Now, as she sat in quiet reflection, the park around her buzzed with the hum of life – children playing, birds chirping, and the distant murmur of the city.

Emily closed her eyes, taking in the sounds and scents of the park, allowing them to transport her through the memories of her journey. She thought back to the person she was when she first embarked on this path – uncertain, seeking, and unaware of the profound changes that lay ahead. Now, she was a catalyst for change, not just in her own life but in the lives of those around her.

She reflected on the spiritual awakening that had ignited her transformation. The early days of struggle, the moments of doubt, and the exhilarating breakthroughs – each step had been a building block in her journey. She had learned to embrace her vulnerabilities, turn her fears into strengths, and find peace in the present moment.

But her transformation extended beyond the spiritual realm. Emotionally, she had evolved from a person who sought validation and approval to one who found strength in her own self-worth. She had learned to navigate the complexities of human relationships with empathy and understanding, turning conflicts into opportunities for growth and connection.

Intellectually, her journey had been equally transformative. Emily's mind, once consumed by the practicalities and pressures of daily life, had opened to a world of new ideas and perspectives. She had delved into philosophical texts, explored different cultures, and engaged in thought-provoking discussions, each experience enriching her understanding of the world.

As she sat there, enveloped in her thoughts, Emily realized the interconnectedness of these transformations. Her spiritual growth had fueled her emotional maturity, which in turn had broadened her intellectual horizons. It was a holistic evolution, touching every aspect of her being.

Opening her eyes, Emily gazed at the park around her. The same place that had once been a refuge for her solitary contemplation was now a symbol of her connection to the world. She understood that her journey was not an isolated pursuit of self-improvement; it was a part of a larger tapestry, where each individual's transformation contributed to the collective good.

With a deep sense of peace, Emily acknowledged that her journey was a continuous process of learning, growing, and evolving. Each day presented new challenges and opportunities, and she was ready to embrace them with an open heart.

As the sun began to set, casting a warm golden glow over the park, Emily stood up, her heart filled with gratitude for the journey so far and excitement for the path that lay ahead. She knew that true service to the world began with one's own transformation, and she was committed to living this truth, one day at a time.

Walking out of the park, Emily felt a profound connection to everything around her – the trees, the people, the very air she breathed. She was a part of this intricate web of life, a thread woven into the fabric of existence. Her story of growth, learning, and love was a testament to the transformative power of the human spirit. And as she stepped back into the flow of life beyond the park, Emily carried with her the knowledge that every step, every encounter, was a part of her ever-unfolding journey.

"Can a journey truly end when each step is a new beginning?"

The cool evening breeze carried with it the faint scent of blooming flowers, a subtle reminder of the ever-changing cycle of nature. Emily pondered on this, drawing a parallel to her own journey. Like the seasons, her path of self-discovery and growth was a dynamic, ever-evolving process. Each experience, each challenge, was akin to the natural transformations around her, contributing to the continual shaping of her being.

She thought about the various milestones along the way – the first moment of true mindfulness, the deepening of her emotional connections, the expansion of her intellectual horizons. Each breakthrough was significant, not as an endpoint, but as a marker of her evolution, evidence to her commitment to continuous growth.

The sound of leaves rustling in the wind brought her back to the present. She gazed at the effortless flow of nature – the trees swaying gently, the birds soaring in the sky, the stars beginning to twinkle as night fell. This harmony of nature was a beautiful metaphor for her journey. It was not about conquering milestones but about moving gracefully through life's ebb and flow.

Embracing this notion, Emily felt a deep sense of peace and comfort in the continuous evolution of her self. The journey, with its twists and turns, its highs, and lows, was not a path to a fixed destination but a lifelong journey of becoming.

Emily carried with her a renewed appreciation for the journey ahead. She understood that the true essence of growth lay in the journey itself – in each step taken, in each moment lived, in each lesson learned. Her path was not a linear progression towards an end goal but a spiraling ascent of continuous self-discovery and transformation.

Emily felt aligned with the rhythm of life around her. She was a part of this vast, intricate web of existence, her journey a single thread woven into the larger fabric of the human experience. In this realization lay her strength and serenity, for she knew that no matter what the future held, she was on a path of endless learning and growth, a journey that was as boundless as the night sky above.

"In the quiet park where paths diverge and meet, does the reflection in the pond reveal the journey, or does the journey become the reflection?

As the city around her transitioned from the vibrant colors of dusk to the soft hues of twilight, Emil walked slowly through the busy streets, immersed in a state of deep contemplation. Her inner journey—a journey that was as much about the paths traversed as it was about the destinations yet to be reached.

With each step, Emily felt a profound connection with the rhythm of life around her. The rustling leaves whispered ancient wisdom, the gentle breeze carried stories of distant lands, and the stars emerging in the evening sky were like beacons guiding her way. In this moment of harmony with nature, Emily realized she had reached a state of peace with the ongoing nature of her personal development.

This realization was not a sudden revelation, but the culmination of her experiences, reflections, and interactions. She thought about the challenges she had faced, the obstacles she had overcome, and the triumphs she had celebrated. Each of these moments, whether they brought joy or sorrow, had contributed significantly to her journey, shaping her into the person she was today.

Her mind then wandered to the people who had been part of her journey—her mentor Mrs. Kaur, whose wisdom had guided her; her friend Alex, whose own journey had paralleled hers in many ways; and even Michael, whose initial skepticism and eventual transformation had taught her the power of empathy and persistence. These individuals, and many others, had been instrumental in her development, offering support, challenge, and perspective.

As she walked, Emily embraced the idea that her path was one of perpetual growth. She understood that each experience, each interaction, was an opportunity to learn, to expand her understanding, and to evolve. This acceptance brought with it a sense of liberation—a freedom from the pressure of reaching a definitive endpoint and an appreciation for the journey itself.

As she walked on, the tranquility of the night enveloping her, Emily carried with her a serene acceptance of her ongoing journey. She stepped back into the world with a renewed sense of purpose, a heart open to the infinite possibilities that lay ahead, and a soul at peace with the perpetual nature of her personal development.

"Where the end of day whispers secrets, can the journey inward illuminate the path of true service outward?"

As the evening sky draped itself in a tapestry of dusky blues and purples, Emily Nguyen sat quietly on her bed at home, her mind deep in thought. This tranquility provided the perfect backdrop for Emily to ponder the profound concept of service and its true meaning in her life.

She reflected on her journey, the transformative path that had led her to this moment of realization. It was a journey marked not just by external actions and achievements, but by profound internal growth and self-discovery.

Emily considered the popular notion of service – the act of helping others, contributing to the community, and making a difference in the world. But now, in this moment of quiet introspection, she understood that true service went much deeper than these external actions. It was rooted in the inner transformation that each individual undergoes.

She realized that the most impactful service she could offer to the world began with her own transformation. By nurturing her own spiritual, emotional, and intellectual growth, she was better equipped to contribute positively to the lives of others. Her journey of self-improvement wasn't a personal quest; it was a crucial part of her ability to serve others effectively.

Emily's mind drifted to the changes she had witnessed in herself. The challenges she had overcome, the insights she had gained, and the inner peace she had found – all these were not just personal victories. They were tools that enabled her to engage with the world in a more compassionate, understanding, and effective way.

She thought about the times she had been able to help others, not just through direct action, but through the wisdom and empathy she had acquired on her journey. She recalled conversations where her words had brought comfort or insight, and actions that had positively influenced those around her. Each of these instances was authentication to the fact that her inner work had a ripple effect, extending far beyond her own life.

Emily felt a profound connection to the world around her. She understood that every individual's journey of transformation had the potential to contribute to the collective good. Each person's inner work, their personal growth and self-realization, was a vital piece of the puzzle in creating a better world.

"In a dance with the stars, where dreams weave the future, can a heart full of hope light the path yet unseen?"

In the quiet comfort of her apartment, with the night embracing the city in its silent hold, Emily Nguyen stood by her window, her eyes gazing into the starlit sky. The room around her was steeped in tranquility, the soft glow of the lamp casting gentle shadows against the walls, creating a space of reflection and anticipation. In this serene setting, Emily contemplated her future with a heart full of hope.

As she looked out into the night, Emily's thoughts ventured forward, imagining the path that lay ahead. She envisioned herself continuing her journey of growth, each day unraveling new layers of understanding and wisdom. The future, like the vast night sky before her, seemed filled with infinite possibilities.

She imagined the experiences yet to come, the people she would meet, and the lives she would touch. In her mind's eye, she saw herself applying the lessons learned from her past to new challenges, using her knowledge and empathy to contribute positively to the world around her.

Emily thought about the projects and initiatives she could undertake, ways in which she could share her journey and insights to inspire and support others. She pictured herself organizing workshops, participating in community events, and perhaps even writing a book to encapsulate her experiences and learnings.

Emily's heart swelled with the desire to make a difference, to leave a positive imprint on the world. She saw herself as part of a larger movement towards a more mindful, compassionate society, where each individual's growth contributed to the collective well-being.

As she stood there, lost in thoughts of the future, a gentle breeze wafted in through the open window, bringing with it the fresh scent of the night. It was as if the world was whispering to her, affirming her hopes and dreams.

With a deep, contented sigh, Emily stepped away from the window and prepared for bed. As she lay down, closing her eyes, her mind was alive with ideas and plans for the days to come. She drifted off to sleep with a smile, comforted by the knowledge that her journey was an ever-evolving story, rich with potential and brimming with hope.

In her dreams, she walked paths of light, each step a dance of joy and discovery. The future awaited her with open arms, and she stepped into it with confidence and a heart full of hope, ready to embrace whatever lay ahead.

"In a world where paths diverge and converge, can the sharing of one journey illuminate countless others in the dance of life?"

In the luminous glow of the early morning, Emily sat at her desk, her fingers poised above the keyboard of her laptop. The room was bathed in the soft light of dawn, creating a serene atmosphere that was perfect for reflection and writing. Outside, the city was slowly waking up, its sounds a gentle reminder of the world moving forward. In this moment of quiet, Emily felt a deep connection to her purpose – to share her story and inspire others.

As she began to type, her words flowed onto the screen, each sentence testimony to her journey. She was writing a blog post, a narrative of her experiences, challenges, and insights. Emily knew that her story had the power to inspire others, to show them the potential for transformation that lies within embracing one's personal journey with openness and courage.

She wrote about the early days of her journey, filled with uncertainty and a longing for something more. She described the pivotal moments of realization, the struggles she overcame, and the profound changes she experienced. Her words were honest and raw, painting a vivid picture of her path to self-discovery.

As Emily plunged deeper into her story, she shared the lessons she had learned about mindfulness, compassion, and resilience. She spoke of the importance of being present, of embracing change, and of finding strength in vulnerability. Her narrative was not just a recounting of events, but a sharing of wisdom gained through lived experience.

Her blog post also highlighted the people who had influenced her journey – from the wise neighbor who had guided her in the early days to the friends and colleagues who had supported her along the way. She wrote about the interconnectedness of lives and how each person we encounter can shape our path in profound ways. That each encounter was sacred and could hold the key to our enlightenment.

As the sun rose higher, casting a warm light into the room, Emily concluded her post with a message of hope and encouragement. She urged her readers to embrace their own journeys, to seek growth and understanding, and to be open to the transformative power of their experiences.

Once the post was published, Emily sat back in her chair, feeling a sense of fulfillment. She knew that her story, with all its ups and downs, could be a message of hope for others. It was a chronicle that spoke of the possibility of change and the beauty of embracing one's journey with courage and an open heart.

In the days that followed, Emily's post resonated with many. Comments and messages poured in from readers who were touched and inspired by her story. People shared their own experiences, their struggles, and how Emily's journey had given them hope and a new perspective.

Among the responses was a message from a young woman who had been at a crossroads in her life. Emily's story had inspired her to take the first steps on her own path of self-discovery. There were also words of gratitude from a man who had found solace and strength in her words during a difficult time.

Emily's story had become a source of inspiration for a community of individuals seeking growth and transformation. Her journey, shared with openness and authenticity, had ignited a spark in others, encouraging them to embark on their paths with courage and hope.

As Emily read through the messages, she felt a deep sense of connection with her readers. She realized that her journey, with all its challenges and triumphs, was a powerful statement to the human spirit's ability to grow and transform. Her story had shown the boundless potential of embracing one's journey with an open heart and unwavering courage.

"In the silence of her sanctuary, can the rhythm of her breath weave a melody that echoes through the tapestry of countless souls?"

Emily sat cross-legged on a plush, comfortable cushion placed thoughtfully in the center of her living room, her hands resting lightly on her knees, palms facing upward in a gesture of openness and receptivity.

Around her, the room is arranged with a minimalist elegance, each item carefully chosen for its significance and beauty. The walls are adorned with art that reflected her journey – vibrant paintings symbolizing growth, framed quotes about resilience and change, and photographs capturing moments of joy and discovery. A small shelf holds a collection of books that have guided her along the way, their spines worn from frequent reading.

In this serene setting, Emily closes her eyes and takes a deep, grounding breath. The air is filled with the subtle fragrance of jasmine from a nearby incense burner, enhancing the atmosphere of tranquility. As she exhales, a sense of profound peace and contentment washes over her.

Her mind, once cluttered with doubts and fears, is now clear and focused. The challenges and trials that had once seemed insurmountable are now viewed as valuable lessons, steppingstones on her path to self-discovery. The emotional turmoil that had clouded her thoughts has given way to a deep understanding and acceptance of life's impermanence and complexity.

A smile graces Emily's lips as she recalls the milestones of her journey – the breakthroughs in understanding, the cultivation of mindfulness, and the deepening of her compassion for herself and others. These memories are integral parts of her, woven into the fabric of her being.

Emily's thoughts turn to the future. She feels a sense of excitement and anticipation for what lies ahead. With each experience, she has grown stronger, more resilient, and more open-hearted. She knows that her journey is the continuous unfolding of her potential.

Emily rises from her cushion, her movements graceful and deliberate. She stands by the window, looking out at the city in quiet contemplation. She is a figure of serenity and strength carrying with her the wisdom, compassion, openness and understanding that comes from the courageous journey to discover self.